Praise fo
Magic is a Shift in

D0977607

"It's hard to imagine a writer interweaving this variety and number of subjects so organically and effectively. In *Magic is a Shift in Perception*, Sharon Gannon muses upon quantum physics, alchemy, choreography, feminism, capitalism, linguistics, Eastern thought, biology, speciesism, fairies and love, all of which blend beautifully into a crafted whole that bursts with insight. The book is as much memoir as poetry, as much philosophy as either. 'We cannot tell the whole truth in words,' Gannon writes, and she's right. But equally true is her declaration that 'If you have the ability to listen, you can hear that the whole world is alive.' The world is alive in Gannon's writing, in her 'curvy, cyclical, musical and magical' book."
– GRETCHEN PRIMACK, author of many books of poetry and non-fiction including *Kind, Visiting Days, The Slow Creaking of Planets* and *The Lucky Ones* with Jenny Brown

"Sharon Gannon's poetry integrates what have been her lifetime concerns — artistic expression, social awareness and a spiritual practice of uniting worldly substances — bodies, trees, and planets — with universal spiritual energy. But more than that *Magic Is A Shift In Perception* is a human record, the document of a remarkable woman's life in the last part of the twentieth century and the beginning of a new one. From the streets of the numerous cities where she's lived to the inner musings of her mind, Sharon Gannon's book travels infinite distances and tells the story of the journey."
– KAZIM ALI, professor of creative writing Oberlin College and author of *The Far Mosque* and *The Fortieth Day*

"Sharon Gannon's poetry encompasses five decades of a life richly lived, from performing in the avant-garde subcultures of Seattle and Manhattan's Lower East Side to the mastery of yoga, which her teaching has helped disseminate across the globe. Her poems are intensely felt and carefully expressed records of her passions and enthusiasms, ranging from metaphysical discourses to celebrations of nature and memorials to particular cats she has known and loved. Readers will enjoy her insights on numerous subjects, her flashes of wit, and her free-flowing lyrical style."
– DANIEL PINCHBECK, author *2012: The Return of Quetzalcoatl* and *Breaking Open the Head*

"It was Sharon Gannon who first taught me that Freedom is a Psychokinetic Skill — the best definition I've ever heard of true avant-garde dance, theater, music, poetry and therefore also one of the political slogans I've tried to live by. This is the poetry of a true tantric anarchist. Om Tara."
– PETER LAMBORN WILSON, Teacher at the Jack Kerouac School of Disembodied Poetics and author of *Ec(o)logues*, *Sacred Drift*, *Vanished Signs* and *Escape from the Nineteenth Century and Other Essays*

"*Magic Is A Shift in Perception* is a beautiful tapestry of poetry and notes woven together with Sharon Gannon's passions of fun, creativity, spirituality, and deep care for all life. This book is a portal from the personal to the infinite taking the reader on a journey that opens and expands the heart, mind, and spirit."
– JULIA BUTTERFLY HILL, activist, poet and author of *Legacy of Luna*, *One Makes A Difference* and *Becoming*

"For over five decades, Sharon Gannon has been leading the way with her wildly original blend of yoga, activism, and creativity. Now we can add poetry to this powerful trifecta. In *Magic Is A Shift in Perception*, Sharon takes her place alongside mystic yogini poets Mirabai and Lal Del with her honesty, wisdom, passion and compassion as she charts a hard-won path to liberation. "God is none other than you/ And you are it, all of it," she writes. How lucky we are to have Gannon's long-awaited book of poems to remind us that magic, bliss and freedom for all living beings are not just possibilities, they're our birthright if we're brave enough — and fierce enough — to claim them."
– LEZA LOWITZ, author of *Yoga Poems: Lines to Unfold By* and *Yoga Heart: Lines on the Six Perfections*

"In her life and her work, Sharon Gannon brings the role of the poet and the yogi back from the periphery to the center. And not for her own sake, but for ours, so that we might value again the beauty that we have within us and let its light illuminate our world. Sharon Gannon is the poet as shaman, as mythmaker, as activist, as spirit guide. Her insights are drawn up from within her depths with astonishing honesty, her bravery is an inspiration. In *Magic is a Shift in Perception*, she is lighting a flame. Pass it on."
– RICHARD JAMES ALLEN, author of 8 books of poetry on spiritual transformation including *The Way Out At Last Cycle*, *Thursday's Fictions* and *The Kamikaze Mind*

"In Sharon Gannon's remarkable collection of wonderful poems and their accompanying notes we are treated to an honest and insightful portrait of an artist in search of her own light and sharing that light as it is found. This is an important and impressive collection of work revealing both process and result."
– PHILLIP LEVINE, author, poet, poetry editor of Chronogram Magazine and President of Woodstock Poetry Society

"*Magic is a Shift in Perception* documents, the life of a mystic who experiences a range of feeling so wide it holds together the death of a family member with the death of a bird who drinks poisonous water. Sharon Gannon looks up at the sky, down at the dust, across the set table and toward the poet who returns from war unable to pick up a pen. Through intense observations and the author's faith in poetry, a vast distance is brought together in a single point revealing what is shared and hidden under the surface of our lives."
– RUTH LAUER-MANENTI, author of *An Offering of Leaves, Sweeping the Dust* and *Fell in Her Hands*

"In *Magic Is A Shift In Perception*, the decades become seasons and words take flight through soul stirring passionate poetic reflection interlaced with luminous narrative. Through this book, Sharon Gannon has created a lasting monument and essential contribution to the world and all seekers of truth. It is an inside lens, delicate snapshot, and potent description of the physical, emotional and spiritual transformation and landscape that unfolds when yoga, poetry, activism, music, and art combine. This book is pure magic."
– HawaH, visionary, poet, and editor of *The Poetry of Yoga Volume I, II*

"Sharon Gannon's *Magic is a Shift in Perception* is a bold and beautiful book that lifts us into the origin of its words through the weave of memoir and poetry, journeying through decades of magic seen through the bright discerning lens of poetry. This is a book with light embedded in dark ink and truth glowing in the spaces, reminding us of the power of words to bind and heal, much in the way yoga can unite and restore. This is more than a book of poems, it is a gift of one woman's life — a rare poemoir! May we read it again and again in the state of honesty that her magic imparts and encourages."
– SARAH HERRINGTON, author of *Always Moving* and *Om Schooled*

"Sharon Gannon's *Magic Is a Shift in Perception* deserves its rightful place in the canon of mystical poetry — along the lines of Rumi, Hafiz, and Blake. But Gannon's poems aren't lost to the dusty fragments of history. Donning the paradoxical masks of prankster artist, spiritual activist, and postmodern guru, Gannon adeptly punctures the often brutal, and occasionally beautiful, world of our techno-industrialized society to illuminate the greater divine reality calling us home."
— JONATHAN TALAT PHILLIPS, author of *The Electric Jesus: The Healing Journey of a Contemporary Gnostic* and co-founder of Evolver and Reality Sandwich

"Sharon Gannon's vivacious spirit jumps off these pages of poetry straight into our hearts. Her book *Magic Is A Shift In Perception*, is an intimate, vulnerable and wisdom filled portal into five decades of a women's life. These poems and accompanying biographical notes are at once intimate and universal and sing a great song of courage, creativity, loss, searching, finding and remembrance. What I love most about this book is after reading it I feel I have known Sharon since she was a young spunky girl and that she is now the dearest of old friends. This unique and timeless offering is at once gritty, down to earth, deeply insightful and full of heart as we journey through the life of a contemporary modern mystic."
— JOHN de KADT, musician, recording artist, poet and storyteller

"Sharon's words carry the supreme essence of great poetry, she has caught the ecstatic and pulsating, unfathomable depth of the human heart."
— DEVA PREMAL and MITEN, recording artists

"Read this book and marvel at Sharon Gannon's ability to capture life in language and then turn around and explain how she did it. Sharon was my first teacher on the mat and now she is playfully teaching me again. Along with her outsider status reminiscent of Anais Nin comes the illustrious gift of creating spontaneous verse, but most importantly, of allowing herself through yogic detachment to analyze and annotate her own work. Shouldn't we all be allowed to do these things?"
— INDIA RADFAR, poet, author of *The Desire to Meet with the Beautiful* and *Breathe*

Also by Sharon Gannon

Freedom is a Psycho-Kinetic Skill (1982)

Cats and Dogs are People Too! (1999)
(Italian translation available)

Jivamukti Yoga (2002)
(with David Life)
(German, Italian, Russian, and Spanish translations available)

The Art of Yoga (2002)
(with David Life)

The Jivamukti Yoga Chant Book (2003)
(Chinese, German, Italian, Japanese, Russian, Spanish,
and Turkish translations available)

Yoga and Vegetarianism (2008)
(Chinese, German, Italian, Japanese, Russian, Spanish,
and Turkish translations available)

Yoga Assists (2013)
(with David Life)
(Italian translation available)

Simple Recipes for Joy: More Than 200 Delicious Vegan Recipes (2014)
(Italian translation available)

The Magic Ten and Beyond (2018)
(Italian, and German translations available)

The Art of Norahs Nepas (2019)

Yoga and Veganism: The Diet of Enlightenment (2020)
(audio book also available)

Magic is a Shift
in Perception

Magic is a Shift in Perception

Poems 1972-2019

A memoir of sorts

Sharon Gannon

©2020 By Sharon Gannon

All rights reserved. This book, or parts thereof, must not be reproduced in any form without permission. Contact info@jivamuktiyoga.com

Typeface: Alegreya
Library of Congress Cataloging in Publication Data
ISBN 978-1-71-546934-4

Gannon, Sharon
Magic is a Shift in Perception
Poems 1972-2019, a memoir of sorts
(ebook and Audio book available)

Photographer credits:
Front Cover: photo booth picture by author (Seattle, WA. 1980)
Back Cover: author's suitcase, photo by author (NYC, NY 1983)
Facing Title Page: Randy Hall (Seattle, WA. 1976)
page 9: Randy Hall (Seattle, WA. 1975)
page 31: Sue Ann Harkey (NYC, NY 1983)
page 191: Eddie Stern (NYC, NY 1992)
page 223: Val Shaff (Woodstock, NY 2008)
page 297: Guzman (NYC, NY 2013)
Page 396: Val Shaff (Woodstock, NY 2008)

Book design and layout by David Life

Dedicated to David Life

Contents

(Poems listed numerically. Go to Index of Titles for page number.)

**PART 1 1970s ROOTS — Deconstruction:
Prune Back Hard to Establish a Better Root System**

**PART 2 1980s SHOOTS — Reconstruction:
New Growth, Recreating Myself**

PART 3 1990s FLOWERS — Reorientation:
Attraction, Drama, Romance, Uncertainty, Musing, Memories

PART 4 2000s FRUITS — Manifestation:
Something Useful

PART 5 2010s SEEDS — MYSTERIES:
To be unpacked and re-cycled

Foreword

by JOSHUA M. GREENE

Those of us who know and admire Sharon Gannon in any of her numerous incarnations — yoga master, vegan crusader, singer, dancer, poet, muse — know that when we pick up her latest book there will be penetrating reflections on the universe, mirrors held up to our follies, and valuable insights into navigating the human condition. And yet, to read *Magic is a Shift in Perception* is to be jolted into fresh surprise. In lucid phrases and deft verbal blends this versatile polymath bares mind and heart, from the early years of her awakening to her flowering as a mature teacher of the ancient art of yoga. It is a journey that echoes classical spiritual transformation; but here, perhaps more than any other memoir in recent memory, we have the gift of mystic poetry which harkens not back to remote times or places but forward into a potential future yet to be realized. It is a treasury by turns intimate, idiosyncratic, highly individual, and utterly modern.

Sharon presents herself unmediated by concern for appearances, and the candor is stunning. Unaffected despite the exoticism of her life's trajectory, she bequeaths to readers an eager appetite for self-awareness. In lucid commentaries to each poem she reveals her experiences on a bohemian path, the transformative role sensuality has played for her, and a restlessness to know God that energizes her every moment. From the opening lines of the first poem, written in 1972 ("We see the everlastingness in everything that's passing"), to the closing lines of the book's last, written in 2019 ("May we all die to our mediocrity and be reborn in our entirety") the author demonstrates a rare gift for condensing profound truths that, in the hands of a lesser writer, would fall into self-absorption. It is a gift that carries into revelations about her worldly life. Sharon converts symptoms into significance. She joins self-examination with philosophical investigation. She knows how to follow subtle movements of her own feelings, how to criticize them and honor them. Even in her most extreme moments, such as the fate of a child, her brother's death or a close encounter with her own, she avoids the allure of excessive writing and gives meaningful, moving form to the chaos inside her.

Sharon was born in 1951. By the mid-1980s, when most post-war Baby Boomers had hung up their beads, shelved their bellbottoms and swapped idealism for careers, she knew what the upstarts of her generation had failed to see: "Keep climbing the best is yet to come" (poem #101: *The Best Is Yet to Come*, 1987). By the two thousands, that victory over acquiescence had ascended into a commanding role in social/spiritual activism (see for example, *#152: Widening Lanes*, or many of the works post 2007). By now she had come to see herself as one with all beings: part of a majestic stream of life that compels us to actively participate and which she is as comfortable describing in Sanskrit terms as she is with references to contemporary artists, jazz musicians and journalists. Hers is a mysticism that leads not to solitary confinement but to worldly engagement and the articulation of millennial truths in a thoroughly modern vernacular.

The writing takes disarming turns, as in the poem titled, *That's It* (2010), which catapults the Ramones in the Himalayas with uncanny humor:

> It's gonna be alright
> It's gonna be alright
> Darling, its gonna be alright
>
> But who is it?—that you are talking about?
> that's it—it's that!
>
> And you can't name that any better than that
> Any better than it, cause that's it
> —Tat Twam Asi...

No other poet comes readily to mind capable of merging parody and compliment with such ease. It is a quality that pervades *Magic is a Shift in Perception*, the kind of wry journeyer wit that we find in concept albums such as The Band's *Big Pink*, Dylan's *John Wesley Harding* or the Beatles's *Sgt. Pepper*. Sharon challenges readers to see themselves in her confrontations with the world, to move with her away from conditioned life, to breathe with her the clear air that fills the lungs of the *jivan-muktas*, spirits who are free even while still in physical form.

There is a bracing, crystalline reality to her writing, as in mountain streams. We can be grateful to gaze into these waters and find, staring back at us, ourselves.

JOSHUA M. GREENE is a professor of Religious Studies, Hofstra University, filmmaker, and author of many books, including: *Here Comes the Sun: The Spiritual and Musical Journey of George Harrison*, and *Gita Wisdom*

Why a Memoir?

Everything in our lives revolves around identity. We spend the first part of our lives trying to find an identity and the rest of our lives doing our best to defend that identity. We are attracted to certain things, people, situations, music, books, food, clothing, lifestyles, etc., because these fit in with how we would like to see ourselves and how we would like others to see us. But of course we can become imprisoned within our identity. To evolve as a person we must grow, and to grow we must let go. To the person who longs for spiritual realization, the biggest obstacle to overcome is *avidya*, the misperception of who you really are. The goal of life is to realize that you are not your body, mind or personality. You are not the mortal self, you are the eternal Self, a part of the Divine and your nature is joy. The small self, the individual soul is known in Sanskrit as the *jiva*; the eternal soul is the *atman*. When the jiva ceases to identify with it's limited nature and surrenders to God, then they are known as a *jivanmukta*, a liberated soul. But you cannot truly surrender something that you don't know, and while of course I have "known" the facts about "my" life, I have not known them in a way that would enable me to see them with perspective and to mine them for deeper truths and thus allow me to be released from them.

To live an examined life is to reflect upon the possible motives that conspired to form your present identity — your perception of yourself and others. We do not exist separately from the rest of the world. We are interconnected. If we live to enhance the lives of others, by doing our best to contribute to their happiness and freedom, then eventually but inevitably there will be a shift in our perception of who we are and who we think those others are. When we say yes to that — the magic begins.

In order to facilitate a shift in perception that allows a greater sense of self to emerge, one must first come to terms with one's self as an individual person, and that means becoming comfortable in your own skin, and with the experiences of your life. To that end, it is helpful to organize, finish, and put closure on things. Writing a memoir is an exercise in such reflection. This book began as a retrospective book of poems. I have consistently written poems since 1972, written by hand or typed and stored in messy notebooks. Organizing the poems into this book involved not only transcribing and correcting typos but a reexamination of each poem, pulling it into the light, sitting with it, and at times trying to decipher what it meant then and also what it might mean now. I had to really listen to these poems, whereas when I wrote them, I didn't always take the time to do that. Through this process of examination, the notes organically emerged and with them the introductions for each decade, revealing the unfolding of my identity through a poetic lens. The poems, along with the notes and introduction sections provided an account of my life — points of reference from which to tell my story and so the book morphed into a memoir of sorts.

I have divided the book into five parts, based on decades, titling them Roots, Shoots, Flowers, Fruits and Seeds, which reveal something about how I see myself on my journey as I look back through each of those time periods. Of course the introductions don't provide every biographical detail and the notes do not explain everything about the poems, but a memoir by definition does not attempt to tell every fact. The reader can, of course, choose to ignore the notes and read only the poems. The poems, as well as the notes, are numbered in chronological order. There are three indexes at the end of the book, organized by Title, First Lines and Subject. I hope that these indexes will provide the reader with a way to easily reference the poems.

Often when I am reading a retrospective book of poems which has been complied by an editor where the poet has long been dead, the editor offers context for the poem, including personal and/or autobiographical background, and explains some passages or words that might be obscure to the reader. When I have read books like this, I appreciate the information but I also wish that I could have read what the poet himself or herself had to say about the poems and not merely take the editor's word for it. So because I would like to read a book like that myself, I felt that I should write a book like that.

What is Poetry?

Working with sound is what poets do: using language, yes, but not in the conventional way of trying to say something about anything. Everyone knows that you can't truly describe anything merely by talking about it. Whatever you say will at best be only your own view of it at a particular moment, and reality is more than your immediate perception of the sequence of moments that create time. But nonetheless something essential about how things and feelings come about can be revealed through sound, more so than through sight, smell, taste or even touch. All that appears as physical matter derives its source from the non-physical realm of spirit and sound comprises that world of spirit. Sound is enchanting and can magically enchant you, instigating a shift in perception.

Perhaps poetry is like arranging flowers of sound. By moving sound shapes in particular ways one can create a sensual atmosphere, in the process causing oneself, and perhaps the listener/reader, to stumble upon or at least approach the pulse of being, if only for a moment. This awakening of the senses brings about insight, and insight is where a poet's passion lies. Insight, not love, is the greatest power of the heart. Without insight there can be no realization of love, because the inclusiveness of love depends on the power of insight. Through insight connections are made; you "connect the dots" and then dis-ease and separation can dissolve. But insight is graceful; it cannot be made to happen. Nevertheless, there are things you can do to facilitate the arising of insight. Harmonizing with beauty is one of those things. The elements of beauty are contained in poetry because to succeed a poem must align itself with beauty, which is the essential power of Mother Nature. She is the matrix of being, and she manifests beautifully through music and meter.

In poetry, it is not enough to just say something or to express what is on your mind or even what you *think* is in your heart. A poem must be more vital. It must strip you bare and it must not be elitist. It should facilitate the arising of insight in the reader/listener, and it doesn't have to speak in a mundane language that everyone can readily understand, because to understand implies that you are separated; you are "standing under." Understanding belongs to the realm of the intellect and intellectual, rational comprehension is not the goal of poetry. Poetry seeks to move the mind *and* heart and in doing so pull them together.

The poet, like the yogi, strives for the realization of *Nada Brahman*, the

Sanskrit term referring to sound as God, or God as sound, although perhaps not all poets would feel comfortable saying so. *Nada Brahman* is the first and most primal original vibration emanating from the eternal One from which all else manifests. This is expressed in sound by OM, the syllable that defies literal meaning. OM is the name of God. OM actually means nothing: no thing. OM, transcends religion because it is basic to human speech, being composed of the simplest sounds that a person can make by exhaling a breath. OM is actually made up of three sounds: *AA* (opening the mouth), *OO* (closing the mouth somewhat to form a circle) and finally *MM* (closing the mouth and putting the lips together to hum). The sound OM is so essential and beyond religious sectarianism that the closest meaning in English would be the word *Yes*, implying radical positive inclusion. In the yogic scriptures OM is referred to as the *pranava*, which means "that which is always renewing." OM, the essential poem, is the eternal fountain of life, continuously rebirthing poetry — succinct complete and utterly mysterious.

A poet is a radical. The word *radical*, like the word *radish*, derives from the Latin root *rad*, meaning "root." A radical is someone who attempts to get at the root of a situation, to peel away all the superficial layers and uncover the essential core. The poet is a radical who taunts the apocalypse and is willing to stand uncovered, revealed for all to see and to hear. A poet is driven to speak from some essential place devoid of self-consciousness.

As romantic poet Percy Bysshe Shelly says in his 1821 essay, *A Defense of Poetry*: "Poetry and the principle of the self are the God and mammon of the world," meaning that the opposite of poetry is egotism. Shelly continues to expound on the meaning of poetry: "It is at once the centre and circumference of knowledge; it is that which comprehends all science, and that to which all science must be referred. It is at the same time the root and blossom of all other systems of thought; it is that from which all spring, and that which adorns all...It is the odour and color of the rose to the texture of the elements which compose it, as the form and splendour of unfaded beauty to the secrets of anatomy and corruption."

Charles Eliot Norton, a professor of art history at Harvard University at the end of the 19th century, speaks of poetry "as a spirit that exists not only in literature, but in art, in music, in human activity, and doubtless in the whole of life — something almost the same as beauty itself, that magical presence which one from time to time feels surrounding him or herself everywhere, not quite out of sight, not quite out of earshot, but for the most part unheard and unseen amid the roar of the world and the grinding of our own egotisms."

Even though Shelly and Norton expressed their thoughts on poetry a long time ago their observations remain current today and are echoed in the words of contemporary poet HawaH in the prologue to his *The Poetry of Yoga, Volume I*, in which he says, "Poetry and Yoga are as inseparable as ocean and sand. Together they create a mirror glass reflecting the enlightenment inside of us. Yoga turns us inward as we discover...the spirit; poetry channels expression outwards pouring the shape (of spirit) into words." There is definitely something about striving to perceive that which is essential, that which cannot be held, something so subtle and fine, more akin to breathing or to mathematics or to music, that poets feel compelled to connect with and bring to the surface of our material world.

An artist, using whatever medium, first finds a way to dive deep into the speechless ocean, but then must come up to the surface for air, as well as to share their findings with others, reminding us of where we collectively come from. Poetry seems closer to the natural essential order of things; it doesn't strive to be linear, rational or expository. It is musical. It is more invocative than direct. It offers an opportunity to the reader/listener to have his or her own experience. Essays can be effective because as most would agree they spell it out, whereas poems can be oblique. Essays tend to speak to the intellect and poems to the heart. Poems are meant to act as triggers that can stimulate feelings, insights and techniques to stretch reality. The job of the poet is not merely to profess knowledge, but to facilitate an experience — the experience of remembering what one already knows.

If a poet is to be political, they must have a concern for the well-being of the community, the body politic. As a social activist one must find the underlying causes of suffering and bondage in him or herself first, in order to develop the best strategy to contribute to the liberation and upliftment of others.

The poet, like the political activist, must be able to communicate more than his or her own personal anger and frustration. And if a poem doesn't change the world for the better, then it has no purpose. The poet as activist must be willing to drop the artifices of being — the contrivances of personality — and stand on common ground with the world. Ideas of *I* and *me* and *mine* must be questioned, and self-gratifying goals must be let go of. What I'm talking about is Self-rule — with a capital "S". If that sounds a bit like anarchy, well fine, because that is what I intend. True anarchy means Self-rule — not *self*-rule — not guided by the desires of the egoic personality, or small self, but rather to be guided by the innermost collective heart — the Divine Self, which forms the ground of being for all. Violence and fanaticism must be replaced by strong and sweet shape-shifting voices if we are going to build a new world from the quintessential essence, which after all is beauty and harmony and quite wild compared to our domesticated cultured civilization. To turn again to Shelly, "poets are the unacknowledged legislators of the world."

As the French Situationists suggest, "Only as a band of armed poets can we ever hope to overcome everyday fascism." Fascism is imposing one's own ideas on others, disregarding the others' needs and happiness. As human beings we have been conditioned by culture to view all of creation from a fascist outlook, seeing others, including the Earth, as existing solely for our benefit. Our normal method of interaction with other animals, human beings, trees, the Earth, water and air is based on exploitation, domination and subjugation for our own temporary profit or benefit. A relationship that is not mutually beneficial is not a sustainable relationship and will result, ultimately, in pain, dis-ease and suffering for all. Ultimately, it is ugly, not poetic, because it is not aligned with beauty, which is the essence of the collective heart. The best way to uplift our own lives is to do our best to uplift the lives of others.

For artistic expression to be valid, like anarchy, it must originate from the core, the great immeasurable, communal, shared heart that connects all living beings. It cannot be just self-expression; it must at least strive to be Self-expression. The poet doesn't create, they channel. Words come through them. Mysticism and poetry are ancient traditions. The rishis who channeled the Upanishads were poets. The great yogic scriptures, such as the *Mahabharata*, the *Bhagavad Gita* and *Patanjali's Yoga Sutra*, were written in poetic verse. Hafiz, Mirabai, Surdas and Rumi were yogi poets.

The poet's place in society has always been as one who gives a wakeup call, who rings the bell that calls us to remember that which is best within us. The poet pulls us into the rhythms of our soul, which is our connection to the essential beauty and joy of our greater heart; that which is shared among us. The poet does this through the sound and feeling of words, not necessarily through their literal meanings. As Shelly says, "the poet strips the veil of familiarity from the world and lays bare the naked and sleeping beauty, which is the spirit of its forms." Spirit gives rise to form; there are unseen causes underlying all beings, things and situations, and if you probe deep enough there is beauty. Poetry may offer some keys to these mysteries.

PART 1 1970s ROOTS — Deconstruction: Prune Back Hard to Establish a Better Root System

Sometime around 1972 I started to write poems. I wrote them in two red notebooks, which I filled. There were hundreds of poems in those books. I destroyed the notebooks one day because I felt like they were just filled with unnecessary human-ego-made stuff. The poems included in Part 1 are the ones that I could recall from memory some years after. A few of the poems are short because they are just fragments, all I can remember of the originals. But most of the poems are short because I was attempting to write poems that were brief, concise and could be remembered and recited without having to read them from a piece of paper.

The seventies was the deconstructive period of my life. I began to contemplate the same idea over and over. I visualized myself being dropped off near a forest with only the clothes I was wearing and with no survival tools other than what I carried around inside of me. I imagined that I would experience a gradual dropping away of all that was superfluous to my life. What would be left of "me" would be bare bones and then, I felt, I would be able to perceive clearly what I was supposed to do and how I was to do it. The image of taking a piece of paper and cutting it first in half, then into quarters, and so forth, on and on to see what possibly could be left acted as an abstract model for me in my contemplation of zero. Many circumstances rose up to prevent my bare bones forest adventure from manifesting in the way I had imagined it. In other ways it did manifest, but the stripping away occurred over time, over a decade in fact, and it might have started with poetry.

My boyfriend at the time, Bill Wikstrom, a painter and sculptor, introduced me to John Rogers, a poet who lived in a small wooden house, basically a shack, on the beach in Magnolia, a neighborhood of Seattle. He was a member of a group of local poets. They called themselves the "Sons and Daughters of Dementia" and got together every month or so at John's house to read and critique each other's work. He hosted a weekly poetry show on a local radio station. John also worked in a used book and record store in the University district called Puss and Books, where all of us hippies went to buy our records and books.

One evening John invited us to a poetry reading at his beach house. I sat in a corner very shy and self-conscious, but all the same I was enthralled by the passion being openly expressed through the music of the words I heard. To listen to everyone offer commentary to each other that was often quite critical was just as exciting as listening to the recitation of the poems. I returned a few more times, sitting as still as a dormouse in the corner.

John gave me a book of poetry by Edgar Allan Poe and said, "The next time you come to the beach house you should read a poem." I said, "I can't write poems." "That doesn't matter, you love Poe, read one of his poems."

When I came to the reading I stood up and started to read, "A Dream Within A Dream," but I found that after the first couple of lines I knew the poem by heart and so I put the book down and continued reciting, allowed the rhythm of it to come through my voice and body. That evening was a magical shift for me as I took a huge step out of my narrow, self-centered, self-conscious world and sailed upon a sea of sound.

> *Take this kiss upon the brow!*
> *And, in parting from you now,*
> *Thus much let me avow —*
> *You are not wrong, who deem*
> *That my days have been a dream;*
> *Yet if hope has flown away*
> *In a night, or in a day,*
> *In a vision or in none,*
> *Is it therefore the less gone?*
> *All that we see or seem*
> *Is but a dream within a dream.*
>
> *I stand amid the roar*
> *Of a surf tormented shore,*
> *And I hold within my hand*
> *Grains of the golden sand —*
> *How few! Yet how they creep*
> *Through my fingers to the deep,*
> *While I weep — while I weep!*
> *O God! Can I not grasp*
> *Them with a tighter clasp?*
> *O God can I not save*
> *One from the pitiless wave?*
> *Is all that we see or seem*
> *But a dream within a dream?*
>   *— Edgar Allen Poe*

The next day as I was sitting on the front porch of my house my first poem came out. I ran back into the house to get a pencil to write it down. That poem was:

We see the everlastingness
in everything that's passing
We become that everlastingness
through everything that's passing

John gave me a hard-covered blank red book for me to write my poetry in. After I filled that book, he gave me a second book and I filled it too. But one day the dark forces inside of me were winning, and I felt that these books of poems were just stupid, ego-driven, banal reflections. I felt bad about cluttering up the world with more of "my" stuff, so I made a fire in the driveway and burned the books.

Some months after my poetry suicide, with John's encouragement, I picked myself out of the ashes and with the few bits of poetic lines remaining in my head began again to make more stuff. How or why I did that I don't know...I guess I couldn't help myself.

Bob Dylan was the best poet I had ever heard, and he knew how to use his breath to construct words musically into phrases, which became song. That was intensely interesting to me. It seemed that if poetry was to get to the root of the situation, music had to be involved, because music is closest to the realm of spirit and that idea captivated me. After all, spirit is the origin of everything, and who doesn't want to know everything?

I joined a poetry art band called *The New Fauvist Revue* with Bill Wikstrom, John Rogers and guitarist Steve Turner. We borrowed the name from the Fauvist French art movement of the early nineteen hundreds. *Fauve* means wild beast. Ken Nordine and the Last Poets heavily influenced us. We would take turns with the microphone reciting our poems while the others backed us with musical instrumentation. John played drums, Bill saxophone, while I rattled a tambourine. The real step into freedom came with improvisation. To be able to recite original lines spontaneously, not to read from a piece of paper, became my goal. I was willing to fall on my face thousands of times to get there. I knew that to be able to do this successfully I had to establish a strong connection to a core place inside, a subtle yet rich place of source. My experimenting with improvisation in poetry converged with my budding practice of meditation, which I would do by reciting the mantra "let go," aligning the words with the inhalation and exhalation of the breath.

Words move, and all movement happens by means of breathing. The breath is life itself — spirit. What causes the animation of form is spirit, and spirit is sound. Matter is sound slowed down so that the eyes can see it Everything is sound.

The next turning point occurred during the mid-70s when I had reached the depths of despair in my self-loathing. Some years before, in 1972,

I had given birth to a daughter and given her up for adoption. The grief and guilt I felt was traumatic and terrible. It culminated in an attempt at suicide involving throwing myself into on-coming traffic during rush hour on the busy street near where I lived in a house with Bill, my brother, Marty and sister, Ivy. My sister, standing in a second floor bedroom window, saw what I was doing and ran down to the street. Pulling me out of traffic, she slapped me and asked what I thought I was doing. I was too overwrought and self-involved to even answer amidst the tears. She said sternly and with great maturity for a young woman of only nineteen, "If a driver of one of those cars was to hit and kill you how do you think they would feel for the rest of their life?" That question pulled me to my senses because from within my self-centered bubble I had never considered that my sadness and suffering might be having an effect upon others around me. I decided then that I would try to do something with my life to inspire or uplift others, and I dedicated myself to acquiring artistic skills, which I thought I could use to achieve that goal. That meant discipline and daily hard work, which I embraced through self-study first involving reading, writing, music and painting.

Soon, under the guidance of Randy Hall, I added alchemy to my studies. He taught me how to observe, using a microscope, the crystalline shapes of biochemical cell salts. A breakthrough happened one day as I was waiting for the water on a slide to evaporate. I fell to daydreaming thinking about our neighbor and his dog who lived downstairs and wondered where he takes her for walks. After a few moments, I realized I had lost my concentration and directed my gaze back to the slide to see that the water had dried and the crystal shapes of the salts had clumped together to form a very recognizable picture of a man and a dog! That was an *aha* moment revealing to me the power of our thoughts, even unconscious ones, upon physical reality. I was all the more determined to purify my mind of negativity and train myself to consciously focus on positive thoughts. Around this time Randy introduced me to the local Theosophical Society Library, where I began to work, furthering my studies in mysticism. It was here that I started to read yogic texts.

In 1974 I enrolled as a dance student at the University of Washington. At that time I was very disconnected from my body and couldn't figure out my left foot from my right. Although I was the worst student in the classes, I was one of the most persistent. Unlike most of my classmates, I wasn't enrolled in the program to become a professional dancer or teacher; I was there for therapeutic reasons. I was trying to save myself from killing myself. The teachers and other students didn't take me as a serious contender or competitor but took pity on me — the terribly thin girl who couldn't dance well but seemed to always be there. I was at the ballet bar for my first class at 8 a.m. and went home most nights after rehearsals at 10 p.m. I just always showed up, and all of that practice paid off in the end; it changed me. The discipline required by the arts I was studying magically shifted my perception. In the tradition of Alchemy there is a saying, "Through repetition, the magic is forced to rise."

1. 1972 Subject: Time

Everlastingness

We see the everlastingness
      in everything that's passing
We become that everlastingness
      through everything that's passing

1. Notes: The changeful nature of time allows us to know eternity, the changeless reality. It is only through experience that we can come to understand this process. Without time there is no experience, nor even existence. Time is a gift from nature that prevents everything from happening all at once. Time gives us space to comprehend reality. This is the first poem I ever wrote. I remember waking up one morning and reciting it out loud. I then sat on the front porch of my house in Seattle and with a pencil wrote it down.

2. 1972 Subject: Portrait

Kershawn

Kershawn Kershawn
      Metal plate in head
      and sling on arm

2. Notes: Kershawn (gurr-shawn) was a neighbor who lived down the street in his sister's house. Born in Ukraine, he had immigrated to the U.S. in his twenties and become a citizen. He had voluntarily enlisted in the military to go to Vietnam as a way of proving his patriotism. When we met him he had just been released from an army hospital where he was treated for multiple war wounds and depression. I remember him as a large man maybe six three or four with reddish hair and skin, an unkempt wiry beard and very puffy hands with short swollen fingers, minus one thumb. More than half of his head had been blown off, and because of that most of his skull had become a shallow, convex bowl lined with metal. His right arm had also been badly injured and was in a sling. He had all but lost the use of his right leg and walked by supporting his left hand on a cane, dragging his right leg along. He had been a poet before the war and now was unable to hold a pen to write anything, and this along with other circumstances made him frustrated and angry.

To ease his frustration and anger he took drugs. Before the war he assured us he never took drugs and equated the drug culture with the "good-for-nothing, lazy hippies who were destroying this country." When I knew him, he spent most of his time with us hippie types. He bought his heroin from the people who lived next door to us and liked to hang out at our house for a bit of art and poetry. When I would sit on my front porch I could see him as he left his house hobbling to get his drugs and I wrote a poem about him. Those three lines are all that exist from the original poem, but they seem to stand on their own as a portrait.

3. *1972 Subject: Life*

Kesey's Kids

A bold move
Why not?
        we just want to say, "Hi"
Come on in, here's a plate of spaghetti
        We were just talking
about sheep and government creeps
Do you know the pranksters?
        Hey, Krassner get up and let the kids have
your seat
        What brings you to us freaks?"

Talking till the moon rose high

In a sleeping bag under a tree
    sunshine wakes us up
Norma Faye offers coffee from a cup
    as we watch Kesey's kids go off to school
Sometimes a bold move can land you
    in the middle of a great notion
Or on a bus named Further

3. Notes: This poem tells of a time when I visited Ken Kesey, author of *One Flew over the Cuckoo's Nest* and *Sometimes a Great Notion* and his friends, the Merry Pranksters, of whom writer and comedian Paul Krassner was one, at his home in Oregon. In June 1971, I embarked on a road trip with my friend Marty Hevly. We hitchhiked from Seattle to Los Angeles. When we had been dropped off at a gas station one early evening somewhere in Eugene, Oregon, Marty said to me, "Wow, we are in Eugene. Wouldn't it be great to run into Ken Kesey — he lives around here, I think, in a place called Pleasant Hill, or Pleasant Valley, something like that." "Well," I replied, "Let's do it, let's go find him." "What, just knock on his door?" "Why not? The worst he could do would be not answer." "He might consider us annoying trespassers and call the police or take a hose and spray us away." "I am positive that Ken Kesey is not going to call the police. C'mon, let's try. It will be fun."

We inquired at the gas station which way was Pleasant Hill. "Up that way a few miles." We hitched a ride pretty quickly with a guy in a pickup truck, "Where y'all goin'?" "Do you know where Pleasant Hill is?" "Yeah sure. You goin' up to Kesey's farm?" Marty's mouth dropped and he shot a look of disbelief at me. "Yep," I said, "that's where we're going." "Fine, it's on my way home, hop in." We were dropped off and walked the driveway to the Kesey home, knocked on the door and were greeted by Norma Faye, Kesey's wife, "Yes?" "Is Ken Kesey at home?" we enquired. "Are you friends of his?" "We're fans!" "Ah...okay, wait here," and she closed the door. After a moment or so she came back and graciously said, "You're in luck, all the Pranksters have arrived today. We're having a bit of a party. Come on in and join us."

The last line of the poem mentions the famous psychedelic painted bus named *Further* which Kesey and the Pranksters drove around. The name, I am guessing, was a tongue in cheek reference to the Gates of Hercules, which according to Greek mythology marked the extent of the hero's travels and bore the epitaph "nothing further beyond," as Hercules was thought to have discovered the end of the world. Then in the sixteenth century, after the discovery of America, which obviously lies beyond the end of the world, the Spanish King, who was also the pope, created a new coat of arms from the image of the Pillars of Hercules, but this time with the Latin words *plus ultra*, inscribed on the banner, which translates into English as, *Further Beyond*. For indeed America was further beyond what the old world had imagined. This image of the Pillars of Hercules continued to morph over time and has become our U.S. symbol for the dollar: $.

4. *1972 Subject: Culture, Perception*

Truth Lies

Where does the truth lie?
The truth lies in all things
All things lie apart from the truth
All things lie a part of the truth

What is the truth?
No one knows
But together we can know
You are me and I am you and
We are lying in this thing together
Like fishes in a sweater
Together to gather two-gether
We *are* this thing *together*

4. *Notes:* The absolute truth is impossible to perceive with the thinking mind. The mind knows what it knows only through the process of thought, which is made up of words and images. Words and images are lies, because they only provide a partial glimpse into the truth they represent. We cannot tell the whole truth in words. Only the whole in its entirety is true. But through the recognition that everyone, everything, every moment is precious and valid to the whole, we can come close to knowing what is whole, what is true. This poem is a reflection on the conflict between Nature and Spirit. Many

religions tell us that spirit is truth and that nature lies, seductively deceiving us. I am offering the idea that this isn't so and that nature and spirit are inseparable — to know one is to know the other — but in order to glimpse the truth in nature you have to see it as more than a mere collection of things.

God is truth and everything is God, including the creation — the natural world of seemingly separate forms. We overcome separateness through togetherness. The most telling sign of intelligence in a person, is shown through their ability to make connections. An intelligent person looks for sameness not just differences.

No one of us alone can know the truth; each of us knows our own facet of it only. By attempting to put things together we can begin to perceive the truth. Separating and standing apart will only yield more alienation from the whole, which is the truth. So communication is the key to uncovering the truth. Through listening communication is possible, and one must be receptive in order to listen. Through communication we come together and communally we can know the truth by realizing our being-ness together *as* the truth.

5. 1973 Subject: Portrait

My Brother

My brother has stars for eyes and
A mouth that cries
Real blues
Tears linger on hairs
Real long lashes
Cut and bleeding gashes
A bluebird flies
As rainbows ride
Above the
Rhythms of his beating heart
Twenty-two equinox baby you
Best chance for freedom
Sad to see a turtle imprisoned

Marty-man rubber band sailor tan
Which wisp of smoke will you float
On tonight
When you go to the stars
A bluebird flies
As rainbows ride
Above the
Rhythms of your beating heart

5. *Notes:* My brother Marty embodied the essence of the lotus, which rises without pretension out of muck. His totem animal was the bluebird of happiness, who could transcend tragedy, similar to the lotus. He was a gifted blues singer, his birthday was September 22, and his eyelashes, were very long. Endowed with great empathy, seeing a turtle imprisoned in a zoo aquarium could cause him to cry for days. I speak of his bleeding cuts and how he was able to sublimate his suffering enabling him to fly high beyond rainbows.

6. *1973 Subject: Poetry*

Zebra

The zebra is innocent
Black and white as penguins might
But seldom do
There is no need to
Up there on the polar cap
In fact what can hap'
To call attention to
The purity of these creatures' souls
And the integration of their coats
I'm told
Shine in reflection
Illuminating the selection

The contradicting contrasts
Growing out from hides
And billowing over bodies of dilection
Pray for the slain where the black and white
Gets rained on by the blood of innocence

6. *Notes:* Some poems come from ideas that I am trying to work out, while others just appear and I more or less transcribe what I hear, this poem is one of those. The poem taught me something about writing — words on a page — positive and negative, black strokes on a white background that come to mean something terribly important, at least to the writer. "The zebra is innocent" because I am just using her to create an opening line to allow the rest of the poem to unfold. Things only appear as they do because we contrast them with other things. Poetry is an attempt to dissolve the rigid boundaries imposed by the thinking process, which separates things into camps of black and white, or thises and thats. In stretching those boundaries, poetry can blow your mind, allowing you to escape the prison of predictability. And yes, *dilection* is a made-up word.

7. *1974 Subject: Perception, Yoga*

Iguana Eggs

Iguana eggs
You eat them
All of these
Find them
Into the desert
Go seek

7. *Notes:* When you have a clear intention and you deliberately remain focused on that intention for some time, you will experience an opening into an area of realization that you would not have been able to arrive at without that focused intention. While taking a class in Indian Culture in college, I saw a documentary film about the *Ashvamedha*, the Vedic horse sacrifice, where a horse is killed then brought back to life by means of mantra. According to the

filmmakers, it was the last such legal ritual of this type allowed before the British outlawed such Vedic practices in India. Today it is agreed among most Hindus that a ritual like this cannot be performed in our modern times because no one is able to recite the mantras effectively to accomplish raising the dead. Regardless, I do not support the ritualized killing of any being and visualize the day that all human beings view the killing of other animals for any purpose as unethical and indefensible. Because this film showed a beautiful and noble horse at its prime being killed, it certainly could be akin to a pornographic snuff film in which someone actually is murdered while the cameras are rolling. I found that to be horrible and unforgivable. Notwithstanding that, I was able to draw something positive from what I saw in the film beyond the killing of the horse. What was especially noteworthy for me, at least as far as inspiring a dance as well as this poem, was the preparation of the site where the ritual was to take place.

The film showed a priest clearing a plot of land. I remember his intense concentration: after he chose the plot, he removed all small bushes and plants, as well as all protruding stones. The area was then leveled and swept with a fine broom by another person bending low toward the ground. It took two or three days to sweep the area to a smooth surface, which was then sprinkled carefully with water so that all the dust settled. Next a layer of cow dung was smoothed and leveled over the surface and left to dry completely, which took some days. Then large baskets of small, flat stones were brought to the site. Another priest appeared and began placing (*nyasa*) stones purposely. He did this while continuously chanting mantra, placing each stone on the ground along with elaborate hand mudras. It took him several weeks to complete the laying of the stones, which were to form the foundation for the ritual to take place. He had an expression of acute, focused intention on something that could be seen as mundane — just putting some stones down on the ground. I imagine if we were to do this today, we would probably just back a truck up to the site, pour some gravel, cover with concrete then level it off. It reminded me of the power of intention and its ability to create a particular atmosphere. I imagine that such elaborate religious ritual preparation prior to the intentional killing of an animal somehow alleviated the guilt that must accompany such an act. We should not forget that the precursor to our modern-day slaughterhouse was the ritual sacrifice/slaughter of animals in temples and consecrated ground as depicted in this film.

I wrote this poem after I saw the film. I also used it as the basis for choreographing a dance of the same name, *Iguana Eggs*. At one point in the dance all six dancers had to arrive at a designated spot on the edge of the stage; stand completely still; lean forward; incline their bodies toward the audience; make eye contact with just one member of the audience; silently repeat the poem a certain number of times (for each dancer it was a different number); gaze intently into the eyes of that audience member; then move into the next dance phrase.

8. *1974 Subject: Nature*

Tears

Have you seen the tears on a window pane?
Water condensing into drops of rain

Have you seen the apples swim?
Inside the shoes with everything

They were there like a couple
Of chairs in the hallway

8. *Notes:* Feelings are not the sole property of human beings. All of nature, everyone (animate) and every thing (seemingly inanimate) feels as well as communicates. If you have the ability to listen, you can hear that the whole world is alive.

9. *1976 Subject: Mysticism*

Silver Needles

Silver needles falling from the sky
I don't think so
I could feel though
Electrified
Slowly now

Paint my throat with iodine
Up and up and around and through
My vision caught the heavenly hue
There were two mountain goats
Introduced to me
Their names were Dee
And their name was A
Oh tell me please, and
I asked the way,
"Sure-footed for sure is the
Only way
Slowly now through the night
Continue past the day
Go to all space
Become so dense you are transparent."

9. *Notes:* During this decade I found it difficult to eat food. I didn't want things inside of my body and was trying to clear out my mind as well to get to the "bare-bones" of the matter. I was very thin and naively attempted to increase my thinness by painting medicinal iodine over my thyroid gland as well as eating very little. This fasting state induced visions. Often, I would see a shower of shiny silver needles, falling through the air above and just to the right of my head. Some sort of insight or charge of creativity always followed this vision. This poem is about those needles.

10. *1976 Subject: Nature*

Atoms of Air

There are atoms of air in your lungs
That were once in the lungs of everyone
Who has ever lived and is living now
We are breathing each other

10. *Notes:* I must have read the idea expressed in this poem somewhere. During this time I was studying alchemy, and I liked reading science as well as pseudo-science books. I had a great interest in nature and in the question of what makes the various forms of nature appear various. I was trying to find the "universal solvent," or what connects everything to everything, the motivator, the cause, or what makes form, form.

11. *1976 Subject: Alchemy*

Who Calls the Walker

Who calls the walker
Here or there
Moving along without a care
The one who knows that
Will know how to alter
A river's water

11. *Notes:* Reflection on God as the ultimate doer. All is God's doing; there is nothing done outside of God.

12. *1977 Subject: Portrait*

Owena

Owena
Oweena
Oh wane nah
Oh wee one...none
You came to me
You came through me
At four thirty
A one and a zero
You and me

How could I hold you?
How could I give you?
Away from me
Oh wane nah

12. *Notes:* Owena is the name I was going to give my baby daughter. It is the name I have always called her in my mind. I know it is an odd name; I am not even sure where it came from. Owena was born on August 10, 1972, at 4:30 in the afternoon. I gave her up for adoption. I knew before I signed the legal papers that I would never get over the loss, that it would shape my life. I regret that I did not have the courage to keep her close to me. I regret so much that I cannot ever express through words thought, spoken or written. How I let this happen is still a mystery. I don't know if I will ever solve it, but I keep trying to be the kind of person that she may one day want to know.

13. *1977 Subject: Nature*

Sand Dollar

Part One: The Sea
Lightening illumines frothy blue
Wet tongue relentlessly lapping
Insatiable appetite for a shore of grits
Never satisfied big mouth spits out the many
And the few diamonds
Phosphorus in the night light
Again and again
Only to take another toothless bite
They say the sea is wild
That's probably why we have been trying to
Tame, ride and empty her
Since we first learned how to float a boat
The idea being: when there is nothing left
The spirit is quelled, contained in its vacancy

Even so nighttime is always better at the beach
When the sun has gone to sleep
Better time to hear the surf tormented shore
And lament all that has been lost
Because you could not hold
Within your hands anything for long no one can
Watch what you love seep like golden sand
Through your fingers to the deep while you weep
Go ahead and cry to God for all the things
You cannot keep

Part Two: The Ghosts
Shakin' wakin' lyin' on top of the sea
Watchin' waitin' in a circle of three
Amateur occultists for sure are we
But nonetheless we will do what we can
A painter, a cat who eats tomatoes, and me

Dancin' drinkin' fightin' over she
Two died taking the lives of one another
Now their lust for her long forgotten
They fly as the wind sweeps them so many times
To the rooftop surface of the Sand Dollar
No guns or knives tonight
Only wind whips

Part Three: The Shell
On one side the Easter lily
Its center is a star
When this crusted eye breaks open
Five white doves await release

Echinoids, sea cucumbers, lilies, urchins and starfish
Soft inside hard as bone when left to die

Sand dollars are mermaid money
Ghosts: shells of things once alive
Taken out of their element now found
Dry on dry land
Stars they were of their own lives
With phalanges five they walked the sea
Out-fitted in maroon-colored suits
Waving moveable fuzzy arms which scoop
Liquid food into a watery heart
Whose job it is to circulate this seafood
Into the internal watery-circulatory system
Of this interior sandcastle of existence

What could it mean to be so watery?
A substance in a flowing condition whose shape
But not volume can be changed
Living forms are mostly water
It is what makes movement possible
People are always morphing into others
Isn't this what eating is about? Love for that matter?
Eaten alive by love, to drown in its watery grasp
Eat your heart out, as they say

The very best time for collecting is
When the tide is out
After a heavy storm
Many skeletons have been dredged up
By the increased wave action.

You can find them nestled flat against the wet sand
Fragile discs still longing for another chance another
Round of it
What can we see for the future of the sea?
I see a world where there is no *Seaworld*

13. *Notes:* The Sand Dollar was the name of a motel in the small coastal town of Pacific Beach, Washington, where I lived with Bill Wikstrom and Eva, the cat, during the summer of 1973. I was still mourning the loss of my baby. In Part 1 there are references to the poem "A Dream Within A Dream" by Edgar Allen Poe, which tells of a lost love slipping through fingers like grains of sand. The motel was very near the beach where I would often walk alone both in the daytime and at night.

It was in the parking lot of this motel that we first found Eva, a black and white kitten. Bill and I lived on the top floor of the motel and received free rent in exchange for managing the place, which had six tenants. We had been told by one of the tenants, a Native American who was also a member of a local Shaker community, that the place was haunted by two ghosts—men who had fought and killed each other on the roof of the motel about 40 years before. During certain nights, and especially when there was a storm, we would hear the ghosts fighting. This was very scary to us.

The Sand Dollar Motel was so named because of the numerous sand dollar shells that could be found along the beach nearby. Sand dollars are part of the class of marine animals known as echinoids, spiny skinned creatures also related to starfish and sea urchins. When alive they are outfitted in dark red skins with moveable spines, but by the time the skeleton washes up on the beach, its velvety covering is long gone, and it is difficult to believe that the hard-bleached shell was once alive. The shells resemble coins and are thought by some to be used by mermaids as their money.

14. *1972-79 Subject: Poetry*

First Lines

Freedom is a psycho-kinetic skill
Fantasies of the past reduce the future to last
Dreams are punished by their fulfillment
Are we more than the sights and sounds of our culture?
Letters on a page mean something because the reader
    believes the language
There is no difference between yes and no
    is this true? Well, yes and no
What is looking is what is looking for

Matter is momentary interaction of waves/of fields/of states/of grains
Matter is sound, slowed down, so that the eye can see it
We cannot eliminate ourselves from the picture, we are a part of it
When we look, we see ourselves
We are only transmitters, locked in an endlessness
Death is not knowing how to join beginning with end
Death will be the last thing to die
Re-fuse
Who gave us God-given rights?
There is no god but you
We are the gods, we are the image makers
What makes form, form?
The maker of the form is the form
Is it hunger or is it greed, who is determining your need?
Sex is a dis-ease, Sex is separation
    alchemy is the yoga of sex
One plus one equals one
Re-member the future
Become independent — dependent inward
When all know "IS" why make it?
We are *in* this thing together — we *are* this thing together
The spaces move closer together, to gather two-gether
Life and death are much the same, life is quicker
Christ was divine because he admitted the fact
Meet me on a bridge, the corpus callosum
I am not a sandwich; I know who the Bee Gees are
Response-ability — the ability to respond
Let us come to our senses, they have been waiting for us for so long
Thought gives way eventually to solid objects
Performance is not dis-play, it is play, actual experience
Do not represent transformation, be transforming, be-living, believing
Life is a representation of life
When time will be no longer
No longer have to explain why

We see the everlastingness in everything that's passing
This is the world, this is the whorl, round and round we go
Atmosphere means around a sphere
    hear here
Bodies are weighted, they watch the clock
Desire issues necessity, necessity mortality
One thing we happen to see is how it happens to be
You only must go to get there
Living is cultivating a garden of desire
Habits are not distractions from life they are the stuff of life
The worth of a habit is in its stabilizing effect upon time
To become so dense you are transparent
The mind is the matter
The ground of being is dissolving out from under our feet
    we must turn upside down to feel stable
The reaffirmation of mystification is impractical art
Art is reconstruction — art is the retelling of Is
It is all plastic, it's malleable, it moves
The need to know no need to know
Dis-aster means away from the star
Apocalypse means to uncover, reveal, unveil and stand naked
To evolve is to roll out — entropy is turning in
Eternity is happening now

14. *Notes:* Most often a poem comes to me in the form of a message, as I wake up in the morning and hear the first line. This poem is made up entirely of first lines, each originally intended to be developed into a poem. Some of these first lines made their way into poems, some never went further than this, and some merely sparked ideas for other poems.

PART 2 1980s SHOOTS — Reconstruction:
New Growth, Recreating Myself

The 1980s were a time of great growth and transformation for me. During the 1970s, suffering from the traumatic loss of my baby, I found eating difficult, because I could not bear the feeling of anything inside of me. Needless to say sex was also abhorrent to me, and due to emotional stress and weight loss, my menstrual cycle stopped. But then, near the dawn of the new decade, during a dramatic total solar eclipse my period mysteriously returned again after a seven-year absence. That overnight incident instigated a psychokinetic transformation that propelled me into the next phase of my life and a decade of intense artistic creativity that involved public performances.

I made a conscious commitment to live a productive life, not in spite of what I had gone through, but to try to transform what had been difficult, challenging and traumatic into something artistic, which optimistically and perhaps naively, I felt might be beneficial to the world. I felt that through art one could give back something uplifting to the world.

During this decade, I focused on artistic pursuits, painting as well as performances involving, music, dance and poetry. Fortunately during the previous years I had developed good "study habits." Each day I spent a certain amount of time sitting at my art table writing and painting. Through this practice I developed a body of work. I didn't feel as though I had done enough if at the end of the day I hadn't produced at least one poem or one painting.

In 1980 after six years at the University of Washington, I graduated with a degree in dance and performed my senior piece at the Dance Student Showcase. The piece was entitled *Iguana Eggs* after a poem I had written (see #7). It featured live music from a local Seattle progressive rock band led by my poet friend John Rogers on drums, with his wife Helena playing guitar. To say we rocked the house would be an understatement. Never before had the hallowed halls of the U. of W. Dance Department hosted a live band of this type. The choreography, performed by six dancers — two men in white sleeveless t-shirts with black tights and four women in black slips with bare legs — was smart, surreal and sexy. The makeup was dramatic with whitened skin and purple lipstick.

I think my dance professors were a bit shocked, but they were also proud of me, as they had borne witness to the power of art to transform a shy, anorexic girl who had nearly committed suicide, into a mature choreographer. The graduation piece was my own coming out after a long winter. I felt like a butterfly emerging from its cocoon. The sad, helpless victim was gone. Coinciding with this creative outburst was a charged sexuality and charisma that I hadn't anticipated. I was becoming more attractive; people were noticing and approaching me.

The night of the dance concert, writers, dance critics and art explorers Gary Reel and his friend Jae Carlsson were in the audience. Gary wrote a review, which appeared in the New York Art Magazine *Art Express*, proclaiming that I had created the best choreography of the post-modern era. Both of these highly sophisticated and educated men became devoted fans, and together with several other like-minded friends we quickly began to develop an intense artistic community which resulted in many projects, including two magazines, the band Audio Letter, music and dance concerts, operas and the Salon Apocalypse. Many of my friends considered themselves political activists, and often we would go out with cans of spray paint to graffiti poetic messages on walls and park benches. I got good at creating slogans like: "There is no god but you," "Freedom is a Psycho-Kinetic Skill," "How is your response-ability?," "Go to all space," "What makes form, form?" and "Are you feeding dog-meat to your dog?"

After my graduation from the university, explosive, creative ideas poured out of me and I was fortunate to have the enthusiastic support of skilled collaborators to work with. My student advisor, avant-garde musician, Stuart Dempster and I began to perform together. Kathleen Hunt, Kat Allen and Lisa Ravenholt, dancers who I had befriended at the dance department of the university, continued to collaborate with me on performance projects. We created *Moon Food* — a dance company named after G.I. Gurdjieff's notion that life on Earth was a garden that provided food for the moon.

Around this time I met Sue Ann Harkey, a photographer, who had moved to Seattle from Wenatchee, a town in Eastern Washington. She wasn't a dancer but that didn't matter because we decided we would become musicians and began developing a band we called Audio Letter. Neither one of us was a practiced musician, but we really wanted to say something and felt that music could be the best medium for us. Exactly what we wanted to say and how, we weren't sure, but felt confident that we would find out through improvisation. It was a courageous step and we were filled with a sense of adventure. Sue Ann focused on guitar, developing a unique sound, while I supplied vocals and a bit of violin.

Steve Starwich, an inventor, created an electronic musical instrument for me that he called the sharona-phone. It was a 10" x 8" metal box with a strap that I could wear like a purse over my shoulder. It had two knobs that controlled volume and pitch; it was similar to a theramin, although much simpler.

Throughout the 1970s I had been living with artist Bill Wikstrom, but after graduation and my artistic "explosion," I gained the confidence to leave the relationship and move out of the house we shared together. I settled into a loft in downtown Seattle at 84 Seneca Street, which belonged to my old friend and alchemy teacher, photographer Randy Hall. The space was one large long rectangle room, with old wood floors, exposed brick on three sides and almost floor to ceiling windows. A small corner of the loft was my living space, a wooden-frame narrow bed, a table, a chair, an electric hotplate, and a saucepan, which I used to boil water.

Shortly after we broke up, Bill became romantically involved with a gifted painter, Isabel Kahn, with whom I became very good friends. Isabel had studied some yoga and she was gracious enough to share some of her experiences, teaching me many yoga asanas. During the early 1980s, Isabel and I, along with my dancer friends, Kathleen Hunt and Kat Allen, collaborated together and performed some very innovative performance pieces that incorporated yoga, painting, poetry, music and dance. Often Bill would create painted sets for these performance pieces.

Audio Letter became very active and we were playing two or three gigs a week. This was the punk rock era and we were known for our political messages, but we also had a bit too much mysticism and artsy-ness about us to gain a lot of respect from the hard-core scene. Even so we had a growing cult following. It was during this time (early 1980s) that I met Perry Phillips and his friends, who were all highly intellectual, politically oriented, left-leaning young men. I fell in love with Perry and we became deeply involved romantically as well as politically. Our relationship challenged me to rise to a level of intellectual and literary fluency that I had neglected to develop before. I wanted to be able to stand my ground with him as well as his academic friends who had studied philosophy and could quote Marx, Engels and Hegel. They were really keen on the French Situationists, especially the writers Guy Debord (*The Society of the Spectacle*) and Raoul Vaneigem (*The Revolution of Everyday Life*) whose points of view fueled their enthusiasm for political/social revolution. Even though these young men professed to be anarchists, and were bent on challenging societal norms, in particular capitalism and sexism, on a personal level they seemed to still be suffering from the disease of misogyny. Though, I will say in their defense, that they were trying to cure themselves. Still, as a woman, I suffered my share of the normal macho disrespect prevalent at the time. They often accused me of being too conventional because I preferred monogamy, wasn't gay or bisexual, attended ballet class, wore my hair long and un-spiked, and didn't smoke pot. To my favor, I listened to the Clash, but my eclectic range of music also included Mozart, classical Indian singer M.S. Subbulakshmi and The Incredible String Band, which to them were all too retro, certainly not up to the urgency of the times. But nonetheless it only fueled my drive to meet their rational, pragmatic intellectualism with emotional, spiritual and artistic skill.

In 1980 Perry gave me a manual typewriter. This gift was a major step in my formative years as a writer. Before that I had written my poems and essays in longhand, usually with a pencil. Typing gave me a new dimension to explore. I loved the rhythmic sound of the machine and the smell of the ink cartridge and how you could print copies using carbon paper. What I wrote looked more serious, more professional when typed out, also it could be read easier by others. Around this same time another friend gave me the *Oxford English Dictionary*. This version of the massive *OED* was the "compact edition" — condensed into two heavy volumes. Because the reduction of the type size was considerable a magnifying glass was included with the books. With the *OED*, not only did my spelling improve but the study of words and their etymology became my new obsession. Now with a typewriter and a dictionary I became more and more immersed in the cerebral world of ideas and articulating my findings through the art of writing.

Sue Ann and I, along with writers Jae Carlsson and Gary Reel, dancer Kathleen Hunt, Perry and two of his friends, Deran Ludd and Eric Muhs, embarked on an experiment and collectively formed an art/political study group that met weekly to discuss current events. We titled our meetings *The Salon Apocalypse*. The word apocalypse comes from the Greek word *apokos*, meaning to uncover or to reveal. I interpreted it as to become stripped bare or essentially exposed. The underlying implications of the word apocalypse were appealing to me, as I was striving to get to the bare bones, the roots of things and did not want to settle for living superficially, dwelling in symptoms, whining, complaining and blaming others or the world for my discontent.

The Salon Apocalypse discussions revolved around a specific focus. We took up heavy themes like murder, famine and greed. The salon was an attempt to create a community of like-minded beings who wanted to find ways to interact at a deeper level than what is commonly available in normal society — deeper than the ordinary dinner and/or drinks, which can quickly become mundane, where there is usually little room for creativity, and intellectual or spiritual growth. We had observed that often conversations at parties seem to involve talking but not necessarily much listening. The goal of our salons was to challenge the normal modes of communication, which we did through poetry, song and dance. Participants were encouraged to contribute to the discussion, not just by talking, but through artistic means, being careful not to fall into mere professing or performance for the sake of self-expression. We were striving to break down communication barriers and move into a more interactive, shared place that could lead to a broadening of knowledge and insight.

These salons yielded more than just inspiring conversation and performance. Two magazines, which we self-published, came out of these salons: *Group 28* and *Patio Table*. The magazines were sold in a local political bookstore, and we also gave them away to friends and others who we thought might be interested. We created a self-publishing company, called *Citizens for a Non-linear Future*, and under this heading we printed our stories, essays and poems, as well as made home-made cassette tapes of Audio Letter music. Also, in 1982 two of our friends, Peter Mumford and Chris Gray, helped publish a collection of my poems and essays in a little booklet called *Freedom is a Psycho-Kinetic Skill*.

The next turning point in my life occurred in 1982 when I naively went with my *Salon Apocalypse* friends to see *The Animals Film*. At the time I didn't know what the film was about but I was excited that musician Robert Wyatt, drummer from the Soft Machine, had contributed the soundtrack and actress Julie Christie was the narrator. I sat in the theater for two hours and twenty minutes while my life was altered forever by this British documentary, which probed the relationship between human beings and other animals. The film explored the cruel, sadistic, exploitive and inhumane ways that we human beings perceive and treat animals, how we use them for food, clothing, entertainment, and medical experimentation without any regard for their happiness or well-being. Non-human animals are not respected for the persons they are and are viewed as no more than objects — things to be exploited for monetary profit or careless whim.

My ignorance and misconceptions were shattered by this film. With my eyes and heart newly opened, I was forced to rethink art, as well as the purpose of the artist and what I was doing with my own life. If I wasn't contributing to stopping the insanity I saw depicted in this film, then I knew, without a doubt, that there was no value to my life. After this experience, I vowed to find a way to contribute to the eradication of the culturally accepted cruelty and exploitation of the other non-human animals with whom we share this planet. I had been an on-again, off-again vegetarian for years.

After the film, I became a vegetarian, though still putting milk in my coffee and tea, but shortly thereafter a committed vegan. The film caused me to realize that slavery is not over; animals are slaves. But it would still take me some years to find ways to effectively and artistically communicate the abolitionist/animal rights message, which asks of us all to extend unqualified kindness to non-human animals. It was frustrating to me that my friends, though seeing the *Animals Film* with me, did not feel moved to change their eating habits or to speak out on the subject. I was easily intimidated and remained silent about animal rights for a while, although with Audio Letter we did perform a song from one of my poems (see #18) where I sang about rendered dogs and cats being a common ingredient in pet food. I tried to focus on developing musical skills, which eventually I felt would empower me and give me the tools I needed to speak more effectively about issues that mattered to me — like the animals.

Shortly after the experience of seeing the film, I fell down some steep stairs and broke a vertebra in my spine, which resulted in a frightening paralysis of my right leg for two weeks. Perry paid little attention to my injury and the lack of support from him during this time made it all the more possible for me to say, "Yes," to Sue Ann when she suggested that we go to New York City to see what possibilities destiny might have for us there. It was clear that Perry and I were slipping away from each other and Eva, my beloved cat companion had died, intentionally poisoned by my landlord. There was more and more contempt leveled against Audio Letter in the Seattle press and among the local artistic intelligentsia. It all added up to me feeling that there was little in Seattle to hold me there. My back injury did heal enough for me to travel, and when it was time to go I did.

In the spring of 1983, Sue Ann and I went to New York City with a few of our *Salon Apocalypse* friends and our band Audio Letter. During our trip, we played a gig at the Life Café, which was a venue for new music owned by David Life on the Lower East Side. After the tour Sue Ann and I, encouraged by our newly made New York musician friends, John Zorn and Elliot Sharpe, returned to Seattle to pack our belongings and move to New York City a few months later. On June 1st, with my suitcase painted with the word APOCALYPSE, I moved, with Sue Ann into a small apartment on East 7th Street — a 6th floor walk-up building where Allen Ginsberg had once lived. At first to support my artistic work I was a bicycle messenger, which was a frantic, dare-devilish, short-lived job. But soon after I got a job at the Life Café, first as a cook and then as a waitress.

The Life Café was a artist/poet's café. New York City artists, poets and jazz musicians hung out there. Every Tuesday night was Poetry Night. There would be a featured reader and then an open mike. I read my poems on those nights. But I felt out of place with many of the other poets who fueled their poems with drugs and alcohol, talking about evil politicians, corporations, lost love affairs, decadent lives and normal everyday master/victim stuff—things that didn't interest me much. Although I had been part of the punk movement in Seattle, the Sid Vicious/Rimbaud/Verlain type of poet's life was not what I wanted to pursue. In fact I felt a strong inclination to overthrow the nihilism of self-centered drug-fueled expression. I yearned to communicate something of deeper truth and felt that in order to do that one must go beyond surface-level emotions like anger and lust. I suppose I saw myself as "old fashioned" in the sense that I am moved by beauty and not by ugliness, idealistically aligning myself with Keats who said, "what the imagination seizes as beauty must be truth."

Another reason I left Seattle was because I thought that many of my close friends were courting darkness and decadence and I did not see that as a future for myself. I was in no way tempted by the so-called romance of gratuitous sex or drugs or living in squalor or glorifying sickness as a political protest statement. I didn't agree with some of my friends that personal self-debasement was a valid critique of our current societal state. Perhaps this was because I knew a little about how karma works from some brief studies of Eastern philosophy and yoga during the time I lived in Seattle, so I did not find it satisfying to play victim and put all the blame on the government, parents and big business. I wanted to explore art as mystical revelation, that would somehow contribute not only to an upheaval of our present culture but also to sowing the seeds of a new way of life in which compassion and connection to nature and the Divine would be paramount.

Within a few months after starting work at the Life Café, my spinal injury flared up and kept getting worse and worse. Tara Rose was a yoga teacher as well as a waitress at the café, and she suggested that yoga might help relieve the pain in my back. I started attending her yoga classes, and soon, in an almost miraculous way, the yoga practice that she taught did heal my back. David and I worked long hours together at the café, and within a year we became intimately involved. This created an upheaval as David was married but soon to be divorced. David and I started to take Tara's classes together, and that began a series of creative, poetic, musical, and performance collaborations that continue to evolve to this day.

My dance partner Kathleen Hunt moved from Seattle to New York City so we could continue to work on developing our choreography together. We collaborated with David and Sue Ann to develop our performance art as mystical exploration. But this venture would be short lived, because Kathleen was drawn back to Seattle and by the end of the decade I was moving away from music and performance art and more toward the study, practice and teaching of yoga. Through delving into the mystical philosophy of yoga, especially by immersing myself in the study of *Patanjali's Yoga Sutra*, I was beginning to cultivate the understanding and the voice I needed to be an effective animal rights activist.

In 1986 David and I spent four months in India traveling and visiting many ashrams and meeting extraordinary yogis and a few saints. Although not every person in India is an enlightened being, the society certainly does respect a person who dedicates their life to seeking enlightenment. From what I had witnessed, everyone on a spiritual path was also totally devoted to living as compassionately as possible. For most people this meant extending kindness to animals and so they didn't eat them. Never before had we seen so many vegetarian restaurants. The highlight of our first Indian trip was meeting Swami Nirmalananda, the anarchist swami, vegan, yogi, activist and poet, meditating deep in the wild jungles of South India, feeding birds and sharing his modest home with a deer named Bambi!

David and I returned from India in 1987 and opened the first Jivamukti Yoga School on 8th street and Avenue B (renamed Charlie Parker Place), down the street from the Life Café. We would continue to travel yearly and sometimes twice yearly to India. Through the study of scripture and the physical practices of asana, pranayama and meditation, I started to realize the potential power of yoga to not only heal myself, physically and emotionally, but to heal many of the cultural ills of our time. Previously I had felt passionately that through art our culture could be healed and elevated, and I had devoted myself to becoming an articulate artist. But after discovering yoga, I moved away from purely artistic pursuits and focused more and more of my time on the art of yoga. I felt convinced that yoga had the power to dismantle our present culture, a way of life founded upon the enslavement of animals and the exploitation of the environment. The practice can free us from selfish concerns and provide us with the keys to happiness by teaching us that happiness is inside of us and comes through us when we bring happiness to others. Through yoga I was discovering the tools to live harmoniously with all other beings as well as with the planet and I yearned to share my discoveries.

Over the course of this decade my destiny as a spiritual teacher was emerging. At first, I resisted the role as it was in conflict with my desire for a quiet contemplative life with time to pursue art and spiritual development. Being a public figure, a teacher, that people came to for spiritual advice was a heavy responsibility that I did not feel up to task with. I felt I needed more time to devote to study, learning and practice and wasn't ready to enter into the extroverted "real world".

My relationship with David was fraught with contradictions. We were strongly attracted to each other, shared similar spiritual interests and were artistically matched. But after a brief romantic period it was obvious that our relationship was fated to be something more than conventional. By investing our creativity into artistic and spiritual pursuits, that eventually culminated into the development of Jivamukti Yoga, we realized it would be best to forgo a normal romantic partnership and go for a higher love. We would find another way to be together, aligning ourselves creatively for what we perceived as a greater good, for ourselves and the world.

The eighties was certainly an explosive decade for me. I went from living in the drizzle of quiet, rainy Seattle to moving to the artistic hot-bed of New York City's Lower East Side and together with David Life plunged deep into the study and practice of yoga. This was a productive time, primarily due to the many creative collaborators I was blessed to associate with in Seattle as well as New York. It felt like being part of a springtime growth spurt — a community shooting up like green stalks seeking sunshine and fresh air.

Many of the poems I wrote during this decade reveal an awakening of political awareness, sexual feelings as well as spiritual yearnings and how I attempted to resolve them in my search for how to live a useful happy life.

I Saw You Walking

Somnambulistic Narcoleptic
Somnambulistic Narcoleptic
Somnambulistic Narcoleptic

I saw you walking down the street
I saw you walking down the street
I saw you walking
I saw you walking
I saw you walking

15. *Notes:* This became a song for the band Audio Letter. Musically the band was creating a cacophony of atonal sound, so I stood motionless, opened my mouth, and in a dead-pan fashion let the repetition of these words, with their images of walking dead, cut through the din. The poem reflects on the condition of the atmosphere in our technological time. We naïvely pollute the etheric space with a dense web of electronic messages that bombard and damage the delicate instruments of our bodies. We are creating, perhaps ignorantly, a race of desensitized zombies.

16. *1980 Subject: Love*

On a Strand

On a strand on a single strand
Of a hair
You call an eyelash
I saw the whole unfolding
In your hair
On a single strand

16. *Note:* A love poem I wrote for the boy I wanted for my boyfriend at that

time, but who really wasn't that interested in me. I worked it into a song, which I sang in a few Audio Letter performances. It is clearly an homage to William Blake and is inspired by a line from his poem *Auguries of Innocence*: "To see a world in a grain of sand...and eternity in an hour...." It also obviously draws from the Marc Bolan song *Jeepster*: "you got the universe reclining in your hair..."

17. 1980 Subject: Culture

Babies

It starts with a kiss and it ends with a this
They were small and they were squishy we called them babies
In a thousand would be worlds
In a million could be years
I like you
You remind me something of my vision
While I'm awake I cannot dream
While I'm alive I cannot die
They were small and they were squishy we called them
Ba...bies...babies, babies, babies, babiessssssssss

17. *Note:* A poem that became an Audio Letter song. An unsympathetic look at unplanned and unwanted pregnancy that is often the result of engaging in sex irresponsibly and gratuitously.

18. 1980 Subject: Speciesism

Dog Food

Are you feeding dog meat to your dog?
This story starts at the dog pound

The dogs are gassed
 after exhaling their last
 are loaded into trucks
 driven downtown to the
 rendering plant
Then, they take and they separate
 the toes from the paws
 the liver from the spleen
 the tongue from the esophagus
 the middle ear from the inner ear
 the heart from the aorta
 the sartorius from the knee
 the trapezius from the clavicle
 the dermis from the epidermis
 the intestine from the anus
Boiling this all together in big vats
 stomachs, hair, ovaries, testicles,
 tibias, fibulas and fats
 cerebellums, noses, nipples,
 kidneys, ganglions, marrow,
 thyroids, teeth and axions
Condense it down and package for transport
 To the dog food factory
Put into cans of *Purrfect* and *Putrid Delight*

18. *Notes:* The rendering of euthanized pets is a common practice in the world today. The rendered "product" is used by commercial pet food manufacturers as one of the prime ingredients in dog and cat food. When you read on a pet food label the words "meat by-products" it can mean the rendered remains of dogs and cats. I learned about this first hand from Steven Jesse Bernstein, a friend of mine, who had worked in a rendering plant in Seattle. This poem became a song for Audio Letter as well as the topic of a poster campaign I conducted to inform people of this practice. Some years later, in 1999, I wrote a book about the subject, entitled *Cats and Dogs are People, Too!*

19. *1980 Subject: Mysticism*

Tasty Taste

There's grey matter and then
There's white matter
Matter, matter, matter, matter,
There was a nose upon the face
That typified all the tasty taste
There are green savannas and pink plateaus
I want to go sit over there
Tables talk to chairs
Because they're there
It's not the structure of the words
It's the combination of the sounds
We can breathe
We have the ability
We are the snake
Spiral spirit make
DNA
Tasty taste
Go to all space

19. *Note:* An effort to improvise in rhyme, revealing a story and continuing the visit to the two mountain goats — code names for DNA, whom we first meet in a poem I wrote in the 1970s, titled *Silver Needles (#9)*.

20. *1981 Subject: Love*

Telephone Call

I got a telephone call
        from someone I never saw
The voice was sweet

like unwashed feet
But the content
of the conversation
was best saved for another time
You see I have no inclination
toward this kind of verification
you see I don't even have a T.V.
Like I said the voice was sweet
like unwashed feet
Now I'm not sure about all this steam
you see I always use straws
if you know what I mean
It's like a tube
the valves are on the inside
they only go one way
and there is no night past a day
It's all like crispy cell-oh-fane
behind my ears and out my brain
soaking up the rain
I know you know
yes I know you know
I saw the screen on your front door
I know you know
yes I know you know
On your front door what is it for?
On your front door what is it,
Four?

20. *Notes:* The heart plays many roles — as a pump, as a second brain, as the center of the soul and also importantly as an organ of communication. The speaker in this poem yearns for someone to talk to who may know the language of the heart and feels that they have found that someone because they have seen through the veil of *maya* — the screen of illusion. On the screen door is the number four, which provides a clue as to how the foundation for a relationship can be built. Four represents a square, a square is made of two triangles that fit together.

Eat Nothing

When there is
Nothing to eat
Eat nothing

21. *Notes:* Many of my friends at this time of my life were angry activists, who spent a lot of their time blaming others for the bad conditions in the world. They liked to write political slogans on public walls as well as on the walls in their homes. The negativity and complaining created a difficult atmosphere in which to come up with creative solutions to the world's problems. I saw my friends as providing me with opportunities to hone my skills of communication. They were a challenging bunch for sure and did not take well to my spiritual views. They looked upon many of my art endeavors as frivolous. One day I was visiting them at a group house they shared. I wrote this poem as a slogan on the kitchen wall next to their refrigerator. It was meant as a logical statement: if you can't find anything to eat, then you will eat nothing. I felt that the slogan invited questions to contemplate like: What is nothing? What is eating? My addition to the already very graffiti-ed kitchen walls was not embraced warmly. Someone commented, "This sounds like something Marie Antoinette might have written, you are so bourgeois, Sharon!"

22. *1981 Subject: Time*

Time Poem

They were walking down by all those trees
That used to grow there along there a long time ago
But neither one of them remembered the trees
That had grown there along there a long time ago
Someone had told them one time, before they left the house
Someone had called out to them

"Remember those trees that used to grow there a long time ago"
One of them didn't hear the one calling out to them
Telling them something about trees
Down there where they were going to be walking
But neither one of them knew why they had been called
To remember about the trees
And it takes so much time
And there's so much time that it takes
And it takes so much time
That time always takes
But no one ever blames time for the taking
You always think that it is someone else that took
And not time that took
But then you always say
It takes so much time
So that would mean that someone else
Took and not time that took
You always say it takes so much time
So that would mean that someone
Took the time away
But where is this time to be taken?
And where does it go
And where would it be placed?
I never did see where the time was hiding
Is it hiding or is it just imprisoned somewhere
And if we knew the right pattern we could find it
And if we knew the right formula
We could make our own
We could make our own time!
I mean it's this thing about time
I mean take it take it like it was a thing

It's this thing about time you know
Take it take it like it was a thing
Like it was a thing you could take it
I keep coming back to this
It's about time
You can take it like it was a thing
And I have a lot of time
I have a whole lot of time
As far as I can see
Everyone else has the same amount as I do
So everyone has a lot of time
We all have a lot, a lot of it
A lot, like a sectioned off area — a place
That time was a space
That would mean that time was an area
A place that time was a space
So time is space!
So we all have a lot of time and we all have a lot of space
We have a lot of space and we have a lot of time
Now I want to keep coming back to this thing — space
I mean I keep coming to time, time is crucial
I mean I keep coming back to it
But this thing about space
I don't have to keep coming back to it
I-am always in the space.

22. *Notes:* Written while I lived in Seattle. I was visiting a group house where some of my friends lived. A bunch of people were sitting in the living room. The conversation was about improvisation. Someone asked if my band, Audio Letter, was into improvising. I shared that even the lyrics were improvised on the spot. This person challenged me, saying that they didn't believe that that was really possible beyond a few vocal sound effects. I countered that while it is difficult, it is actually possible. I tried to explain improvising lyrics on a given subject was a practice in and of itself. Someone asked if I could do it right then, in that room, and I agreed to try. My friend Eric Muhs, who had an

interest in physics, suggested the subject of time and space. There was a small cassette tape recorder on the table. I stood up and said, "Okay, here goes," and this poem came out, very stream of consciousness. Eric recorded it so I was able to transcribe it later. It is fun to read, because it has a good rhythm, which is always helpful when improvising lyrics.

23. 1981 *Subject: Love*

With You

We stood on the ground space was marbles smooth and round
still is with you
Logic is hard
Intuition swift and timely
I saw you curled around some shell you were kissing
The breaking of the smoothness of the breathing of the shell
You listened to your blood as a medic for advice
I saw you alone I was alone I saw you as you were alone
Still with you
Mercury slippery unbelievably smooth in weight
Even ever on charged transferring
Scoop up and gently solidify
There are dreams in violet hue the color of space
Hands make the true appearance of the scream of nothing
Hear no bracelets and let no ears break
You broke through to me
with you alone
Mirrors are of quicksilver mercury double image
The sum of it safety in numbers one plus one equals one
Our car flew over the top of the world
It was cold I had to take off my clothes
A song fell from your fingertips and smiling lips
The mind is told in everything we do

Splinters of wood are not good tickets
Roses and sand don't work either
We could see these things as real work to do
Arms wrap the heart legs wrap the mind tongues unwrap the secret
At first everything seems twisted
Then it all starts to move in long waves
Alive like flames
Reaching up
Away we flew out the window
with you

23. *Notes:* The first time I experienced a sexual orgasm, the universe of infinite possibilities seemed to open up. I felt that I had been privy to a miracle, and I fell in love immediately with the boy — my savior — the one who had lifted me from a mundane to a magical realm filled with boundless, ever-expanding potential. I naïvely assumed that my boyfriend also saw it the same way, but alas, that wasn't the case, for him it was nothing special. The fact that we could have such diverse experiences together at the same time was confusing and hard for me to process. But what to do? I decided to let the confusion be and tried to channel what I could understand into a poem.

24. *1981 Subject: Culture*

We Live in a Culture

We live in a culture, we live in cultures,
Where people have forgotten
Forgotten who they are
Forgotten that they are the gods
So we have judgments or degrees on form
On what is form, on what is real,
On what is real-al-ity

We have separation
Dividing separation into two separate concepts of separation:

Outward: the manifestation of form,
Which is time, tempo, degree
How white is something?
How black is something?

How female is something?
How male is something?
When something contains enough something
Then it is called something
The determining factor here is
How much?
How much white, black, female or male
Does the thing contain or exhibit
If the thing contains enough according
To the specific cultural specification
Which it dwells in, then it will be made
A white, a black, a female, a male,
A live reality within that culture.

What is culture, but a grouping of thoughts and forms?
Who makes reality,
But the thoughts and forms of the reality?
The minds and the matter
The minds are the matter

Not only is there outward separation
Of the forms of thought into degrees of duality
But in the very nature*
Of the making of the form

What makes the form, form?
There is a belief that the maker of the form
Is somehow different or separate
Or other than the form

This alienation of form from maker
Maintains dis-ease
Maintains ignorance and a lack of
The ability to connect
There is no response-ability
People will look for what is right and wrong
What is good or bad
To the loudest voice outside of themselves.
There is little development
Of reflection or connection
For the skills of response-ability
Are left undeveloped and open to manipulation.

We are the image makers
The maker of the form is the form
I am the form and I am forming
I am life and I am living
As above so below

I see dis-ease in my culture
I see very little love outside of need
No joy or freedom born of ease
Of merger or the ability to know what you feel
Love is not manipulation
Love is not victimization of form
Love-less-ness is a ness where there is so much separation
That value of the separation possible better viewpoint is lost
In adherence to a power struggle to dominate or be a victim of form
People have forgotten the nature of form
And the illusory aspects of matter.

This is a loveless world as long as there continues to be such
Rejection of the ability to make an insightful connection
To feel as others feel as real as your own
As long as response-ability is given to something or someone else

As long as freedom or knowledge is withheld or
Given like it was a gift, a thing
As long as it is forgotten that the maker of the form is the form
We are in the lair, mutely waiting cause we have forgotten how to sing

24. *Notes:* *The root of nature is *nat*, meaning to bring forth. This poem
emerged spontaneously as the lyrics to a song set in waltz time at an Audio
Letter rehearsal. The rehearsal was recorded and afterward I was then able to
transcribe it.

25. *1981 Subject: Mysticism*

Transcendence

Transcendence is an apocalyptic event
It takes the past as it leaves the present
Change is always the same
If you care to look deeper into it
It is form passing into form
It is orgasmic
It is the expansion of truth and reality
Through the phases of duality
Like the moon it moves from necessity
Guaranteed full promised monthly
This is bold like love is bold
Naked revealed
It has no body and nobody can have it
Love that is... has no body
And nobody has love
Love is the body
Blood, the intoxication the invitation
To this apocalypse
This standing naked
Psyche stripped is the flesh

The matter is the mind
Thought is form
Words come next
Few make new most make do.

25. *Notes:* We are more than we think we know, so we must go beyond what we think we know to understand who we are. In this poem, I was trying to convey something about the origin of matter being larger than and out of the range of reason. I was attempting to direct the focus to the Supreme doer: *That* who is sublime and beyond all grasp. To catch a pre-verbal glimpse of *That* demands nothing less than apocalypse — one is required to stand naked, uncovered and exposed. But contrary to our present culture's negative view of the body and nature, I wanted to express something about the sacredness and necessity of the body, of life itself, in this process of transcendence. What are we really transcending? What are we really aiming to go beyond in order to invite the mystical experience — a revelation of how and why things come to be?

26. *1981 Subject: Life*

The Weak Shall Inherit the Earth

The weak shall inherit the Earth
Let them have it they need it

We didn't have much money
So we spent a lot of time

I spent a lot of time in my room
I didn't have my own room
I had to use the bathroom

My mother had lots of lipstick
Many colors lots of lipstick
I don't want to wear the lipstick

26. *Notes:* Our time on Earth gives us many opportunities to work out our unresolved karmas — issues with life, others and ourselves.

27. *1981 Subject: Perception*

In the Bathroom

Underwater you can hear
Whatever one is thinking
Underwater you can drink
Whatever you are thinking
Underwater you can think
Whatever you are drinking
Underwater you can drink
What everyone is thinking
I could sink
Anyone can go sinking
How to sink without drowning
In the drinking of thinking
Underwater I can hear
Whatever you are thinking
Underwater I'm not drowning
I am only thinking and
I can hear time sinking
Time thinks drinking
Time drinks thinking

27. *Notes:* As a teenager I lived with my family in a small houseboat on a lake in Seattle, Washington. I didn't have my own room, so I would spend a lot of time in the bathroom. It was the only room in the house with a lock on the door. I would lie in the bathtub and sink to the bottom where I felt I could hear my own thoughts more clearly, but because of this I started to get ear infections. Consequently I looked for other ways to meditate.

We Are Life As We Live

A neurosurgeon
I cannot find from where the form, forms
Living-ness is gone from the cadaver
Consciousness has fled the cortex
To know all together
Each a container for everything
It happens as a hologram
Locked in an endless-ness
We are life as we live
We are precious
We are the participants
There is no difference
Between Yes and No
Is this true?
Well yes and no

28. Notes: I was attempting to portray process as a precious non-commodity endowed with infinite possibilities, celebrating the wisdom of Mother Nature as Life itself, forever wild and unaccountable and in the deepest truth, invisible to the rational eye.

29. 1981 Subject: Culture

No Longer Have to Explain Why

I despise all you would-be assassins
Your fantasies of annihilation
You ride in the train and you look out
      the window
You sit in your rooms and you watch

the movies move
You are masters of the view
You are the victims too
We are annihilation, we are precious
No longer have to explain why
We are caught in a conspiracy of crystallization
All built from a thought — full
     of condensation
No longer have to explain why

29. Notes: I was frustrated with my group of friends who spent so much time complaining and cynically criticizing the government, politicians, corporations and family, while they themselves were sitting in comfortable chairs in front of television sets taking drugs and eating junk food. To me they seemed to deny their participation in the picture they were criticizing. By writing the poem and then singing it in Audio Letter, I came to an epiphany that relieved me of my frustration with my friends through the realization that I no longer had to explain *why* to them or anyone. The ideas expressed in the poem are derived from quantum physicist Werner Heisenberg's concepts concerning the observer and the observed. The very act of looking at something pulls you into the picture and alters it. Although looking back in these notes I can't help but notice how I naively neglected to take into account myself as an observer and how my own negativity was affecting the picture I was seeing.

30. 1981 Subject: Alchemy

Speaking

Thoughts, which are of the air,
Become spoken words through the element of fire
     by means of friction
Meaning becomes apparent by rubbing against something else,
Then cooled to crystal through the medium of water,
     the saliva necessary to speak.

30. Notes: With this poem I am describing the alchemical process involved in the transformation of subtle thoughts into spoken words.

31. 1981 Subject: Time

Could You Agree?

Could you agree that you and me
We were running and we couldn't see
The sidewalk cracking
Trees exploding
People were smashing
Against each other
And the sky was shimmering
We were running and we couldn't see

31. Notes: Running is a metaphor for speeding up time. At first, things go by in a blur, but as the speed increases things can even appear to disappear altogether! This poem tries to describe the experience of coming into the eternity of the present moment, the moment when time stands still, which can happen to two people who are having an intimate experience. The world of past and future dissolves as lovers embrace, falling into the present. This phenomenon can have more universal application as well, whenever the "doer" disappears into timelessness.

32. 1981 Subject: Time

Like A Fish

You know I love you like a fish
It's weather proof don't get me wrong
I am not speaking as I am
Fortunately I am dust
In gratitude a pillow

Perhaps a tuna
We are in this thing together
We are fishes in a sweater
Anklets are so tiring
Rendezvous perspiring
No one here gets out alive
Life and death are much the same
Life is quicker
Matter is sound slowed down
So that the eyes can see it.

32. *Notes:* When the problems of life seem overwhelming and without solution, it might be helpful to retrace our steps back to the oceanic experience and set out again, to remember that time causes matter to materialize and that nothing material is really real; it only appears so because it is sound vibrating at a particular rate of motion, which enables our senses to pick up the image. The phenomenon of life is indeed so musical,

33. *1982 Subject: Culture*

For the Society of the Spectacle

I have defined by contact the mighty ulcers
Environmental stimulation forging into the gelatin-like tissue
Which is the grey matter
The brain waves have ways of
Acquiring identities
A mass of filed measured and sectioned
Nouns
The continuous production of images
The continuous production of images
Inspiration received
Issued into the waiting jumpy river of synaptic charges
The underlying current is slow

The underlying current is steady
Fed by the spring of nostalgia
For a pre-conceived
Pre-fetus of a cultural utopia
Fed by the flash of neon advertisements
Fed by the other people with their other things
Inspired by the desire for identity
Inspired by the desire for identity
To make oneself a part
A class-less society will have no need for art
A class-less society will have no need for sex
For the constant defining of and by separation
Civil-lie-za-tion is separation
Disease
Sex is disease
Separation
Art is the re-telling of IS
Art is re-construction
When all know IS
Why make it?
Art-Society-Sex
will be outdated ideas
But for now for now
For the society of the spectacle
Defined images are useful
Let us get in order
Let us make some order
Just us
Justice
Just us
Who finances you?
Images, images, images
The maker of the form is the form
Images, images, images

33. *Notes:* This is the first of a series of prose poems that were published by some friends in a limited-edition booklet in 1982 with the title *Freedom is a Psycho-Kinetic Skill*. The two poems, #34. People and #35. Cool and Cold were included in that publication as well. Each poem has to do with how culture is defining the way we see the world around us and ourselves as a part or as apart of or from that world. In the poem I ask the question, "When all know IS, why make it?" IS refers to ISIS, the ancient Egyptian Goddess, also known in other cultures as SOTHIS, Mother Nature and Prakriti. I am suggesting that if we actually took the time to delve deeply into nature and attempt to understand life we might find more pleasure in our connection with our environment and the other Earthlings with whom we live, rather than distancing ourselves by exploiting the Earth, reducing Her and all other life forms to material objects for exploitation, sale and consumption.

34. *1982 Subject: Culture*

People

People look at what they can see
People are afraid
People are afraid of being
People are afraid of being responsible
People are afraid of responding
      Responding is an activity
People are afraid of activity
      Life is active
People are afraid of being alive
People are afraid of being
People are afraid of being wrong
People are afraid of losing
      To lose is not to have
People are afraid of not having
People strive to have
      Not to have is wrong
      To lose is wrong

> It is wrong not to have
People spend the first part of a life
> Acquiring an identity
People spend the rest of a life
> Defending and maintaining
That acquired identity

34. *Notes:* I was really talking about myself but felt that perhaps what I felt was also felt by others, that these feelings were not coming from who I really was, but from the culture that I had accepted as my own and that I had allowed to define my identity.

35. *1982 Subject: Culture*

Cool and Cold

Cool and cold
Radiant Arabian baby
Abyss and apocalypse
I moved on
Even on a day like this
we can discuss your wish
Ways and means of realizing
enlightenment
the path is a maze...
Zing
Some time is no time at all
even in the deed indeed
their tasks of being
Have stopped
Have never stopped
It is like this
It was never like this
Becoming so dense

You become transparent
Walk right through the fence
I was looking
As I was seeing something
I remembered that I was
seeing something
Because I had forgotten
That I was it already
Cool cold
Radiant Arabian baby

35. Notes: A stream of consciousness poem that evolved out of the phrase: "cool and cold radiant Arabian baby" and that unfolded into this surreal, oracle-like message concerning the defining aspects of our culture where individuals are viewed as separate from the whole and material reality is thought of as the only existing reality.

36. 1982 Subject: Portrait

Electric Ladyland

Alright so you keep it private,
but having been to electric ladyland,
I wanna show you something beautiful —
        just a glimmering glimpse.
Days gone past and these will too.
Oh yes, yes the angels hover over us,
        through us too.
We have access to more than the cube,
        formed by those angles.
We have access to the angels,
who live behind the corners of everyday.
Days gone past and these will too
Just let me have this one, alone with you.

You sacrificed your life for me —
      or so it seems to be.
As I remember, the brain floods with the
cool ecstasy of electricity —
      as the wind cries merrily,
"Hurrah I awake from yesterday, not to die —
      but to be reborn."
As fire becomes water, oxygen triumphs.
And it's too bad, if you deny
that the will of God, is not your own —
and everyone else's combined.
Let us just get with it everywhere,
and forever, however long it takes.
Tears of joy or sorrow are much the same —
both are wet and wash by.
So down and down and down we go,
as Neptune spears us onward,
the green becomes the red.
Prometheus plays guitar —
      because it sounds like heaven said.
The voodoo child speaks in semiotics,
      "We can all be free —
      but we have to want to be."

36. Notes: This is a tribute to Jimi Hendrix. While I lived in Seattle in the 1980s, I felt I had to keep my fascination with Jimi Hendrix private. His music was timeless to me, like Bob Dylan's poetry, but mystical, psychedelic, timelessness was not a concept that was easily accepted by the intellectual scene with which I was associated at the time. I was also in a punk rock band and to listen to Jimi was just about the most un-cool thing you could do.

Is This a Bridge Exactly?

Then what is it connecting to what?
They waited, they're weighted,
by what they cannot see

Is there water beneath this bridge?
Maybe a couple of feet perhaps?
Or several miles?

They waited, they're weighted
by what they cannot see,
and this decides,
defines what they will be

You see, they cannot see,
and that decides,
defines what they will be

You see,
they cannot see.

37. *Notes:* This is another poem that emerged as an improvisational song I sang with Audio Letter and then transcribed.

38. *1983 Subject: Portrait*

Eva is Dead

Eva is dead
Poisoned he said
We shave our eyebrows

This morning in mourning
As the ancients used to do
Wrapped black and white
In blue for the long night
Under a tree by the water
We stay we pray
While the sound pulls her
Into the dark journey
Toward the light
She used to eat tomatoes
With us on the sand by the sea
I have decided to really go
Now gone is she

38. Notes: The event that caused me to make the final decision to move from Seattle to New York City was the death of Eva, the cat, my companion for nine years, who was poisoned, I believe, by my landlord who wanted me out of the house. I had read somewhere that ancient Egyptians would shave their eyebrows as a show of mourning when their companion cat died. Eva, an irresistible, lost, black and white kitten had come to me out of the sea. One day I found her sitting in the parking lot by the beach where we lived on the coast of Washington State. We did not have much money for food. She didn't seem to mind and ate what we ate, which was vegetables. She taught me so much about cats, about people, about those who come from and return to the sea. When she died, we took her body and buried it on a bluff in West Seattle by the sea, the subject of the poem #39, that follows.

39. 1983 Subject: Portrait

Buried at Sea For Eve-R

She has closed her eyes to see
The skeleton of my favorite cat is wrapped
In a blue sweater and buried in the ground
Under a tree on a cliff by the sea

I'm going to go and get those bones
Get on a plane and bring them home
There is no such thing as ice
It is just a rate of motion
Something like glass
Did you ask about the great liberation
Study retains concepts, best to make a sieve
All of the nothing shall belong to you four-ever Eva
Four like a square four-eve-r
Flatland fland f...land flannel land oh man!
Oh breezy sea
See sea for how we see the thing and itself means
Nothing no-thing what-so-eve-r
She came to us from the sea
With whiskers dripping out of the water
We gratefully welcomed her our daughter
A thunderbolt of white across her chest
Now wrapped
Where she is at the moment
Sitting in the warmness of understanding
Standing under
Mirrors and glass and silver that lasts

39. Notes: This poem is about Eva's burial, on top of a cliff in a park in West Seattle overlooking Puget Sound at sunset. Perry and I took her body, wrapped it in a sweater and gently placed her material remains in a hole under the vast sky. It was a day of great sadness, confusion and regret as well as gratitude for having known and loved her. After her death I decided to go to New York City.

My First Birthday In NYC

I want to tell you about the train
But it is not you that I call it is someone else
That I know will talk to me
And it isn't a train, it is a firetruck
All the people are outside on the sidewalk
There is a fire across from my sixth-floor window
Yes, it is mine now, my floor, I live here
The gutters of the street are red with the blood
Of pigeons, their small bodies blown up by the cruel
Throwing of thousands of firecrackers by all these idiots
Who live on this street with me now
The street is mine now, my street, I live here
The fireman sprays water on the burning building
Outside my window
I block off the sight by quickly closing the shutters
Collapsing on the bed
I look at the pictures on the wall
I was so sure you would have come by now

40. Notes: This poem is a letter of longing to my boyfriend Perry, whom I was missing terribly at the time. I wrote this poem on my 32nd birthday, which is July 4th. Sue Ann Harkey and I had moved to the Lower East Side of New York City from Seattle, Washington only a month before. The local drug lord, who happened to live across the street from us, would "provide" for the neighborhood several times a year to celebrate various holidays. In honor of July 4th he gave away what seemed like thousands of firecrackers. For a full week preceding July 4th, he and his friends would meticulously line up firecrackers end to end down the middle of 7th street, position themselves one person on Ave. B and one on Ave. C and then at the same time light the "end" firecracker. For the next 20 minutes or so, we would all hear the explosion of each firecracker one by one as, in a domino-effect the explosions moved closer to each other, ending in a finale at about the spot where our building was. Everyone would then clap and cheer. The street would be enveloped in hazy smoke and frenzy. All of the animals, pet dogs and cats as well as the wild pigeons and other birds would be in a state of terror and anxiety for the whole week. Sue Ann and I went to a 4th of July party on the roof top of a building on Clinton Street to view the fireworks that the city would provide. But I was terribly homesick and missed my boyfriend, who was back in Seattle. I could not seem to get into the party vibe that was in full swing, so I left early and rode my bike home. The poem I wrote was an account of what I found when I came home. I had only been gone from Seattle for a little over a month and yet it felt like I had been separated from all that I knew and loved for an eternity. It hurt that our separation didn't seem to matter to my boyfriend. It was my birthday, after all, and he hadn't even called or sent me a birthday card. I was living on this street, which was one of the biggest drug distribution centers of the area. Ave. B was a dirt road. The police were on horseback. People were killing pigeons for fun by blowing them up with firecrackers. I felt I was living in a nightmare.

41. *1983 Subject: Love*

There is a Room in My Heart

I will be away for some long time
Accept this as I am trying to tell you the truth
The truth is always hard to tell
Because of its all-inclusive nature
To really tell it,
I would have to be talking endlessly
Into many days and nights

To tell of love's joy in the sadness of yearning
Is to express longing
Is to confess gratitude for the grace of feeling

To say that my heart is empty
And my days are filled with

Thoughts of you cannot be close to
How it is

My heart is never empty
It is always playing home to a secret
It is filled with love for you
It is love for you
This heart is a room for you

The breathing there in that room is quiet
Because of the muffled sweetness there
The world can watch, but it will never see

As I move about with feet bare and the touching
Of these hands on many people and things
As the words speak, they never tell directly
The sounds of my heart
How clever those words and actions have become
In their disguises
It seems that the sounds of the heart room
Must filter through somehow
The sweetness there is too rich and strong
To be held back
It would ooze through fingers that act to enclose
I am sure

This constant visitation of the images of you
Of the smell of you while the world goes on
Is very interesting and feeds my curiosity
How can this be?

Everyday has its comings and goings
But the room is always there
And you are always there — here in the room

And I can remember to say
Do not love anyone or anything
Let love, love you
The best you can do is to be love itself

That is meant to be the message for
I will be away for some long time
So I said, but
How can that really be?
Where can I go?
Where can you be?
It is all here always
We are us and you are me and
I need to know how that can be

41. *Notes:* It is a blessed gift to have a pure sweet memory that is eternal, to recall in times of distress or weakness. A place to take refuge. Sweetness has the power to sustain and nourish; it is eternal. To have something like this that you carry around with you inside your own heart is valuable because it is private and exists "far from the madding crowd." It cannot be touched by the mundane, and you never have to defend it, explain it or prove it to anyone. You know you have it and that is evidence of its worth and value to you. Let the whole world collapse around you, it would not affect the room in your heart.

42. *1983 Subject: Culture*

His-story

From the C to the C
From the B to the B
From the A to the A
From the D to the D he... he... he... hisssss story
I don't believe His story

Patriarchy misogyny homophobia patriotic idiotic
His story is not Her story or my story or Our story
For it is a story lacking We
The whole patriarchal system would be upset
If women controlled the basic means of production:
The production of human beings
The womb-man, the which, the Wicca, the witch,
Isis, Inanna, the virgin, the whore and pussy galore
We can touch we can kiss we can spit and we can lick
Do you want to hear me scream? Or moan for more?
He's the star of his own movie, the one on the floor
The one with the quest
I can only enter the stage at his request
Provide at best a romantic interlude
I'm supposed to like my psychic prison
Rejoice in my task
Like my bondage and do what I'm asked
How can you be surprised if I'm tired of all this?
Sex is dis-ease
You ask me to be quiet oh come on, please!
Sisters hear me
Undress your bondage
The graven image that enslaves you and us
Apocalypse now
Let us stand naked and drop this pretense
Let the men crawl on the floor
Looking for us in a room
With piles of discarded skirts, panties and heels
The wicked witch is dead
Nothing is left but her broom

42. *Notes:* I was trying to write something that addressed women's liberation and abortion rights. I had also made collage posters that I wheat-pasted on walls, windows and bus stops in graffiti fashion around the city. One was a picture of a naked woman walking along a beach wearing only a rope

loosely draped over her neck. I had cut out the picture from a *Playboy* magazine. My heading read, "APOCALYPSE NOW," with subheadings, "Undress Your Bondage"; "The Graven Image that Enslaves"; and "Where a Man Belongs — With the Image He Has Created." Also, next to the picture of the naked woman, I wrote the question, "IS THIS PERSON NAKED?" implying that even the naked image of a woman has been reified into a fetishistic commodity to entertain men. At the bottom of the poster was a brief dialogue in the form of a movie script, reading:

MONSTER: Friend?
DR. FRANKENSTEIN: Oh no! You are my creation.

Another poster addressed the issue of abortion. A woman was lying on her back on the floor, which looked like a hotel hallway. The woman's legs were spread apart with her feet toward a doorway where a silhouetted man stood. The woman's arms were stretched over her head, a bottle of perfume lying on the floor near her left hand. The text read, "The whole phallic-powered, patriarchal, homophobic structure would be upset if women could decide their reproductive futures — that is, if women controlled the basic means of production, the production of human beings." The heading read in big letters, "CAPITALISM IS AN ESCALATOR TO DEATH."

There was a study done where men were asked if they were threatened by strong women, if so, what was it exactly that they feared women would do? The majority answered, something to the affect, "Laugh at me". A reverse of the question was put to a group of women, most responded, "Kill me". These two types of fears speak to the tension between the sexes in our culture.

43. *1984 Subject: Mysticism*

Fullness

Fullness taken from fullness, fullness alone remains
It is this and cannot be changed by the cut of the knife
Into the pie or the circle from the square
You can go back
But remember you cannot be there when you do

For you are here now always
Sleep in the dreamless sleep of never going or coming
And you will never come or go
It is when you begin to float
To find that the boat
You are on is adrift on the waters of a dream
Look down at your own two bare arms
Can you recollect
These terms of your existence are your own
Assumptions of space of time
Compromise always but without fear
If fear appears hold steadfast to your own
Let go of all and receive everything
You step from the boat onto a shore of soft mud
Feel cool wetness ooze between your toes
Sink to the ankles root like a tree there
No difference between ground and where you begin as feet
The thought is then a bird then the bird becomes
A thought of flight which pulls the roots from the mud
It is always one thing or another
A continuous stream, a river of events
Birds soar from your head
You also soar from your head
Which appears way, way down there on the ground
Next to the river
Magic rubs the lamp of sight, smoke forms
Set your mind on ghosts you will surely
Come to know one
Then become one too eventually
Set your mind on birds and those too will become you

43. *Notes:* There is a mantra from the Yajur Veda (which also appears in the Isha Upanishad): *Om purnam adah purnam idam, purnat purnam udachyate, purnasya purnam adaya, purnam evavashishyate.* The English translation goes something like this: "That is whole, this is whole. From the whole, the whole

becomes manifest. From the whole, when the whole is negated, what remains is again the whole." So we can never escape, because It is everywhere, and we are It. As meditation teacher John Kabat-Zinn says, "Wherever you go there you are!" So best to take care with your imaginings, or not. Anyway, you get to see only as far as you can see.

44. 1984 *Subject: Mysticism*

Angel Angle

At an intersection
All meaning begins at an angle
Four angels with their bodies of light
Create the gates of mercy and might
Angels angles this is the world
Math, meter, music, mother,
Help me find my way out
Like all walls
What is inside and what is outside
Depends on which side you are on
If you want to know why
The answer is to figure out how
You only must go to get there
It's the rhyme of the universe
The reason of time

Separation appearing separate
You appear as your question
You could be the answer
You may be living condensation
Of merging separation
Windows covered in dark plastic
Tiny tears for light to stream
I wear this plastic and try to become plastic

Malleable form
Awakened desire may not arouse devotion
Ginkos have no ovaries
That is refreshing to know
All meaning begins at an angle
Also refreshing to know
Angle angel this is the world — for a while
Thank goodness, angels straddle both sides

Making love to a plane crash
Speaking with a tongue bandaged
Angles angels this is the whorl
Out of a sense of practicality
My breath becomes
The plaster on these walls
The angles of my limbs
The gates of angels
Meaning may only be the beginning
But let the music of the architects begin

44. *Notes:* The two words angel and angle are so similar that they must share things that most of us never consider. Like all things mystical, secrets abound, coded in symbols waiting to be discovered. The occult may appear hidden, but it is never hidden too deep. All secrets can be revealed to those who have the courage and curiosity to look beneath the surface. In geometry there is a great moment when two lines intersect to form an angle, and from this meeting whole universes are created. This poem calls for a reconstruction of meaning, a way to live beyond good and evil — a call to go back to the origin, which always begins at an angle where two seemingly separate lines meet. Angels live at those points, and that could be refreshing to remember because angels after all are devoted to service; they will help you if you can call on them. But to be able to speak to angels you have to know something about their language, and that has to do with geometry. The architecture of the natural world is structured out of sound, which can be understood through mathematics or music. Geometry is the work of angels. Angels — or angles — are our guides helping us navigate through the chaos and difficulties of life to find meaning in the mystery.

Go Into the Fire and Pull the Children Out

The thing is you got to keep talking just don't stop
Letting the words kind of go, like through you like you are traveling
With them like you are them because, you were with them
in the beginning.
In the beginning where there was no time, as we think we understand
it, the point where time was a space, where it shared in its being-ness
the space that moves out and becomes a dimension of itself and this
process can be seen through the medium of space.
Anyway so like I said you got to keep talking, turning yourself inside
out to expose, to play with the plasticity of your being-ness,
this is the apocalypse.
This is transcendence.
Transcendence is an apocalyptic event that propels time.

We have a right to speak, to touch by speaking, to be friends.
Keeping talking, don't stop to think
or to judge what it is that you are saying
and what it may mean,
because that will inhibit the magic of the image you are making,
which is made up of such fine stuff that it cannot be seen
but perhaps described later.
Although I do know that you will get the feeling of it
while it is happening if you are truly being with it —
being with the movement of the process.

But before you start just remember
that what you have to do is to keep going.
Don't worry about being truthful—about telling the truth.
To be really truthful a description would have to be endless.
We are all lies, we all lie separated, apart from the truth,
and yet the beauty, the incredible beauty of our existence

is the marvelous-ness of the definition of our definition,
of our individuality.
The helpful-ness that each and every-one of us as separate aspects
can reach and touch to the others.
The limits, the great wall, the skin, the great wall of skin.
I think we are dealing with time and space here.

I must go into the fire and pull the children out

They are us and you are us and we are in this thing together,
two gather together. I think it is about justice, like I said,
we have a right to be friends, just us. People are afraid of freedom
for it is the limits of their identities that give them a feeling
of what is what, and sometimes it is just too overwhelming
to see further than the definitions, but such a waste.
And yet I know that it does take preparation and caution,
one does not want to lose oneself, after all. Oh I don't know!

But I do know that we have to keep talking, speaking affirmation,
basic affirmation for being,
then I think some amazing motion can begin.
It is strange this fascination with staying
and yet this is the work to be done, the work of freedom.
We must be fearless. We must remember that people cannot be rushed
cannot be pushed. When they are ready they just simply go.
I believe that we can assist each other and that is what we are about,
for, we are each other.

I must go into the fire and pull the children out.

Sometimes the children are the forms of my own mind
but sometimes they are not. They are in the defined limits
of another's mind and I am able to recognize them.
We are thankful to be blessed with the skill to re-member.
We must know the chains of our hearts, as our own hearts
and we must know our own hearts as not our own.

All right, I do want to say just a little bit more here
about time and its relation to space.
Time begins at a point where it is simultaneous with space,
it then moves away from itself, through succession,
it takes on dimension. It moves, from zero.
Because space is curved it is destined to come back, again,
and it has then, indeed gained, again.
It will come back to meet its beginning, but then move out again,
due to this relationship with time space is brought through
to an altered more evolved being.
There is a humorous irony here, where time
attempting to consume space,
actually becomes space and loses itself as it was.
But then again time moves out, rolls out, from that meeting point,
continuously. That is evolution.
My question is, what propels this motion and where is it all going?
I will contemplate this as it is thus far in my limited mind
and thank you for listening,
I hope I did not take up too much of your time.

The thing is we have to keep talking.
We need one another to be able to
Go into the fire and pull the children out

45. *Notes:* This prose poem is a transcription from a cassette tape that I made as a letter to David. I wanted to write him a letter without using paper or pen so I spoke into a tape recorder, then I gave the tape to him. I meant for him to listen to it privately. Soon after, I got a call from a waitress at the Life Café, who said that David was playing some strange tape of me talking about very strange stuff. To my horror, he had taken the tape to work with him at the Life Café and was playing it on the stereo system. I think he thought that I had made him a music compilation. Well so now, as it was then, it is here for anyone to hear.

Together

Are you sleepy now? It's time for bed
I am so tired now; my eyes are near-stuck-shut and
I can just barely hear the pitter-pat of the
Un-cut toenails of that skinny dog on the roof

Still-ness like the inside of a piece of fruit
Can you get inside, like in-the-side
Of the dog
Not until we...all and
You are me and we are us and we are
In this thing to-gether
Can we get inside
So that the in and the outside
Are happening in the same side
The same place...same time
So what I am saying is that all the things
So what I am seeing is that all the things
We have made all the things
Yet we see these things
And they look like they are apart from us
But they are a part of us
They are us

Pink, pink, pink,
Little Inky Dink Jr. of the inky-dinks
Little Horsey and Spotty-head, Mrs. God
They, all of them said, they told me they said,
"Alive some think they know
that it would be better to be dead"
and yet

pink, pink, pink:
"The dead know one thing, I think;
it is better to be alive."
And anyway, Mrs. God and I two-gether
we are the sphinx
To see as well as not to see
We have made the buildings
Laid the concrete
constructed and designed the metals
took them out from the inside of the Earth
and put them on top of it
Mountains and bees and birds and we
are those too
Oh the precious gems of metals!
And where is the heart of the golden diamond
anyway?
Let me talk to that one later
But at the same time

These too they are us and you are these
All those things
And you are us
and we are everything and nothing everywhere
Everywhere is where the skill
the ability
the response-ability
For all that is
is the is,
all that is, is

Is this urgent or not at all that urgent?
You can't go "back to nature"
It is wherever you go!
And where do I live?

I'm alive where-ever I go
Coffee or tea? What shall it be?
The leaf or the bean?
Are you leaving or are you being?
Close your eyes,
It's all filled up.

46. *Notes:* This poem reflects on the exploitive nature of contemporary society that can't leave anything alone to live out its life in its own place and asks, where are we going with it all? The poem incorporated snapshots from my life at the time. There are references to "Ozzie," a beautiful greyhound who was David's dog companion for many years. The stillness inside the piece of fruit is a premonition of Ozzie's death. Every year during the "dog-days" of summer in July, David and I would perform an outdoor ritual in order to celebrate the return of the Dog-Star Sirius. In one of our "Cymbolism" performances we had an "All-Species Parade" for which David made a papier-mâché dog's body that resembled Ozzie and I got inside of it and together we made a sphinx. The "Dog-man" was a local homeless man who lived in our East Village neighborhood. He had a pack of dogs who all seemed inbred. They could be seen every day making their rounds. He had names for each one like Inky-dink and Spotty-head. The last verse of the poem explores some common questions that we all get asked, for example, "where do you live?" and the proverbial waiter or flight attendant's, "coffee or tea?" The poem responds with Zen-like insights inviting the questioner into a more expansive universe of possibilities.

47. *1984 Subject: Alchemy*

Lukewarmness

Lukewarmness that is a word
That I have never liked to say
The sound of it bothers me

Lukewarmness sounds like

A certain every-day-ness
Under-bed dust taken for granted

Curtains and veils and carpets of skin
Great walls of skin
With each description a closing in

Alive in a representation of life
Dying a hyper-death
While complaining of boredom

All metals are essentially gold
And would return to their golden
State if they could

Your secret desires
Will be granted in full
Once you know what they are

We us you and them
The sum is the hydrogen sun
From which all energy comes

Increase entropy of the outside
The internal can begin to roll out
Evolution is not mundane

47. *Notes:* Life is full of possibilities; boredom is boring. We never know how much time we have left in our finite lives. Life is usually over before we know it. Full engagement is the only remedy. Life provides opportunities for transmutation. An alchemist can change a base metal into gold because gold is the essential nature of all metals. In a similar way a yogi can transform from an ordinary person into an enlightened being because enlightenment is the essential nature of all beings. But it is up to each one of us to realize and to act upon the opportunities that are presented to us every day.

How Much?

We live in the dis-ease of self-division
My head, my hand, my body, my feelings
Proportion how much determines intensity
Intensity demands attention
Noisy wheels get oiled
Pain is painful because of how much
We have neurological systems dedicated
Exclusively to measuring pain
Take a needle, extract fluid from an injured
Throbbing swollen foot
Inject it into an uninjured hand
Pain will cry out from the palm
demanding you to look
Oh wondrous thalamus connecting us
To the reticular activating system
Let us join together near and far at once

48. *Notes:* A brief reflection on proportion, which is an aspect of time and measurement. Sensation registers as painful according to the portion of it.

49. *1984 Subject: Life, Perception*

Scientist in a Box

It means not only to uncover, but to reveal, to veil again
They went out
Over there to initiate themselves
From making it live to believing they had made it a living thing
I watched them as they worked

I played with plastic
My watch was plastic
The thoughts of myself are moldable plastic
Able to style themselves by the hands of themselves
Changing is no change at all
It is only just reorganizing steps
Everyday life reminds me to make a member again
Of what was in the thought, which made up the veils of my mind
A long time ago
As time succeeds the limits of thought tell me of when
So that I may remember again
That I have always contained this
As it is now
Becoming so dense I am transparent
As a scientist watching I remembered I was ignorant
Falling into the tremendous temptation to look in a box
Such an old mistaken practice
Cloaked in the veil
Of anything will do
That is any *sensible* thing will do

49. *Notes:* A scientist by definition is a specialist in systemizing knowledge derived from observation and the gathering of facts. If that scientist only looks at life from a three-dimensional perspective, their findings cannot possibly be conclusive, because reality is broader than our five senses can perceive. In the poem I'm being critical of the type of science that is content to merely rearrange and reorganize the same old ideas. The poem proposes that we are only limited by the limits of our imagination and asks the scientist to think out of the box — to become humble in order to step into the wonder of nonsensical possibilities. And suggests that if they are unable to do so, they risk being confined to a tight unimaginative box, unable to see past the limits of physical senses.

Lime Slime Glue

From this limbo of the planets
Lime slime glue
Any stone consisting wholly or partially of calcium carbonate
Is an imposition on the limitlessness of what is real
Art a-parting, a parting into two
Art a-parting, a parting into two
Frames, frames — let's have a standing place
A static space a stage
Who endures only as long as the actual?
For it is in the actual contemplation of the actual that
Actually lasts to actualize
Inspiration is to breathe on and on
Expiration is not perishing but becoming
Thought limits and separates
Transmute the walls of thought the moments of time
Atmosphere around a sphere there is no desperation here
Is time the enemy of mutation?
Do me a favor
Stop the clock
Do we know what we know?
What do you mean, what do you mean?
They all believed they had descended from trees
Dear little lizard talks a thousand splendid schemes
Understanding is the science of standing under
The moon is a different color
It is calcium calcifying making images
Relaying back again and again
I cannot die now
I have to go to work

50. *Notes:* The poem reflects on planet Earth as a realm of existence, as the *bardo* or in-between state. But perhaps not the planet, the real planet, but the planet as we have come to define it within the narrow limits of our understanding of time, thought and matter or lime, slime and glue respectfully.

51. *1984 Subject: Time*

Watching

Passing the time like some machine
Is a perfect way to forget
Even if you never did remember
But if you can be diligent even while asleep
You will remember then that it is play, which
Assists time into space
So that time can become space
Glimpsing is lovely and wonder-us
It can keep us forever watching
Glimpsing at the visions so ecstatic
Saint Theresa would weep with burning pain
Hermione watches through windows pained
Gliding over the whitened leaded frames
I cannot continue to dance while she watches
Movement is the intermediary between
Time and space, they have their communion
Through it and it is their communion two-together
You become the master of the view
You become the victim of the view anew
Frozen on a windowpane

51. Notes: How to move past the limitations of the self must have something to do with suspending time. When you see something with your eyes, you bind yourself to the future of telling someone else or of remembering. How to come into an actual experience of the whole, unlimited, beyond thoughts and images? Through play, not work (as it is understood in our culture), there is a chance to break through. The poem references Saint Teresa of Avila, who was said to live in a state of perpetual ecstasy, perceiving her worldly physical pain as Divine communion and in doing so suspending time. Bernini's famous sculpture of her definitely conveys a frozen moment in time. There is also a reference to a book by the Seattle-based writer Steven Jesse Bernstein (1950-1991), titled *Hermione*, and with it a recollection of my confusing, intense, difficult and brief relationship with him during the early eighties before I moved to New York City.

52. *1984 Subject: Life, Perception, Time*

Space is Curved

If you possessed a very high-powered telescope
you could look through it and see the back of your head or through
even your head and into the vision itself.

Isis the old mother giving birth to the father
Secreting her vital fluids through eons
of movement of time of metabolism
Which is life, actually life and death together
But the contracted word life is used to mean both life and death,
but we are to remember that both are meant,
just as man is used to refer to all of humans
attempting to delete the embryonic sac that once contained us,
the womb the womb-man.
It is by gathering two together that we are we.
But it is said to be a matter of convenience to refer to them, to us
like this and so we are to remember what is supposed to be meant.
But all of that goes along with history,
which is his story, the father's story.
The matriarchal age of Isis is long past,
it passed when she gave birth to the father her sun.

Picture this: the vital oil, spinal fluid, viscus fix us, the coiled serpent
wound at the sacrum like the osseous rings of a tree, rising up,
rise up Osiris
The age is upon you, so says Isis, the mother-wife-sister
with the cobalt voice of orgone mists,
as the moon with one-sixth the gravity of the earth retreats
and allows the sun to spread the golden polar reflection
of the blue-orange nectar, the oil, the christo, christos, christened one,
which means having been given a name.
Once something is named it stops moving, it can then be forgotten
or better yet inverted, so the Christ is robbed of process
and becomes a noun.

The multitude of solid objects that are thought to make up what we
know as reality are more like the edges of the shadows of a fuller reality
which bleeds past the definitions of this third dimension.

And so we have had upon us the reign of the mother and the father and
still numbers increase moving into the reign of quantity, to more and
more. The age of the Hour is upon us. The mother and the child unite
and produce their own child: Horus.
The hour has come, it is their time, it is ours.
Our quest is to know time, to no time. To move it into a space of its own
so that it becomes itself. So-that, so-this, is Is, becomes itself, herself —
the truth.

Taurus earth horns crescent silver of the silver moon see how the
orgone blue clad one wears the crown of horns and carries at her breast
the fish who divides double at will, her child, her husband, swimming
in the sea of oil of which he has made through his own toil.
It is now with their child, the water bearer, bearing the father,
this child of the mind of air, the fine work of the weaving of breathing,
inspiration and expiration, on and on with counter clockwise motion
of the star clusters, the mathematics of the sky people, the child will
wander into flame after sucking the rings of Saturn from the udder of

the goat, they hear the bells announcing the hour,
slipping the orbit eyes and two gather, become the fire of the archer
on four cloven feet with the human face, with bow drawn upward and
away, the weapon of far-sightedness.

52. *Notes:* An apocalyptic vision, stream of consciousness, cosmological,
astrological, a trip, an adventure, back and forth in time

53. *1984 Subject: Alchemy, Culture*

The Sun and The Moon

The serpent unites without touching another.
There are two pillars meant for holding.
The sun is but one child
bound as any to its family.

The moon, an issued reminder
much more supernatural —
why of course, we are told she is dead.
The sun using the moon to give itself
purpose, identity and direction, moon-while
the moon, we are told is passive with no ambition.

Are we to accept, repeat and acknowledge this,
as the support for the organizing of the system?
Laying the patterns for this dimensional existence,
the active as the projector
or the passive as the receiver?
The power of fire is said to be in its
projectile emanations of light and thus of life.
Sun worshippers loving white despising the night
hating even the thought of death.
Womb has been labeled as the moon,
just listen to the ballad of the hip death goddess.

Remember, so you do not have to think about it —
never questioning the participant's part
in the makeup of the real.
Things are the way they are because
we are the things that are the way we are.
What is isn't somewhere waiting to be found —
there is no waiting in the universe.
What is, is always how well it can be.
Use the mirror technique of seeing ourselves.
But greater power in time will be realized to
have come of its own time within the chords
of perception while disguised as the wave of time,
the trend — the commonality.
Beyond seeing, beyond the study of reflection
there is a greater magic and means of knowledge.
It is in Being.
Ritual is the meticulous backtracking to rebuilding
through re-creating so that the skills become
alive through multi-levels.
Re-creation should be play, for goodness sake.
The heaviest chains that bind the translator
are the chains of definitions and language.
No one lives outside of their culture
at any given time —
we all feed on the same agar-agar-gelatinous-amino-acid medium
of words, sounds and meaning.

53. *Notes:* The first line references the ouroboros, the alchemical symbol of the snake that eats its own tail. Cultural prejudices are reflected in language and limit the expression of ideas. But one's actual exploration of consciousness is not necessarily bound by language. Investigating language could even be a tool for breaking through cultural confinement. Within the third dimension we are bound by duality, symbolized by the sun and the moon, male and female, the *ida* and *pingala*, and so on, but when we stop talking and drop into the present moment, we can enter the fourth dimension which is symbolized

by the timelessness of the ouroboros or *sushumna*, the yogic central column where infinite possibilities exist.

Is There Someplace Where Everyone Is Invited?

As science was not separated
From the magic of the eyes
Growing out from the tails
Of seven peacock birds

It was how the nails are clipped
And the testes slit
For a couple of days the plants
Turn brown at the edges
After improving the landscape
All as a matter of convenience

Is it only somewhere deep in some wild ravine?
That nothing is excluded and all invited
A place where, as it does, it becomes itself
Without the use of scissors or other sharp objects
Dividing and plucking fur from feathers to skin
Of branches, flowers, roots, fungus, fingers and things

We could do our best to control our biological
Cellular reproduction contract and withdraw
Holding is how not wanting to be apart begins
Not wanting to be living while sidewalks are
Smashed by feet who have forgotten how to listen

Lovely turquoise creature abbreviated
While they sit and dare not place the feet

Into shiny bowls of whipped soft stuff of things
Which ring now and then for all of them
Carry the same burden but even so they can't
Even pick it up while it is crying no one can

Perhaps because it is so very loaded and so slippery
That it goes without itself to begin again anew
Turning in its socket, cracking its scab running, itching
But not to move makes it all the worse

I lose sight of myself when I look too long
The length of it disconnects me from winged ones
Birds are outside the cleaned window
Smelling of the squeaks of fromme
Why did they shave their heads?
She was going to have a baby
We saw her in the movies at the Vampire Ball

Saving time saving senses
Countless ringing metal discs
Dropped on sidewalks taken
Mistaken for quarters
As they walked, they stepped on faces
Of monkeys grasping one another
In acute postures of anxiety
Doing all that they can to tell us,
Who may not have time to listen —
Where we may be going
With all of this slicing and dicing

54. *Notes:* Do there have to be winners and losers for progress to happen? How much time are we really saving with all of our improvements? Can time really be saved, and if so, saved from what? I saw the cover of a small pamphlet entitled "Animals." Inside was a photo of two monkeys in a laboratory cage holding on to each other for dear life, their terrified faces looking straight into

the camera lens. As a species we seem to be obsessed with rearranging nature, manipulating the outer appearances of things, whether they are living or seemingly inanimate. We paint walls, mow lawns, clip hedges, ears, tails, testicles...anything that may be clip-able. We cut living beings up in laboratories in the name of science. We put fish in bowls to decorate the room...all for what? Are we improving anything? Who do we think we are? This poem contains references to Charles Manson's cult, Roman Polanski's wife, Sharon Tate, vivisection, ignorance, stress and apathy. The title of the poem is a question to the human species and to the culture we have created.

55. 1984 *Subject: Alchemy, Nature*

Free Radical Messy Mess

Oxidation of lipids leads to that place
Oh yes
The formation of highly reactive
Mole-lec-u-lar
Fragments
Free radicals
Causing changes tangles entangle-ments
Lattice work woven and prized for its buoyant
Resiliency
It is a criss-cross-linked messy network of
Cluttered nests
As in the beginning acts of a Shakespearean play
The dialogue issues the color of the rest
Sets the time and specific patterns which will ride
Throughout the veins of place
Named and labeled interchangeably with the pace
And so they speak
Messenger listens and gives comment
According to previous adventures within the terrain
Shaping the message into something visible
I am talking here about the DNA/RNA dialogue

Working at construction this is the place where
Thoughts are built and take on weight — atomic weight
Entangle-ment is the strangle meant
Heat salt and motion — these are the secrets of the
Vampire
Pi means to drink
Reduce to liquid
Pour through and down the sink
The problem is one of geometry.

55. Notes: This poem investigates the question *What makes form, form?* It looks into the biological play of cellular metabolism, the protagonists being a group of free radicals who cause a lot of trouble, making a lot of messes in the nest.

56. 1984 Subject: Culture

Living in the Sixties

How does it happen and what do you do
What are you saying to who and to whom?
Forget trying
Simply leave it off
And so they took the road that seems to
        Go that way
They were laying down their science
Which is said to still be in existence
Taken on tapes photos walls and
        What else, books
Writing is not enough unless they can read
Reading not words but what was said
What to do can be known through remembering
Why you are here and that they were there then
Spending not ever longer ever so longer
Then a second on or at it

Assist in the timing of the things
Get them moving and you will become them
But only for an instant and then ever so
Breathing not keeping at anyone at all
It is being leaving every moment and
      Never going
Based on two appearing as three
Let the words get out inside out
We can only assist each other in the
      Transparency
The press out happens at an accelerated
      Rate
This rate that they were talking about
Is only but barely comprehended
Like the veil and the stone waiting
      In the boxes
Yes — more trivia to come more celebrities
More stars and more and more and more
It had to be done through music
The radio sound is the medium of
      Shapeshifters
The music of the second half of the century
Did its job; now anyone can wear the
      Color pink
Also the chemical flood of psychotropics
Initiated a cram-course on neurology
      The brain on a stem
Many of them like a field of poppies on and on
Turn over faster until the thing is able
Has the ability to become itself
The sky is falling over you
The world is titillating dangerously
Into zany zaniness

And so when they looked under the car
That reminded them of a table
They could see that the body was intact
Devoid of any signs of putrefaction
And holding in the hands were grains of
      Golden sand
Crystals while they sleep
Apples and oranges and so within
Calligraphy those flowers have been
      Crushed

65. Notes: During the sixties I did not take any psychedelic drugs, but I appreciated the positive aspects of how that phenomenon impacted culture, especially as expressed artistically.

57. 1985 Subject: Mysticism

The Vision Itself Brings You to Itself

Here I am describing to you
A situation, a place
In a space
Of 10 or 15 minutes in 3-dimensional time
That I was a part of earlier today.
Riding my bicycle next to the FDR Drive
Which is kind of a turnpike
Going forward and kept going
Missed the turnoff
The path becomes no path
I am on a cement strip 2 feet wide
With a metal guard rail on the side
Rushing motor vehicles on the left

I keep going
The rush of cars obsesses me
My balance challenges me
Momentum propels me
Not to stop and change course
I could slip
There are many rough spots in the
Pavement and glass and little mounds
Of dirt and sand and sometimes gravel
I could slip and the bike would slide left
Everything would happen so fast
I used my forward sight,
Projecting my vision 20 feet ahead
As well as right in front simultaneously
It's like walking on railroad tracks
You got to keep your vision
Looking ahead
And if you can
Do that
You can build up speed
The kind that will carry you effortlessly
Onward
Walking on rails or a tightrope
The thing is to project your vision ahead
Clarify it, keep it, maintain it as a movement
Not a thing,
And it, your vision itself,
Will bring you to itself.

57. *Notes:* This poem came from a near-death bike riding incident, which taught me how to project my vision several feet in front of me and arrive at my destination safely.

Coming to Life

Hence forth whither did they come
Will be seen in where they go
For all that we see at any a time
Was once without a show
As above same again so below
But with quite varied weight
The needle the cone it is we
Who can call it these
Beckons in blazing silver light
A met desire which is only death
But life also and thus
The oscillation
To beget limited limitation
The cone being spiral
As it suggests
All with the laws of curvy things
They seem only as they are
And cannot have come from
Any other ring pass not
From here or any other place
Without the movement into space
Remember that as you are
So you are until you are not
Yes and no being with you too
Where they merge only you can know
For to travel with their communion
Is your surest school
The intermediary between the lines
Of time and the tongues of space
Is all that can ever be talked about

Here where talking rules the course
As you do so everyone else does
Remembering the drawing light
Which was the key, the pass
The surest culmination of desire, of need
Need set in motion
Must by its very design
Propel itself
To eat its tail
Desire issues necessity
Necessity demands mortality

58. *Notes:* Much is said about the light at the time of death, but what about the light at the time of birth? The poem speaks of the unseen reality from which material, existence emerges and to which it returns. This reality is made of subtle vibrations of sound and light. Space is curved, and as the poem says, "with the laws of curvy things," what we perceive as real in this material world may be only a shadow of itself.

59. *1985 Subject: Portrait*

Alleluia

Great Handel at the organ with the queen Caroline
Together two gathering children gathering before
All the Esthers, Deborahs, Josephs and Sauls
At an Oratorio, closed hearing taking breakfast in private
Medicine sipped before the court took their places
I suspect David Garrick is waiting upstairs
Brave or simply glorious are they which
Reinforcing themselves through living on the edge
Of the motions of the drama
Taking the old stories okayed by the English King
Lifting the bible into the playhouse, making it sing

The carol sang yes, yes of course, and asked if
Her children could learn music from her friend
When her womb burst, she died and her funeral
Was the grandest of any queen, the musical
Portrait that Frideric painted still tells of Alleluia

59. *Notes:* Catching a few snippets while listening to a radio program about the composer George Frideric Handel, I fashioned them into a poem. There are references to Queen Caroline of Ansbach, who befriended Handel, as well as English actor David Garrick. Esther, Deborah, Joseph and Saul are references to oratorios in English that Handel composed based on Biblical stories.

60. *1985 Subject: Portrait*

Young Bach

Scarlatti at the harpsichord, crossing himself
On hearing the name of George Frideric
Before that, the young Bach was Young
While in Pennsylvania the governor is ordering
People to move out of the hillside caves that
They have been making their homes in, for many years
He threatens to fill the caves with dirt if they refuse to vacate
One hundred years before Martin Luther had believed
The power of music could evolve spiritual consciousness
In his church the congregation sang
You could hear common people transformed into choirs of angels
After then Johann Sebastian was young
In the midst of a musical family until his tenth year
Now both parents were dead
Pachelbel also a Johann was his older brother's teacher
They lived together for five years
Young Bach would steal music out of the cupboard at night and copy it
It took him months as the night was dark

Saint Michael's was a choir school for poor boys like him
He was an organ player self-taught
There was the court
There was the town
There was the church
Living on Cabbage Street with an auntie next
He became the choir teacher
The children would come to school wearing swords acting like clowns
He didn't get on well with the children
Many of whom were older than he
He would call them as many names as they to he
The teacher is asked to leave the school

60. *Notes:* Johann Sebastian Bach (1685-1750), Domenico Scarlatti (1685-1757) and George Frideric Handel (1685-1759) created what we now know as Baroque Music. They were contemporaries. Scarlatti and Handel knew each other and held each other in high esteem. I wanted to write a poem that provided a glimpse into the paradoxical world situation at the time that these composers were creating some of the most sublime music the world has, or will ever, hear. Martin Luther (1483-1546), a predecessor to all the others, finds his way into the poem because of his contribution to the development of the choir, and Young Bach gets a job as a choirmaster. Johann Pachelbel (1653-1706) makes an appearance also, because he was the teacher of Bach's older brother and, through his brother, Bach covertly developed himself as a musician. What struck me was how ordinary these extraordinary artists were and how serendipitous it was that they lived at the same time. There is also a reference to people living in caves, because in 1685, as William Penn was helping to construct the city of Philadelphia, it is estimated that 2,500 people lived in caves dug into the banks of the Delaware River. My god — that is so strange to imagine — people living in caves waiting for a city to be built for them! But not so strange if you equate it to how many of us live inside the caves of our hearts waiting for great music to be composed that has the power to elevate us out of our mundanity into heavenly realms of possibilities.

My Troubles Been Walking in the Sea

Sum time, hear now
Along the inside of the banks
Of all the cities
Take all the money
Take the torch
Take the harp
The bowl
And the garden
A chair is not a throne necessarily
My troubles been walking in the sea
Don't tell, you're tired
Don't tell me
I can't hear it
Here now
Take all
Of yourself
And go
Take the torch
Take the harp
The bowl
And the garden

61. *Notes:* This is a poem about origins, the origin of our culture, of language, time and symbols, and how even though we may try to retrace our steps in an attempt to get to the essence of something, words are only shadows of the truth that we experience. How can we ever speak the truth? What could the words we use possibly mean? The garden is tamed wildness. The water is our origin: it is large, deep and unfathomable by the instruments of civilization. Somewhere inside we know this, and so we throw all of our troubling questions, as well as our garbage, into this mysterious sea.

Smelling for the Past

Notes to an aspiring perfume maker
To know through the nose
Is a way stronger,
longer, than any picture or song
used to invoke memories.
Are we more than the sights and sounds of our culture?
Are we asking of the origin of the family?
Private property?
And or the state?
How are we to know,
no need to know?

Who among us is working on the duplication,
the recreation of scent?
The nosey reification of memories

Yes — we have heard about
That little teacake
Dipped in its tea water fashion
and the lady in pink
But I want more
As I remember that,
that was all on a written page
I was the reader then and so
believed the language
It was seen and heard
As these records go through
that great switchboard
called the thalamus gland
as all audio and visual matter does

Unlike the smelts
whose path is more direct
Call it quick, yes
Why not?
Right to some corralled-like, reef-like
region of the brain-like.

Who among us?
Is there a perfume-maker here?
Are you the one with the sheet of glass?
Allowed to stand while smeared
with butter for so very long
Smooth and even
long like a plane of glycerin
I have heard and also seen
the delicate lilac blossoms
of the lilac tree
lying fluttering among those
sheets of buttered glass
All offering their scents
anxious for their death
the dissolution of form
Why not?
You see they are immortalized
as they are etherealized
Streaming in high clear pitches
of sound-scent
Into the transparent layers of
the no-longer time
Near the ring pass-not
Merged in true-love fashion
among the many nose
And as a by-product,

for all action has its time,
which trails it like a comet's tail
The past is brought back to us and
built upon again
gaining a little bit more
becoming a little more dense
So that we may all become transparent

62. *Notes:* Memories, oh sweet memories! Smells trigger memories like nothing else can. The sense of smell is underrated in our culture. Like the power of music and sound, the power of scent is a mystery in our time. The reference to the "little teacake dipped in tea" and "the lady in pink" is of course from Proust's *Remembrance of Things Past.*

63. *1985 Subject: Culture*

Fading Green

Alright so it was then,
That the whole ball of the signs,
which are the forms of, and according to,
maybe 15 thousand birds of the scarlet dimension
It all, all of it, fell, once on the morning of the last Tuesday of the week
Making this glorious, high yellow sound,
Which touched the tops of new bud trees, winged ants,
Four camels and, the whole flock of those transient thieves
Four women, three men, and then of course, even me
It was then, that we had known, that we were known, to have come
then, And that we were to be there, then, and also ever after that
To make that sound, with a word, would sentence you,
and or anybody else,
To be ceaselessly talking, into the endless time
For it, or any other thing to gain, a truthful description,
The same said description, would have to be nothing less than endless

But then, how, is it then,
That I should begin, to tell you of the sound?
Perhaps remembering, as I am, just now about, to begin, to do
That the same geographical location that I am residing in and there,
whereabouts, is the same space in time that I was when
the glorious sound
Was heard, and since you were there, then too, since it is that you are
here at the same time, now too
Then you too, must have heard
that glorious high yellow sound, then too, also
So I will just re-mind you to re-member it, and get on with
The telling of the touching of the tops:

Secretions of the pituitary can, could have been seen, as the
Brightest vermilion green
The opening being open and the screaming light, streaming in,
Also beside and under, and yes, perhaps even out, that too
Out along the sidewalks and by and for walking,
All walking through the city and even beyond, even that
for all that it touched, did not know that they had been touched, that is
so this was all even on the outskirts of the outside
of the outskirts of the city
I knew this then, as I know it now, and even now
was known to me then
Even as I speak to you now, I have spoken then and here then,
is then and was then too

The green became us, and we became the green
This green and green was close to only being called such green,
From the feeling, the touching, rather than the vision of it being green

For like us, we had no sight at that time, and are only now becoming
Known to be green, through the sight of it
You see we are fading,

Though my theory and those of other ones and one also say that even
This shimmering, shimmering, green,
That can now be so brightly, brightly, seen,
was then so very, very, very green, and we are fading
in comparison next to that, but that
Is only because we can lapse, into loopholes of forgetting and
don't remember that we know, and so
with that, we begin not to know, that we know
and then to say that we know,
fades the green, which is us, even more so,
and even as I speak, I am fading,
fading green, and I am like you, and am you, also.

63. *Notes:* This was originally an improvised song, which I sang at an Audio Letter performance. Later I transcribed it into a poem from the recording. You can hear the "song version" of it on the CD *Neti Neti: the Audio Letter Remixes*. It has to do with our (human) disconnection from Nature.

64. *1985 Subject: Alchemy*

Born Out from Themselves

Out from themselves
The quest is laid bare
Thread bear
How is a thing not its name?
The conjoining of two circles is a mouth
Speak and receive offerings for the future momentum
Why this cruel game?
Does the earth drink water?
The plants are not born of the soil
They have made the soil out from themselves
Of the this then of the that
They told me that green is and also was the color

Of what it was that emanated out from the heads of the scribes
Born out from themselves
We are born ourselves of this earth
Let us go out and dig this dirt
Get ready we are going out
Tonight and perhaps tomorrow
For there is so much work to be done
While the dogs are singing best to listen
Step by step seven or so eight steps from Thebes to Dodona
Octave eight
Like a spider
A man came to our house, the tattoo parlor, he told me as he read his
cards that he called *my* cards that I would travel, and he thought my
name was a spider, so he called me Octavia
So it has something to do with music and sound and mouth and arms
Logos names and making?
It is all being made as it goes
The ship Argo has a speaking timber which tells who is in the cargo
Oak speaks to the little druid whose name is Frieda
She is without pupils
Her eyes that is
No distractions she can see the whole scope
They said she came from Venus and that's a planet you know
She talked with trees
Illness is a condition where options are narrowed
Blinded can't see the scope of we
Out from ourselves we become whole and so well
By including the we.

64. *Notes:* Alchemy is the art of forming form. This poem is an investigation into that process. The poem explores the theory that what appears to an individual in the world comes from that individual's own perceptions. By expanding our perception we begin to understand how everything is made; we can even begin to understand where soil comes, or the causes of illness.

Identity

The identity doctrine must be grasped first
Then the possibility for instant enlightenment

Now this grasping of the first takes a while
What is a while?
It is no more than whatever it takes

I remember it being said once, as I was listening,
That the world loves suffering more than any other pleasure.

65. *Notes:* One must have a well-developed sense of themselves as separate
before they can let go and know themselves as part of the whole.

66. *1985 Subject: Alchemy*

Matter

To etherealize is to realize how to release into spiral motion
Mists of clouds of smoke reminding us it is here and it is there
The joy compounds in satisfaction when you see it and also
Remember that it has always been there and here.

For sentient beings a life can be a recollection of the gathering
Together of things; vast combinations propelling one onward
Riding the ecstasy of something new, which,
you know has always been.

You and what you do matters only because you are doing it
As it is done it is done anew and lives on as a collected stream of vapor.

The simultaneous recollection that you are separate apart from
every other thing and as you know this you become a part of it with
full capacity of knowledge which, can be called nothing less than love.

Movement is just this too, the communion, the bridge, the crossover,
The intermediary between time and space, it is their utmost necessity.

Crave it, desire it with a realized affinity that instigates all motivation
For once set in motion, desire must run its full course
As it does, so does every other thing, which matters,
for we are it, and are at the same time with it.

66. *Notes:* A fanciful musing on the alchemical process.

67. *1985 Subject: Portrait*

Shelley's Heart

They lived, we see them, they are immortal now
Oh who knows what to do, and where to set the blame?
The time was then, it isn't now,
Let me speak of them,
Let me pull some thread to help the weaving of this poem,
He also liked to sew and did things like that, as well as she
He often left his wife and child alone while he visited Godwins at home
What quest did he accept which first earned him his *me*?
Or shall we say first earned them for we?
To Triumph over Life he wore the Mask of Anarchy
As he sang a hymn to Pan, a lament in memory
He did resurrect fairy queen Mab who now lives forever
A tree saved his heart from the burning pyre on the beach
What moved such an action, a will beyond reach?
This large heart was kept in a box in a room

Where his wife sat and wrote letters from a desk with a loom.
Stories are woven into tapestries of sound to infinite degree
If you pierce him then only shall he
Arise from the ashes, a phoenix to be
Some will say this, while others that
The world might become weary of the past
But his heart beats loud and fast
Pressed against my own, where it will break at last.
A heart of a poet is a valuable find,
Able to move one across eons of time
The scarlet dimension, did I already mention,
Where the birds of no wings live?
Blood, scarlet red, still pumps even while dead
We have heard the lute of hope in sleep,
We have known the voice of love in dream
Let livers as well as hearts remain whole and free,
Not punished for trying to enlighten humanity
A poet's words will burn eternally
I know also that there will be a man stepping
On the face of the moon in midstream
Before a woman does — it's told in the meme,
That will be a fact and is to this day
It is an individual endeavor, or call it a project, whatever to squash
The synthesizing faculties latent in the brain, as well as in the heart
Whole civilizations have taken up this quest with mad enthusiasm
Heroes dragging the goddess along by their side
Placing her in a cupboard along with the weapons and supplies

Pretending the keys are lost which unlock
The bio-chemical-neurological chains,
Which have tied our brains into knots
We strive to be quiet, as we have been trained

Pretending that the doors have always be shut, and the keys lost or

Stolen

This goes on and on, this talking of then,

But we will all shut up when

We step into the scarlet dimension, and are greeted by the red birds

Who sing with no wings, of unbound Prometheus and other such Things.

67. *Notes:* This is an ode to the poet Percy Bysshe Shelley, beloved husband of Mary Godwin Shelley. There is a reference to visiting the Godwin home and also a reference to the *"me,"* which is an ancient Sumerian term meaning "the memes, laws or rules of civilization." Shelley challenged the cultural norms of civilization through his art, as well as way of life. He was a radical who followed his heart and never bent well to authority or to cultural norms. He left a pregnant wife to live with the then 16-year old Mary Godwin, daughter of feminist Mary Wollstonecraft, who later became Mary Shelley, his wife until his untimely death at 29 by drowning. He was a vegetarian when it certainly was not fashionable. His ideals of gentleness and nonviolence, as well as his uncompromising adherence to the dictates of his heart rather than the artificial mores of society, influenced during his lifetime and for years after, painters, dancers, writers, poets, philosophers and politicians, including Dante Rossetti, Isadora Duncan, Thomas Hardy, Upton Sinclair, Oscar Wilde, William Butler Yeats, Lord Byron, Henry David Thoreau, Karl Marx and Gandhi.

The poem includes references to titles from Shelley's poems: "The Triumph over Life" and "The Mask of Anarchy" as well as lines: "The world might become weary of the past, O might it die or rest at last?", "My heart beats loud and fast: O press it to thine own where it will break at last" and "We have heard the lute of hope in sleep, we have known the voice of love in dream." In Shelley's poem "Prometheus Unbound", he strives, like the Greek mythological hero of the title, to bring enlightenment (fire) to humanity by insisting that love is the *prima materia* — the essential (heart) solvent, which is missing in humanity. Prometheus's liver, which is eaten by a large bird while the hero is chained to a rock by day, is symbolic of perception — because the liver is linked with the sense of sight. Also the liver functions, of course, as a purifier of toxins — which pollute or cloud true perception. So the punishment is that Prometheus loses his sight by day — he can't see even while the sun is shining its bright light. Shelley wanted to unchain this hero and allow him to be free with his liver and his sight left intact. We might say that Shelley wanted to free this political prisoner (a poet) from an unjust sentence.

The line in the poem that reads, "A tree saved his heart..." is a reference to the last name of Shelley's friend, the writer Edward John Trelawny, with whom he lived together with Lord Byron during the last years of his life in Italy. Shelley died when his small ship sank off the coast of Pisa. His body washed up on the shore and was cremated on a funeral pyre on the beach. Because of Victorian custom women were not allowed to attend a cremation, but Mary wanted her husband's heart and begged Edward Trelawny to take it from the corpse, and bring it to her. She then kept it precious in a box, wrapped in the pages of one of his last poems, close to her for the rest of her life. Afterward, it was buried, as the story goes.

68. 1985 Subject: Speciesism

We Passed a Yellow Dog

We passed a yellow dog, huddled in a doorway
Was he resting, watching or attempting sleep?
We were walking by, we were four people
We were among twenty or so on the streets
Many more of us lived in the apartments
Behind those windows
And yet,
There was only this one dog huddled on a doorstep, alone
Was he resting, watching or attempting sleep?

One of my companions said that
he absolutely hated that dog and wished him dead.
Why, I asked in disbelief?
"Because he chases me on my bike down the street."
As he spoke, I remembered it was a motorcycle
he was talking about, as we all walked down the street,
wearing shoes and stockings on our feet.

Startled by a cab, the cat dashes away from the gutter water

she was drinking, and I go back to what I was thinking,
as I was looking into the water,
which I knew I could never consider drinking.
I remembered we called the cat a *she* and the dog a *he*.

He is a dog and he is innocent
of any wrong you have accused him of,
Why not give him a right to defend himself?
against all the tyrannies that we have inflicted upon him
and all others who do not look like one of us to us?

We are all over the place,
leaving ourselves everywhere, taking up all of the space
There is little else to be seen,
we alter everything to fit our scheme.
Buildings even look like us, we are taking over,
there is precious little else but our own company to keep,
and we seem to want it that way and we are determined to get our way.
Look at the television, people, all about people, human people
everywhere, walking and talking,
Pressed out, perplexed expressed.

The poorest human being, is always one up on the richest dog or cat.
Yes what a cute little thing, but would you love *it*, really?
How far could your affection go,
could you choose the cat's life over your boyfriend's?
Would you even hesitate to contemplate?
Or would there naturally be no question at all as to the more worthy?
After all, you can always replace a pet,
buy another one or better yet
adopt from a shelter.

My friend then said in a complaining tone,
"a dog's life is so care-free, they don't have to wear clothes or watch TV."

Well do we?

Huddled in a doorway alone,
he is a dog and cannot choose his own family or friends
At the mercy of we, who tend to forget that he, may need
a little mercy from time to time,
huddled in a doorway alone.

68. *Notes:* One very cold winter day I was walking down Clinton Street on the Lower East Side in Manhattan and saw a poor dog shivering. He looked so lonely and destitute, without a friend in sight. Later on that day I tried to talk to a friend of mine about seeing this dog. I tried to talk to her about how I was feeling about the dog and how difficult it must be to be a dog in a human centered city (or world) where his basic needs and feelings will go unnoticed. I was worried about the dog, knowing that anything could happen to him. He wasn't safe. He had no one to turn to. The fate of a stray dog was not a bright one. He could be picked up by city officials, silenced and killed without anyone even noticing. My friend did not share my sympathy for the dog. She reacted by saying, "Oh yeah I've seen that dog. He may have distemper or something. He is really mean; he barked at me and I thought he might bite me. He should be tied up somewhere and not be allowed to sit in front of that doorway." I wrote this poem, because I felt frustrated at being unable to help the dog or to even to find the right words to speak up for him to my friend.

69. *11985 Subject: Life*

Day Number Four

Day four and it's a Tuesday
Speed fire mercury
Coffee ascending the descending colon
Lying on our backs together and then on the shoulders
Take all the roads that go north
Remember it is hard at the beginning

Movement is the key to momentum and strength
During these days of water we are purified by the fire of our movement
We keep going, we went up some steep hills
with one speed and a clickety-clackety pedal
I went ahead and he lost me
They were all calling me names because of the veil over my face
I waited by the entrance where a spotted yellow and brown wild cat
Had been hit by a car and was falling back
into simpler corporate beings
The smell was strong like our perspiration these days
He showed up on his red bike looking very elegant to me
We went where the hallway was stone with arches
I gave them six dollars for the two of us
We were walking now, and it was difficult off the wheels
We sit for a few moments in the roman chapel of columns without fuss
David thought the chairs were worth a comment,
being very small and quite straight
I particularly liked the windows, deep set with leaded glass
The light was allowed to stream in
I thought of waking up with him and having those windows to greet us
Walking into a garden but waiting until last,
To see the tombs of all the dead ones with their dead dogs
Are those socks or shoes so pointed and soft?
Limestone so polished, smooth and even on
Glass-cased boxes house a reliquary for a foot made of leather
Painted with scenes from the life of Saint Margaret
The king wanted to marry her
she didn't want to marry the King
she was put to death, what did
she do with death?
Could it have been better than wearing his ring?
There are crystal cases encased with
gold, emeralds and rubies
More and more of them for rosaries

For bones, for hair for arms for toes
Clear from the center of the earth, a crystal unicorn
Hunted speared his bitten flesh torn from muscle while
another one sits captive encircled by a garden
Angel tree a woman with a veil walks past riding an elephant
Saint Francis of Assisi had the stigmata you know,
but everyone likes to talk about,
how he liked talking with birds
Even in Belize the shamans feel an affinity because
bird language is all about flying
I know that that's not all that birds do
But it's really quite enough all the same
It's about momentum again and movement;
the intermediary between time and space
All the manuscripts in the book of the apocalypse when the
Lion returns during the Age of Aquarius the air bearing water
Many lions are here in this Abby of tapestries and columns
Saint Mark is in the reception Hall with one who has a very bushy tail,
So he can cover his own tracks
There are a few tails in here
Drago the Dragon has a serpentine tail and everything has a lot of gold
to remind us that this is a place to contemplate the sun, I'm told
God is the Sun and this tale is very, very old
Gold can be grown and will appear as chloride with crystalline shapes
It turns purple in my test tube around David's eyes,
now purple like grapes
We walked to the Unicorn Café
we had to — all was falling out the bottom of our feet, into the stone
You know Calcium Fluoride is very soft and likes to couple with
other molecules, quite readily it will
We drink iced tea sitting in the shady part of the patio putting
apple juice into our glasses to sweeten the tea, just a little
The happy man at the cash register gave me a refill happily
Revived and clarified we go back inside cloisters of stone and bone

on the terrace there is a plan began to build our own enclosure
will we work our magic with power tools cutting limestone
could we do our own absolutions — why not, we have come this far and
have found each other now
One of the nine heroes is David holding a harp, a sword and a book
He wears blue like orgone and like water
Riding astral emotions of the fourth-dimension step by step we leave,
not fast,
the monastery overlooking the Harlem River,
where the sun is setting,
we become frogs, dogs, monkeys, scorpions, and peacocks on the grass
With loose, lubricated, mucoid released joints,
we find our way to the road
which is not smooth, and it is early evening as we roll on wheels
We do not pass the big blue swimming pool this time, instead we climb
hills and we reach a new fountain of so many giraffes,
who have angel wings
beneath a highly clouded sky and all of it is on top
of a big crab looking like the statue of liberty
The stones are hard to walk on,
much like the Sunday beach of colored glass,
where we could have made a tent
Let's go through the park, smooth pavements for blocks and blocks
It feels like we could ride forever everything is nice, flight like
We are purified by fire to the right is the water lagoon, can't stop
We run into the big race and had to get out fast,
our momentum getting checked by this spectacle,
until we make it to Park Avenue
I am glad David gave me a job at the Life Café, so I don't have to
ride this bike in traffic everyday, only now he gets to feel a little
of what it's like and I'd like him to feel things going through him now
Near the East River it is twilight along the water
like on the first day of the fast and we are better now and we know it, so
we ride up Tenth street unto Avenue C and the guy downstairs pushes

the door open for us as we carry the bikes upstairs into the rooms for
us and then we leave again walking for ice and tea and lemons and
limes and candles
We have returned and there he is, fixing the clickety on my bike
He has blue clothes on, his hair is tied back
twice glazed with Indian Hair oil
You see we found an old bike frame and he is
taking the bearings from another
I made some psyllium seeds and iced tea for us
We have a lot of ice melting fast in the sink as day four ticks and tocks
into day five, we go to sleep
When we are in the Egyptian Section of the Metropolitan Museum
tomorrow I bet we will make plans to go and live in Egypt
As we visited all the old houses on Staten Island, growing honeysuckles
We picked a couple and sipped the nectar and asked ourselves if we
might want to live there, with all the shady old trees and green grass,
remember all the large boats and all those smells the day before?

69. *Notes:* During the summer of 1985 David and I took a vacation. That meant didn't
go to work at the Life Café. We kept pretty much to ourselves. We fasted for seven
days, drinking just water and tea. Every day we drank a colon cleanser made of
psyllium seeds as well as taking coffee enemas. During the fast, we were physically
very active: we went on bike trips around the city, visited museums and practiced
yoga asana, kriyas and pranayama every day. This poem was written on day four of
the fast when we biked up to the Cloisters, then to the Cathedral of St. John the
Divine and on through Central Park, heading home to the Lower East Side.

70. *1985 Subject: Perception*

Some Mushrooms are Blue

The stems are long and some are short
Primarily blue-gray and silver and of course
Some veined gold, which appears tan or brown

All of that is meant for the light you know
When they are dried, they weigh close to nothing if you compare them
to your own physical body of bones, muscles and blood
We wait for days without food, keeping the channels open with floods
of water

They arrive and we dip them in the nectar of flower tea adding just a
tiny bit of fire to encourage the dance in the cauldron-sea
Vapor gathers momentum for the flight
Absorbing the liquid, drunk to their fill, they expand and began to
tumble while morphing and swimming through rivers of intestines,
being touched and sucked languidly by long fingers of snaky villi who
smile as they pass

De-constructed into pure forms of chemical-ether unrestrained and
propelled by nothing less than intention, which in this case was known
to us to be nothing less than love and it is indeed blue, the color that
lifts us up and takes us around and through.

70. *Notes:* On the last day of the seven-day fast described in the prior poem,
David and I locked ourselves in our small apartment on Ave C and ate some
Psilocybin mushrooms. Why did we do that? Sometimes fruit is served at the
end of a meal. We thought this was an appropriate ending for our fasting
week of "no meals." Mushrooms are fruits — the fruiting bodies that fungi
produce. It felt like all of our previous activities of the week should end with
mushrooms — which would symbolize the fruit of our karmas over the week.
We wanted to make a yogic offering by offering the fruits of our actions to a
deep and mystical experience. We saw it as a way to "let go and let god." We
hoped to become better people, humbler, more in awe from the mushroom
experience.

Just as you wouldn't call an apple a tree, it isn't appropriate to call a
fungus a mushroom. Mushrooms are the fruits of fungi, as apples are the
fruits of apple trees. Fungi are complex living organisms that grow mostly
underground unseen. We human beings are also somewhat like fruits in that
what you see — our bodies show the karmic results from our inner and outer

experiences. Those experiences, especially the inner ones are vast and complex involving all of creation and perhaps even more, as in what lies dormant in creative potential.

After some minutes I knew I was moving into the psychedelic experience, but managed to first type out this poem, before words became irrelevant.

71. 1985 Subject: Portrait

Dream Harp

He is sleeping over there now
He is making a harp come out from his dream
It lies propped up against the amplifying machine
He sleeps under silver stripes and lilac flowers
There's a mirror along his side
The blue face of a cat watches above the bed
She just started doing this last night
From his chest go out circles of steady pink light
He is tired and still as they pulse with longing streams
He sleeps feeding from these fluids of dream
He'll read these dreams later when he is awake
Sometimes spending the whole day it will take.

71. Notes: David had a dream in which he saw a little girl playing a harp. When he woke up, he built the harp he had seen in his dream and gave it to me to play. It was beautiful, made of cow horns and strung with piano wire. He even etched a portrait of me in the copper band he used to piece the horns together. He worked many days to complete it. I loved playing it. The sound was etheric and eerie and somehow watery. The line, "The blue face of a cat watches above the bed," is a reference to a painting I did that hung over the bed when he had the harp dream.

Coffee

I would not advise you to drink coffee
Before you know what, you want to do
or it will prove a discourtesy
Build the train and lay down your tracks
First trench the path first
Or there will be wrath
Then flood it with your focus
Consciousness is chemical, moves
electrically so needs a channel
to current its locus.

Drink the brew only if the path has a
good groove
Then the steady firings of the neurons
could be improved
But if the tracks have not been laid in place
or if they were bolted down in haste
The acceleration will cause confusion and the inability to concentrate
You will lose your footing to jittery
and the wheels will become skittery
ATP will be released in chaotic spurts
The engineer will be unable to assert
The vessel will likely capsize
Fall off the track traumatized.

72. *Notes:* While I was in college my psychology and biology professors all encouraged us to drink coffee to improve our ability to study. My mother also encouraged me to drink coffee while I was a little girl. There are even coffee stains on my first communion dress! When I got older, I questioned this advice. Through my own experience in the creative process I have found that caffeine does not enhance creativity, or facilitate insights, though it may help

one concentrate more firmly on a task, but only once that task is known. The level of concentration achieved by the caffeine, however, will not move one to a creative breakthrough in understanding or problem solving. When you ingest caffeine or amphetamines, you stand on unsteady ground, casting your fate to the wind of your karmas. You won't be able to easily tap into your unique ability to creatively chart your own new way.

73. *1985 Subject: Culture*

No Shopping Day

Stay in bed lying down evened out allowing and letting
Only working on those two activities and then...
The thrill:
The time progresses, the sky darkens and you know that the
Stores are all closing one by one

You couldn't buy anything now, even if you wanted to
You must wait until tomorrow and then remind yourself
That today isn't the only bargain day
There will always be another last chance clearance
Or president's sale even if you missed this week there is the next

Keep working at those two activities: allowing and letting
The time progresses, the sky darkens and
You know that you are still alive!
How much can you do without?
Get out of bed take a walk down the streets moving on the sheer
Thrill of having no money in your pockets or bags in your hands
You couldn't buy anything now, even if you wanted to.

73. *Notes:* In an urban area, we live with the constant pressure to buy something, everyday leaving the apartment carrying a purse and coming home weighed down with bags. There is little to see on the streets of a city except shops, restaurants, stores, stuff for sale and requests or pleas to buy.

Two Druids

Alternating fingernails
Two hands folded on folding chairs
Silver and gold painted fingernails
Two people sitting on two folding chairs
Hey, don't you even know my name?
Me of the same civilization's fame
You also are of the same
Sitting on a hillside
Balanced by rods buried deep electrified
A wash of lime please!
A lime wash to bleach the hair and make it
To stand away from the head dyed
Two people sitting on two folding chairs
Over the country they gaze ringside
Two people sitting on black and white squares
Serpents like dragons encircle the wrists
Of the folded hands folded on folding chairs
Gawain or Cu Chulainn, which one are you?
Or are you one and both the same,
Cu Chulainn?

Fingers glide down metal strings
Strung on a horn shaped to a harp
It is the figure of the J which appears
As the long neck of the deer
You can see it in the eye
In the pyramid
Its number is eleven
There now, under the mistletoe
While holding in the hands

The magic egg made round from
Snake secretions plus sand
We're going to win the law suit and be
Met by a prince who has stars in his eyes
Living within the oak trees
Coming out at night
Strange to die under the moon
See them there on the chairs
Off the hill of Tara green and white
Until the sky falls and the sea breaks
Its limits which is always

Like cures like and so
We drink fermented juice as a remedy
For excess gas in the stomach and intestines
And as we see so it seems
The two cannot view one and another
They are polarized on opposite sides of the hill
As they sit they rotate from some mechanism
Within the mound, around and around
Atmosphere means around a sphere
The woods are cut down
Away while stumps stay
Fire to smoke and ice to water
It is hot here and there as they sit
Somewhere we must begin to see more than we know
Watch the cat as she cocks her head to one side
Listening to the grass while time takes a lapse

These two they sit forever it seems
As they do it goes on because they do
What the Hawthorn and the Oak tell us is true
The queen has been abducted
There are vast treasures to be found

To be brought back and forth
What shall we do and when shall we do it
Until we can hear we wait right here
And as we do we work on being and breathing
And we find the essential things eventually
Oh yes, by the way,
The chairs rotate clock-wise,
As well as counter
For all karmas move as spirals
Cork-screwing
Back to the future and out to the past,
At last
At last!

74. *Notes:* This poem is to celebrate optimism as a choice when you find yourself between a rock and a hard place. In the midst of chaos and darkness, not knowing which way to go, just sit still, but do it joyfully and with contentment. Through sitting still one is able to really begin to go somewhere. The basic instructions for meditation are: stop, be still, listen. Consciousness is the means by which we come to know what is. The metaphor of the snake has been used in many cultures to describe consciousness. Kundalini, which means individual consciousness, is symbolized by a snake. Through spiritual practices consciousness, and thus one's perception of reality, expands. When the snake hears the flute she awakens and moves in her serpentine or curvy way. Thus the awakening of consciousness occurs through sound.

The imagery in the poem plays with some of the ways in which the ancient Hindu and Celtic traditions intersect. The poem is entitled "Two Druids" to provide a clue about listening as the essential key to the evolutionary process of real knowing. Legends tell us that yogis, like Druids are deep listeners and shapeshifters. Like snakes, they can change form and re-cloak themselves by shedding their skin. This is a reference to reincarnation as the solution to mortality.

The mythical, handsome Irish warrior-god, Cu Chulainn (pronounced Coo-Cullen), who was known for how his beauty became distorted into ugliness when his anger drove him into battle, makes an appearance, as well as Gawain, one of King Arthur's fabled knights, who was also an herbalist. There are snakes appearing in many forms in the poem, including blue ones tattooed on the wrists with dye made from the woad plant, like David Life's tatoos. The reference to bleached hair is pulled from the fact that many fierce Celts would ride naked into battle with their hair dyed in bright colors obtained from lime and flower pastes. The poem is written as a riddle. I hope I didn't spoil it by giving away too many clues!

75. 1985 Subject: Culture

Sirius

Africa near Egypt
Timbuktu
Fish like ones
The serious few
Came into the atmospheric
Oceans with letters of breath
Messages tumble in the air
Speaking of birth telling of death
'A' begins the alphabet
Symbol of sacrifice
Face with horns turned upside down
With a beginning the rest is set
Gone with dogs
Dog gone dog god gone
Far out gone
Timbuktu
Fish like ones
The serious few
What Is
Is looking for you

75. Notes: The Dogon people of West Africa believe they came from the star Sirius and are decedents of ISIS. I'm interested in origins, root sources; radicals like to explore roots and possible causes for what is. The letter "A" begins our alphabet. "A" is a pictorial symbol for animal sacrifice: it is the head of a goat or cow turned upside down. Many of our human languages of which we are so proud begin with a sacrifice, the death of another.

Ogotemmeli

Ogo-tem-meli
Mali-o-ropa- o-annes
Om-phalos-o-sirius-or-acle
As-are-astar
Am-phibious-ara-rat-ark
Ak-hen-aten
Del-phic- dodana-oak
Tim-ber-dru-id-di-git-aria
Oc-ta-ve-neti-neti
Emme-ya-emme-ya
Po-toe-lo-po-po
O-annes-nom-mo-na-vel
Stone-isis-mave
Del-phic-e-pro-men-eia
Tim-a-rete-ni-candra-ski--kasta
Ogo-tem-meli
Twice-six-ty-sirius
O-sirius
Plei-a-des-flock-of doves
Long-tail-ori-on
Ar-gus-eyes-one-hun-dred
Arc-girdle-io-e
So-this-is-is
Ty-phoon-blind-va-por
Ea-cano-pus-argo-a-mem

Mi-rod-no-ah-no-mo
Or-phe-us-oc-taves
Ep-silon-e-del-phi
Can-is-major- mer-maids
Gil-ga-mesh-en-ki-du
Sumer-sumner-summer-land

76. *Notes:* The Dogon Tribe of Africa are keepers of an ancient mythological system. They have a very sophisticated understanding of astronomy and believe that they have come from the star Sirius, which they say has two companion stars, Po and Emme Ya. Modern day astronomers have discovered the existence of Po and have named it Sirius B, but they have not discovered Emme Ya, yet. Stars, trees, water and fish play important roles to the Dogon. Ogotemmeli is the name of a blind member of the Dogon Tribe whom the French anthropologist Marcel Griaule met when he went to West Africa to study the Dogon in the 1920s and 1930s. He wrote a book that I read entitled, *Conversations with Ogotemmeli,* which came out of his experiences with the Dogon. This poem is a stream of consciousness exercise in which I started with Ogotemmeli, using his name as an invocation, which then unfolded and took me to Babylon, Egypt, Greece, Britain, into the ocean and up to the stars. It is a challenging poem to recite, for sure.

77. *1985 Subject: Alchemy, Love, Mysticism*

Pass The Ring Pass Not

Now we've gone into it, dog-gone
Two snakes speak while entwined
For-eve-are brings the weight of form
The rocket ships are in our mind
The rhythm is in the spine
Where the DNA lies curled in lines
Conversing with the central system

The snakes play and the dogs howl
Sitting in the eye our friend the moon
Floods came as the atmosphere
Loosened and fell from the sky
As a by-product the past is brought back
Built upon again adding what we lack
Gaining a fraction more in its becoming one
Into transparent layers of the no-time
No longer pass the ring pass not
Merged in true love fashion among the none

77. *Notes:* The potential for archeological exploration into the origin of culture, myth, religion and civilization is available when two people come together in the sexual act. Sexual intimacy can be a mystical union, an alchemical experiment in which deep secrets rise to the surface, yielding clues and insights about who the present partners are, where they have come from (the past), and who they need to become (the future). In the poem, Eve brings us all into the weight of time and it seems we will be here until we crack the mystery of time. Integration of body and mind is essential for enlightenment. The body is an incredible vehicle packed with a storehouse of vital information (DNA) on every subject which ever was, a complete library of wisdom. Snakes, are kundalini or consciousness. The destination for these snakes is to meet up with Shiva, who is the abode of joy. Shiva sits in the third eye, the pineal gland, as the illuminated moon of cosmic consciousness. The central system is the central nervous system. Dogs are the messengers who bring news of our salvation, if we could but understand their language. If the coupling is successful, fluids are released, a reference to the universal solvent which will complete the alchemical transformation. True love results in the true sacred marriage, which delights in the One. This true love goes way past "sex," way past the ring, which binds one to the wheel, the wheel of *samsara*, which locks us in the mundane, going around and around, over and over again, fueled by ignorance bound by pride, mistaking what is unreal for that which is real. So let's pass on that and go pass the ring pass not into what is really real...and delightful!

Enkidu Enkidu

Wild one what happened to you?
Traded your joy for that which is new?

You who ate grass and fruits on the floor
Breathing the wind with the birds who soar

Sleeping close to warm hearts who beat
Not even tempted to chew on the meat

Into the forest send miss be havin' Pompadou
With a bright, red apple to tempt her to you

She was paid by the company, the firm who sought
To recruit a brave bear, a monkey could be bought

Under the tent the circus begins
No need for a muzzle or cage, he comes as a friend

Laughing and sniggering they know it is wrong
But can't seem to leave, they're caught in the throng

Pull up a chair and pour out the drink
Time for entertainment, not time to think

Everyone get down and do the funky boogaloo
Enki Enki Enkidu da doo

Party hardy Inky Dink Inky Dink Inky Dink Do
Boogaloo down Broadway with Yogi and Boo Boo

Once the liberator of those caught in a trap
Now you're drinking blood at a table
What are we supposed to make of all that?

78. *Notes:* Enkidu was the vegetarian wild man who lived in the forest with his friends, the animals, in the Sumerian *Epic of Gilgamesh*. After leaving the forest, he became the best friend and strong right arm of King Gilgamesh, the consort of the Goddess Inanna. In the story the king's men hire a prostitute to seduce Enkidu and lure him into the city where he trades his wildness for domestication — becoming acceptable and civilized. It is a story of the takeover of nature by culture and so-called civilization. It is an ancient story about human beings separating themselves from animals into a whole other species, who harden their hearts, wear clothes, cook food and live through means of deceit and denial. It is my feeling that Enkidu appears again in the Indian Ramayana epic story as Hanuman.

79. *1985 Subject: Culture*

Enki Ea

The sweeping rays and did you remember
All of us inside of something like a wardrobe?
The rays of digitaria once yearly sweep
The Earth who is said to be female
And so lies waiting
Lapiz lazuli is the night sky
Who is blue
Who is it bluer than that?
Enki or Ea?
The universe is this plus that
And did you remember the divine laws
Of the abyss?
None can look upon them
To look and to see something

Tells that you have forgotten
That you are it already
And so you are cast out
Separated
And so you are
And as you are we are also
Because
We are you
Enki Ea
The universe is this plus that
Neti neti
It is this it is this
it is not this
That is all
But never all of it
Remember the east is on fire
Utu comes up
Three angled as it goes
And as it goes it comes

79. *Notes:* This poem is a look, actually just a glance, into the rich Sumerian mythology that provides us with the origin of our present world-culture. Digitaria, also known as finger-grass because it looks like a bunch of fingers (digits) growing out of the ground. It has been eaten for centuries by grazing animals. Two of the characters we meet in the poem are Enki, who is the Babylonian water god of wisdom and Inanna, the Queen of Heaven and Earth, the Goddess of love, the morning and evening star. Inanna steals from her father, Utu, the "memes," which are the laws or blueprints of civilization, in order to help her to build the Earth city *Uruk* (which is now about 150 miles from present day Baghdad). She builds this city for her beloved Gilamesh to rule. Ea, like Enki, is a water deity. Ea appears out of the sea half fish and half man. Perhaps he is Matsya, the fish-man, the first avatar of Vishnu, incarnating to restore balance to the Earth? Blue is the illusory color of water and of sky. Inanna is a solar deity, the daughter of Utu, the sun God.

Flying

In the dream they were sitting in chairs
Chairs without legs, sedan-like
Flying over fields of grain

There was a voice coming
from over the shoulder
A tempting resonance of throat and tongue
"You don't need those chairs up here
a thousand miles in the atmosphere."

As they traveled spine-pressed
Reminding them of sentience
Into another dimension yes
With the flesh spine-pressed

If they let go of the chairs
They'd be bodiless

They refused and having done so
Fused again in glorious rejection to
The invitation of the voice
Coaxing them to deny the flesh
As if it were an uninvited guest
...eyeing it all the while.

The body is a preciousness
To someone without one

From inside the head it was heard to be said,
A tempting resonance of throat and tongue

"You don't need those chairs up here
a thousand miles in the atmosphere."
In the dream they were sitting in chairs
Chairs without legs, sedan-like
Flying over fields of grain

It is one thing to fly while leaving the body
But it is a glorious task flying with the body
United in kinetic adventure bridging dimensions
It is this very sort of activity which will assist
The freeing of time from the space
of past present and future blind

Revive the body by breathing light
this flesh is a suit, able to carry
time through all doorways and
arrive into a space of its own

All being is possible
Go to all space
To be free is nothing
But to become free, there,
That could be something!

80. *Notes:* Chairs without legs is my own code term for karma or one's physical body, which is made of one's actions or karmas. Asana means seat. A chair is a seat; it is what connects us to the Earth. Our bodies are made from our past actions — all of our previous relationships with others. If we deny the body we deny the importance of how we have treated others in our past. Through this denial we remain ego-bound in self-centered activity and go around and around on the wheel of *samsara*. The physical body is our vehicle; without it, it is very difficult, maybe impossible, for enlightenment to arise.

The poem celebrates the yogic *siddhi* (power) of flying and describes liberation through the transcendence of time.

The Culture of Sleep

L-dopa, tryptophan, serotonin to eat
Rise up — it's in the clock
Rise up Osiris!
Shaking Parkinson's disease the sense of senility
Time to put it all back together again
What is your fascination,
the color of the needs of your dreams,
society in the guise of you, them and me?
What are the uncoerced desires, can we but see
beyond the constrained, filtered, impelled and obliged?
The construction at its source —
can its existence even be?
Where is this construction site of activity
where phenylalanine, arginine and the
fine white powder of ornithine are birthed?
Don't point me to Philadelphia, Argentina,
to Corinthians, or worse!
Direct me in the direction of where I need to go.
Tell me of thalamitic tribes of T-cells who embark on adventures
traveling the path of the heart.
Let me go too, but how do you know
and how do we go?
You only must go to get there, did you say?
Rise up — it's in the clock
Rise up Osiris!

Ride the serpent, coiled at the sacred,
ascending the site
up and up and around and through
catch in a net the heavenly hue.

Three mountain goats introduced to me
breathing this way and the other
they were said to be
neither nor the quest, but the cup itself
wrought from kindness
enchanted by the possibility of staying late
It is not three things but one
As they spoke, with tongues of frame not flame,
they told their names whilst sitting on the
wrist of the abyss — the train.
Their names were these they did say:
Their name was Dee and their name was A
Oh tell me please,
and I asked the way
Up and up and around and through
again and again each time a-gaining,
over and over again.
Indeed a gaining taking on weight,
atomic weight becoming so dense,
transparency arrives —
simply in its chemical complexities.
It is in the breath, who is spirit
There are as many atoms of air
in two lungs at any moment as there are
breaths of air in the atmosphere
surrounding the whole of the world.
Within six years time,
every breath exhaled is uniformly mixed
as a speck of light falls in delight into
the fiery furnace of a sun bewitched.
There are atoms of air in your lungs
which were once in the lungs of everyone,
who has ever lived and is living now —
we are breathing each other.

The will is alive only as well
as consciousness is chemical.
Be the chemistry, black and dense as fertile soil
containing the potential for all that can be.
Feed the head change the lead
into the gold, the christo
the oil of its oracle the tongue — it's
a natural extension
and becomes divided with the snake
now traveling up uncoiled
to regain again its golden oil.
The endocrine system is the holographic circuit
system fed on light, on starlight, of its site.

Look over there, can you but see
the deftly stepping autolytic enzymes
phagocytic cells of entropy harboring their
cyanide, usually scheduled for release
at the time of the great sleep.
What a pity to be unconscious,
which means without togethering,
during that most special of journeys,
of trips, while the pineal
drops its shade and opens to the light.
Hung body, the pituitary, releasing its drops,
L-dopa, tryptophan, serotonin to eat —
stimulating, reversing the process
of aging to death.

But for now, let's go to the
culture of sleep and so to release
these wild gland bodies — pineal and pituitary
need not be tamed, exploited and milked,
While in the underworld no food shall you take

lest your vital organs atrophy
succumbing to dormancy —
the place where no one cares.

Long and ever on, sleep ever on long
awake you deserve not
Catching the waves rising and falling
is to put back together making it live
It's in the clock — Osiris arise

81. Notes: The dialogue can be hard to follow and very tricky; you think you know who's talking and then the speaker changes; it's like listening to something out of two stereo speakers, it's meant to shake the listener up and send them deeper into the psychedelic landscape of their own consciousness. Alchemy is definitely a theme here. The word *khem* means black, and it is the name that the Greeks gave the Egyptians, as they came from the black fertile soil of the Nile delta. The word *chemistry* comes from this term. Alchemy is the mother of the life sciences of chemistry and biochemistry. The "atoms of air" and "the DNA mountain goats" (from two earlier 1970s poems) make a return appearance in this poem about the mythical dream journey inside the body of consciousness, where one is magically put back together and made whole by Nature, the great goddess, like Osiris was made whole through the power of love by ISIS. The poem is a warning to let sleeping dogs lie. If we ingest, or inject chemicals from the outside of our bodies we may cause the glands, which have the power to secrete those chemicals naturally, on their own within our bodies, to atrophy. The result is that we become dependent, not independent. The alchemist and the yogi want to become independent, to develop inner dependence — dependence on the inner, the eternal soul, the atman, the Self within — dependent upon the grace of God.

Bodies of Smoke

Elements die as people die,
according to the corruption in them
I remember it being said once
that the world loves suffering
more than any other pleasure

To look deeply into the secrets of matter
So how was it before it was this?
Paracelsus said that everybody,
every tangible substance,
is nothing, but coagulated smoke!

There are stories about the birth of fire,
its development and evolution
into subtle and complex forms

We have the so-called great weapons now,
bombs of fire, which hold within, a blow-out

All bodies will pass away and vanish
as a matter of speech into smoke

Out along the outskirts of the large
great grandmother of the stars,
pass that old ring pass not

All of them are all of us
the bodies of smoke and we are all smoking
Changing, changing, nothing changes forever nothing changes

With every breath of fire that issues from my mouth and smoky throat,
I feel and know that time is ending its present reign and moving

Yes time is moving and as it goes it is taking upon itself a spacious
quality, time is moving into space
The smoke from which we come resolves into the smoke
and comes again ashes to ashes, the firebird flies

82. Notes: The poem is inspired by one of Paracelsus's paradigms in which he states that the origin of all that is manifest in physical reality is smoke. I sang a rendition of this on the Audio Letter LP *It is This It is Not This*, where it is entitled *Paracelsus Paradigm*.

83. 1985 Subject: Yoga

It Is This It Is Not This

The world is an illusion it is not real
The absolute is that which is only real
The individual self is an illusion
It is not real
The individual is none other
Than the absolute
Illusions are real too
You are this
You are that
That is that
It is this it is not this

83. Notes: The foundation for the philosophical system of Vedanta, according to the 8th century acharya, Shankar, is stated as "The world is unreal; only the absolute is real." The 16th century acharya, Vallabha, said, "The absolute is real and there is no difference between the world and the absolute." The Sanskrit term *neti neti* means "not this, not this." The yogi who wishes to realize the truth about themselves, the world and the absolute, practices *neti neti* as a method of self-inquiry, first asking questions like *Who am I?*, and then rejecting each answer that appears as divisive to the absolute whole, by invoking the phrase *neti neti*. But, even with this method, ultimately only by means of graceful, loving devotion to God will the real truth be revealed.

84. *1985 Subject: Time*

Once Upon a Time

It was always like this
It was never that other way
Once upon a time
When the boxes were under construction
The doors closed the windows paned
What was left outside was screaming
With visitations only through dreaming
It is as though we should have more time
Age confuses us and confusion ages us
Don't throw your pearls before swine

Fantasies of the past reduce the future to last
Become so dense you are transparent
Habits are not distractions from life
They are the very stuff of it
We do one thing after another
All these activities accumulate
There becomes a number of them, a quantity
And we become inseparable from them
We take on quantity
This is aging and how we pass time

We think we know so well what time it is
What day it is and what we have already done before
And who we have already met
And what we already know
We accept death when it comes
Because it is time
At least when it
Comes to others who are dying
We may ask, How old are you?
How many years old are you?
But how many years dead are you?
Death is usually not measured as much
We have had our requirements
Of what they have told us we need
In boxes of what we have learned
What we believe
Now we sleep
Why not
No one else is awake
Are we sure?
Maybe they are being diligent even in their sleep
Even in their dreams once upon a time
It won't be too long now, not too long
When time will be no longer
And death will be the last thing to die.

84. *Notes:* I was inspired to make a collage poem about time taking lines from other poems, this is the result.

Using It All As a First Step

Using it all as a first step
As actually five first steps
And remembering then that when there is five
There is the potential for ten or twenty
So it might as well be ten or twenty
Or one hundred
For as there is one speaking there is always
At least one other one listening
One always means two and
Two means a multitude
Wisdom eye of the great mirror
Very large or so it seems to be
Being is believing
Be a living being

There are fifty letters in the old alphabet
The hand a star a five
Where there is three there is four
For a while ever so long
A long time ago
Watching is always clinging
Even though one says they are "only watching"
You see the vision is seen by itself
However could it not be?
And the touching is touched by itself
However could it not be?

We are not killing the fair and sweet tasting Earth
The Earth is not immutable
She does not live surrounded

By attendants
This is how I believe
All Earthly beings are being Earth
How could we not be?
And when we die we do not leave
For where would we go?
Any one of us is an example
No more no less of everyone who is
Living now and has lived
We are always in the right place at the right time
There is no place else to be and no time for it
Everything proceeds and recedes
The earth is patient with itself
Or impatient according to the varied aspects of it

Hands and feet with phalanges five and multiples of
Stand and touch upon the ground as starting steps
To where are we going and do we leave behind anything?
To transform the poison of death into the elixir of life
How many steps does it take and for whom and can
You afford to miss even a half step?
But even if you do
It is of no matter
Life goes on
It goes on of itself which is the same as you

Our hands are open
But never empty
They blaze with innumerable degrees of
Same self-light
No matter what we do
But in the doing is the going
Go to all space
Until all is gone through and all is remembered

Then the blessed act of knowing can issue
Which does not have much to do with the separation
Of remembrance, while it is contained there all the same
And always was and is

Can you see the blazing light?
Seeing is not believing
It is only living beings being
But true love happens in the instant of seeing and being
At the same time
In the all of space

85. *Notes:* To understand what everything is and where it comes from, who we think we are and where we think we come from, we must first acknowledge sound as the primal ground of being, then we can take our first baby steps. As babies we take steps and walk clothed in name and form or word and number or space and time or sound and silence. But can any of us really conceive of silence? All of manifestation is composed of sound. Earth is sound: she is the ground we walk upon, the ground of our becoming, she is the music, the math and the matrix — she is our Cosmic Mother, who has given birth to us.

86. *1986 Subject: Mysticism, Perception*

Holy Guardian Angel

The vision itself brings you to itself
Establishing contact with your holy guardian angel
Cultivating your magical personality

The clothing of ideas
With words that clearly express them
Is one of the functions of the mind
Yet few of us self-initiate active thoughts

The mind is a useful thing to have
You should never lose it

From the outside world inward
Through the senses to the brain
The brain then telegraphs the information
To the mind
Which in its turn records it
Grooves are set
That usually closes the incident
Wraps up the experiential package for perhaps ever
The alienation felt as a result
Of having your thinking done for you
By the ideologies of the day
Can lead you to the search for the pleasurable negation
Of that alienation
Which is called: thinking for yourself
It is the pleasure of making your mind your own!

The science of meditation
Meditation is a skill, which can be utilized
To develop fuller potential of the will
You can become yourself
Working in the evolutionary process of all
The planetary evolution
You must begin with the practice of visualization
Projection of an idea so that it will eventually
Take on substance, material weight
It will become a thing of reality
Eventually means that it will work within
The realms of time of sequence of process of growth
Of thises and thats

Diligence and perseverance

Continuance with the project once begun is essential
To the building of the magical personality
With the belief not the hope
That your physical self will merge with the
Projected magical imagined self

Magnetism will eventually attract your will to itself
The substance of the magical projection is protoplasm
Made from your own imagination
It is electrical it is magnetic
This magnetism becoming so strong
Through repeated concentrated effort
That it will have the strength of itself to attract you,
Its originator to it
This power of creation is the power of will
You must take special care in your imaginings

Keep this in mind:
Whereas prayer means asking for something
Meditation means to listen
So begin and let the steps follow

Keep this in mind:
Always work for light
For this is what we all are
We are beings of light

Keep this in mind:
Always work for love
Which is movement
The intermediary between space and time

Keep this in mind:
Work for the nourishing forces

For harmony and beauty
Of vitality and life everlasting

Keep this in mind:
When times of conflict arise
You must be ready to declare your purpose
What your will is aligned with

You must actually be able to say
Joyfully that you work for light
For love for life
Or whatever you know these words to be

Keep this in mind:
There are those forces of entropy
And those forces of inertia
But you can remember magic and
Call upon your holy guardian angel

86. *Notes:* As this collection of poems reveals, magic is a shift in perception. When you are touched by magic you see things differently, your scope of vision widens as your horizon expands. You must learn to practice visualizing good things, what you want to see happen in your future. Through your vision you will be brought to your vision. Whatever you see will come to be. You don't have to be a blank receptor of the sights and sounds around you. To awaken to the pleasure of planting seeds in the garden of your own mind is a great awakening in anyone's evolution. How to get through hard times is a matter of learning how to construct the magical personality, which will act as a bridge to take you to your angel. An angel knows the way to God and may show you.

Meantime

In the mean of time while in the midst of meantime
They would always most assuredly come
To administer to those with the clarity of purpose
Though perhaps, not matched by quality of vision

For May's measure of meandering meaning did merge
On that amazing day in the middle of the meadow
Mentioning mercifully the organ called melodeon
As it melodramatically plays from a megaphone memory.

Melt Mr. Melville, as a member of the classics
Moby memorializes you in merciful metal
Your megalithic form mesmerizes
The metabolism of a muse
Midas was too touched for this mind mire of mischief

May we all part one
from the other and be it
On our separated ways
Walking down the divide
A better day in the middle of May
Was meanwhile never spent much better

Wait a minute minus fifty-nine seconds
I mean wait a second, but didn't say it
Cause it is hard to say what you mean
And to mean what you say in a second
May we go for a second time of it?

Betwixt the two is the mean, the middle

And the in-between
As we lead, we follow and in the doing,
In the meantime, meanwhile
The mean of time is made.

87. *Notes:* This is a stream of consciousness poem. The first line flashed into my mind, afterwards in the meantime, I sat down and typed out the rest of this musing meandering.

88. *1986 Subject: Culture, Nature, Perception*

Sound

Sound became the symbol representing language
    an atomic phenomenon
Into cartoon strips it pictures itself
No casual indifference to ideas
And their lengths
    of time
Sentences have no missing parts and they have
Within themselves the potential for
    wave development
We are all stardust incorporated
SO-THIS speaks from the depths
DNA sentences, constructs of condensed light
Extravaganza for itself same sake stems from
A root where all sources are desire
This desire is
    the desire for revolution
Soil is turned over and meets
The temperature of the sun, its star
Then begins again the work of

covering itself, burrowing
As it goes throwing up whatever and all
For anyone to shift through for clues:
Windbag to Wednesday
Relations preserved in amber
A developed vocabulary is more than the ability
to say yes or say no
Think of us as time-binders as well as space-binders
We sit at the window carved away from the rock
Wall of the sea cave beneath, submerged and locked
We open our mouths for the sounds which are the words
The first structuring of the sleeping jelly
asleep even ever on
Oh sweet jelly and as you rest
Stuck to yourself which is all selves in sleep
Where there is no need to remember
For it is all there
in the waking crest which is always
a little above the water
We practice remembering and as we do, for by doing
We bury ever deeper and so forgetting eventually has its rule
upon the Earth

88. *Notes:* It is hard to imagine what a thought would look like without language. This poem explores the relationship between conceptual thought and the development of spoken and written language and the reality of our world. In the Vedantic philosophical system name (*nama*) or sound vibration comes first and out of that form (*rupa*) organizes itself. Trying to remember origin by remembering the sound of it, as waves developing into reoccurring cycles. The words in **boldface** form another poem within a poem.

The Book of One Hundred Hands

Within the book of one hundred hands
The emperor loses himself
Which one is mine,
In this, this universe of infamy?

Can we ever find what we are looking for,
through the act of looking?
We can hope for nothing more,
Than the sight of it to appear.

Is there no-thing
Beyond the sight of a thing?

The hand open, is an implement
When closed, a weapon.
Making a fist, a measure of ignorance,
Unrefined passion.
A clenching hand holds the notion that
It is possible to lose.

Cruelty, destruction, energy and courage,
This is the vision of power

These are the fives
From the earth, from the water,
From the fire, from the air, from the ether.
The method of Geburah.

Some Caesar stares forward
With blind eyes that see as much

As the emperor stands,
Closing the book of one hundred hands
Removing from his fingers one by one
His rings to place them in a box
Joining the thumb with the first finger
To form a circle
The zero is the nine
This is the vision of,
the machinery of the universe.
Here idleness and independence
Share the same face
"Let me take a course of action," he says
and with this,
He took the book
Of one hundred hands,
Dividing it by five, the measure of the fingers,
And reducing its outcome of twenty to two
He knew the vision of God
Face to face
He found the answer to be devotion.

89. *Notes:* This poem was inspired by a "How-to" art book entitled, "The Book of 100 Hands," which was one of the books in the Life Café library. The poem also references the Kabbalah Tree of Life that I was studying at the time with a man who owned an esoteric bookshop on East 4th Street on the Lower East Side of New York City. David and I did a performance based on this poem at the Ensemble Theater, which was also on East 4th Street, sometime in 1986 or 1987. We recorded the poem and incorporated it into a musical soundtrack, which we played as part of the performance. It was one of the earliest yoga asana dances that David and I performed together.

Beyond

I thought I could go beyond
I thought I could go beyond
The whispers and the shoutings — past the dawn
Cravings and yearnings for it, after all

Delivered from all these could bees
The day is dreary from thinking of wases and wees

Memories poison
The kisses of eternity

I thought I could go beyond
I thought I could go beyond
I thought I wanted to go beyond — all else

But it is now — that I know
That I must pray
To remember to remember nothing
And in just one moment know something
about — all else

90. *Notes:* A poem that attempts to talk about that which can't be talked about:
the meditation process.

91. 1986 *Subject: Perception*

Break the Set and Scatter the Pieces

You draw a line of your own making
Making the line into its line-ness

Take special care with your imaginings
Dreams are punished by their fulfillment
It is this, it is not this
Break the set and scatter the pieces
It looks like a mess
But it is only a matter of time
before the so-called chaos
takes on an undeniable pattern
becoming the shape of something visible
It is then that you may break the set
again another gain gaining
We see the order thanks to training
Well after all this
After the revolution
then what, after?
After the labels and names are placed
upon all that we think is other than us
then how do we move
what will talk be like and to whom?
When all know IS why make it?
The opposite is itself, however could it not be?
As above so below
While below that demarcation, sex is separation
As above this same self-separation
is love but never called
Break the Set and Scatter the Pieces
The child of Isis is upon us
Up and up and around and through my vision
caught the heavenly hue
There is no-thing ever true
A thing is a lie,
a separation from the truth
To see God face to face is to meet a lie,
to meet what lies in-between

In other words, to meet an angel
We cannot live in a world of contradictions,
for we are the world and we are contradictions
We are near and far at once,
seemingly striving to become one or the other
Break the set and scatter the pieces
The child of Isis is upon us, the hour draws near,
fear not I am with you always
Indeed only, I am you
It is only by the motion of this and the motion of that,
this oscillation, like bone
It is all a matter of and by and for time,
Of its own same, same-self, catch it now and allow
the temple to open wide its doors, strip the skin and dance
It is nothing less than motion and motion is time indeed
Apocalypse uncover unveil the sheaths of Is,
the sweaters of Yemaya
Keep things going as they are, and they will continue,
it is the rhyme of the ocean, it is the reason of time,
the skin of the alphabet and
with these letters I thee wed
Cleave unto me only with thine eyes,
the portholes to the liver,
look down and see into the river,
the giver that flows and erodes
It is not this, it is not that
All things are lies
they lie apart from the truth,
they lie a part of the truth
To be really truthful a description would have to be
nothing less than endless,
so we talk on and on into the night, which is the day anyway

If you look at it you will see only your vision and
the vision is never the thing itself, it is you looking at it
Round and round we go,
we wouldn't want to be late for the show
For heaven will be just like you pictured it,
so take special care with your imaginings
The more you see, the more it seems to be
The best we can do is to touch,
one another with the wand of remembrance
Keep on and on with it until we no longer have a longing need to
Atmosphere means around a sphere
Go to all space, speak all tongues
Everywhere you are invited
Go and
make a nest!

91. *Notes:* What is on the other side of the abyss depends on which side you think you are on. Reality is empty and appears according to how you see it. Each one of us has within us the power to change our inner and outer reality, but we must have the courage to break through habits and conditioning and perhaps float on unfamiliar ground for a while until we can put all the scattered things back together again, ideally in a less confining way.

92. *1986 Subject: Yoga*

Come to Sit

Each time we come to sit
We invoke the goddess
For her sigil is the chair
Pubic bone titled forward
Muscles along the lumbar
Vertebrae relaxed

Available to listen
Allowing the in-between discs to
Remain soft and gently cushioned
There between the bones
Shoulder blades smooth and flat
Sliding down
Seventh cervical moving forward
Towards the interior of the neck
Muscles soft and softening
Voice in potential
Skull riding suspended
Hovering over the column of bone
From the hip joints elongating
The femur bones outward toward
Knees continuing the line of the bone
Straight down into the feet which
Act as two triangles
Pressing into the floor
Which is the Earth remember
Anywhere you are.

92. *Notes:* This poem explores the wonder that arises when one brings awareness to the seemingly simple act of sitting down. When I was studying at the University of Washington some teachers came to the dance department to teach the fundamentals of Alexander technique. I found what they were doing to be very fascinating because it involved subtle awareness of the smallest details involved in simple movements like walking, sitting and ascending and descending stairs. It was interesting to me in part because I had been practicing these simple movements on my own for some time already. A few years later, when I broke my back, these practices came to mean a lot to me, as the smallest movement of my spine could generate much pain. When I began to study yoga I learned that the word *asana* means "seat." Asana practice is the practice of consciously sitting, creating a good relationship to the Earth.

On Purpose

We have created words to suit our purposes
With sounds we clothe our thoughts
As we dress our intentions do we recall
The origin of our purpose?
The reason why we live?
Do we re-mind ourselves as we speed toward
Where we are going?
We have created tools to suit our purposes
With machines we clothe our aims
As we drive the tractor do we remember
Why we eat?
When we first named plants and animals
Designated them as food
To be eaten
Were we able to recall why is it
That we work?
What propelled us then
What motivates us now?
What we do is important
Because we are important
Who can waste a moment
At work not done on purpose?
Who can waste a moment
Doing anything for no reason?
When was it that you gave up
Doing things on purpose?
To live a life of intention
Is the best way to sort out
The stuff we need to make us
Truly happy and free us

From mindless activities
Like going to work for no reason
Other than a job

93. *Notes:* This poem investigates the all too normal activity of not doing things on purpose: working at jobs that you hate and wasting your time not doing things that you like, which all adds up to unhappiness, a disconnected life, a person lost, with no purpose.

94. *1986 Subject: Mysticism*

Prayer

For those who suffer greatly from distractions during prayer
I wish to speak to you, because
I know that you are listening
What is it that is so bad?
Who is it that is so sad?
Prayer is asking so
Let us speak all tongues as if they were our own
At once we can ask the water for the lantern the shutter and the bowl
At once we can call for the harp the torch and the garden
All at once we request the chair the throne and the veil
At once we ask for the vision for balance the serpent and the wheel
At once we call to the temple to the heart to the bowl and the tree
At once we call to the phoenix to the crane to the lioness and the cobra
All at once we ask for the eclipse for the hand and the lasso
All at once we listen for the owl for the stone for the energy
To go from words to wordlessness and back again, a-gain
Becoming so dense we are transparent at last
In the west it is water and in the east it is fire
Look over there: they are sweating secrets in their sleep

94. *Notes:* Prayer is asking, and to ask for something you have to have a pretty good idea of what it is that you want — a picture in your mind. By praying we can develop our natural psychic skills of divination. In this way prayer can help provide us with a compass to navigate through our lives.

95. 1986 Subject: Alchemy

Three Fires

Solar fire
Electric fire
Fire by friction
They fall into that order only through
the natural movement of their motion
Everyone needs to know and has the need to know
Existence of being is evidence of this
Few seem to really be reaching towards God
But everyone is striving towards their origin
Some might call that God
Through an examination of the raw materials from which we came
We may begin to break the code and hear the name
And understand from where we came
Away from the one and landed with all the others
who became the others after all
Everyone as separate from the others
Is a specific fiery aspect
While together as one with no other is either nirvana or
nothing more than extinction
No more motion — stationary
But a station is a place and when it rises in the air it is stationary,
An airy station, a lofty place
Seeking is a trip
Through space

Trips take time and are fueled by fire it is light that propels one higher
Going from one place to another is due to the continuous
Motivation to reenter the origin of being
It is the lila, the play of light
The sun is our source but what is behind the sun
Is the one who lives within us
The three fires are all three light
We have come to know them through sight
Thanks to the wonders of fire by friction
We turn on a light and are able to study through the night
When the day breaks it is then we think the sun has returned
But really it never left, we only turned our back on it
As we spun around a curve
All actions can always be likened to a comet
trailed by its tail
It is the tail that gives the action visibility
makes the whole thing known or at least seen
The sun does not beam down upon everyone
Everyone beams the sun
We are the brightness of this star
Old as carbon that we are
There is nothing we can set on fire
Electric fire and fire by fiction are not of our making
But even so, our combustion is the fuel of our own awakening

95. *Notes:* For transformation to happen the element of fire must be present. There are three forms of fire: solar, electric and friction. Friction produces fire when one thing is rubbed against another. Electric fire pulsates in waves. Solar fire radiates in pulses. Ultimately all fire is the same fire; the differences relate to rates of motion (time). Friction is slow, electric is fast, and solar is fastest. The speed of fire is aligned with the speed of light and is perceived by our instruments of perception. This is why a curious person is always trying to find ways to expand their instruments of perception. Our star, the sun, is our source for life, for all motion. All forms of life on this planet are made of starlight. Ultimately we are trying to know our origin. This is why we tend to

seek the light and aim outside ourselves for the sun, forgetting that we hold the same light within.

Mercury, Sulphur and Salt

Of the three they will always and always be
We call them now
come Mercury, Sulphur and Salt
If you care and it is your inclination to look,
then look into and into once again, into
the definitions which are also called
the limitations of these three in form
As the looking increases in duration,
the actual will appear as of the air
It is the air with which we call
the one of the four elements that hold
the properties of the three
Pass the ring pass not and within the unified field
the work of gravity, the by-product of the curvature of space
Electromagnetism which holds the degrees of duality
within their respective spheres of substance and taste
visiting one another and gaining and giving through their visitations
We learn to believe that the thing does not perish as it is produced
but this producing insures its propulsion
The greater and then the lesser forces also number in the game
what and how it is to be explained
in terms of three, only metaphor can be lent to be able to see
the assumptions of the other spaces
beyond the limits of height, breadth and width must cease
through this exercise of contraction and release
Access will be gained to pass through the ring pass not,

the doorways of material weight
Remember weight must not be denied or criticized,
for we are doing more than backtracking through our fate
We are making new,
becoming life as we live
As we listen we become able to hear
As we sense we widen space,
and call upon our agents of magic
come Mercury, Sulphur and Salt
The mountain of our limitation is buckling,
at the foundation of the geological fault
With the fire of sight put into motion,
slippery mercury slithers in delight
As the walls dissolve into thin air,
the atmosphere becomes heavy
Our perceptions are only limited by our imagination,
but the mind's light is quick like mercury
The sight burns through sulphuric fumes
In the desert night we stand on the tip of the pyramid,
while the base dissolves into the canyon's reflections
How we master heat, salt and motion will determine
the limits of our perceptions.

96. *Notes:* For the alchemist, if change is to come about it comes through the application of heat, salt and motion. Sulphur is heat, salt is the foundation, the mathematical grid and mercury is motion. A sodium chloride crystal is in the form of a cube. You start with salt, then when you introduce heat, motion is not far behind. This poem is about the alchemy of expanding perception. If we wish to see more, then we must expand the limits we have placed on the grid of our perceptions. The widened or new vision will appear out of the air.

My Country is Dazzling with Grace

I'd kill nobody in a moment I want you to know that
But do you know what I am going to do?
Earlier today
Some things are quite for sure
With the red shoes on under the warm running showers
of the green sun
From the corner is where it always comes from
Could you give me a clue?
I am a slave here
It's a wild time no longer
Still having been the full effect comes through
Light shows, smell of clothes, beauty loves the beast you know
Beauty, like her sister, Truth, is always tested
No one ever believes them at first sight
Atmospheric change smiling in my room
There are so many of you moving you will be inside me soon
Saxons Saxons close the gates!
My country is dazzling with grace
I am certainly not nostalgic for the past and yet I am no fool
When it comes to building the present with what has gone before
Where else is it supposed to go
Nothing evades the ears or the nose
although the eyes don't always have it right
Names are used to bring a halt, "Hey you there"
The traveler arrives cold, shivering at the bridge at night
"Stop right here, put on this cloak, now look at you, what a sight!"
But we can't very well go back to the place we were standing on,
not under, for we are not standing under or understanding
I want to make that point as clear as I am able
even though I am not and never was able

It is all Cain here, fields of cane, sugar cane
It was not Abel who planted a father's wrath
Cain travels into the land beyond, exiled on the run
I'd like to know what styrax is made of,
whether it is a bark, a resin, a wood, a stone or a sap
Can you tell me, or tell me who can, and I will be on my way back
thank you I like the smell of it as it burns,
Who's to say if I will after I learn, more about it
Tomorrow night I plan to go to the world, but not now, so let's listen;
Here come the bells, my heart is empty, so full of you
Walking upon singing fields hand in hand talking and planning things
Hear the trumpets and all sorts of melodies caressing strings
As the smoke fills the room shaping into phantoms of spoons
Saxons Saxons close the gates!
My country is dazzling with grace

97. *Notes:* A stream of consciousness poem I wrote down, as I was relaxing, full of thanks, burning an exotic incense made of styrax, while pleasant memories drifted through allowing me time to reflect alone in my room, my own mind (my internal country) after a challenging night at the Life Café where I worked. As I recall, I rarely needed anything in the form of entertainment other than my own mind to help me unwind.

98. *1986 Subject: Culture, Perception, Yoga*

Can Any One of Us Have a Private Life?

Revolution of self-theory: new concepts in management:
The person themselves takes over
the decision making for their own life.
With it begins the deciphering of where do you begin
and where do you end?
What is you and what is them —
just what is your own life?

Are we more than the sights and sounds of our culture?
If I look upon you with eyes of love,
where have I learned that look?
What movies and magazines have I already seen?
What attitudes have I read about in books?
Can anyone of us have a private life?
Cars are snarls messing up my hair
causing me to stare along the solid lines
Checking out the broken times the road passes many painted signs
Does love exist beyond good and evil and if so
where does it go from there?

The appointed priest enters the temple of the great.
Kyphi smokes up the room which is the designated place
The smell remakes the mind for the little grapes form
in clusters on the vine
Grapes are community minded always developing in groups
Drinking wine the people of the villages of old dance
once or twice a year.
Nowadays because they have forgotten to remember
the appointed times,
it is any day or evening and so the power of expansion
becomes the power of contraction.

All is open, available for disclosure
sitting in storage behind walls of enclosure
surveillance by authorities do their job of exposure

While deep inside the skull a thread of light extends from the pineal
to the nape of the neck, it is there that you will be able
to enter into the hall and meet Her.
She waits there shrouded by fibers of nerves floating
in endocrine secretions.
Only in a state of trance may one be invited to the dance.

Morning has set me cold with fear for I do not hear you near
Our cat has died in the night we look for her in the mirror
Our fingers do not slip they never could we would not allow it
For we have waited so long for this moment, we look like it too.
How could we not look like what we have done,
in the passing we become

for there is no escape from that
doing makes forever down pat

We should get going, the train is waiting,
it won't leave without us, but never rest assured,
the coal which it burns is made from our own sweet blooded bones.

98. *Notes:* A poem that reflects on the liberating by-products of the practice of yoga, the delight of thinking for yourself and even going beyond thinking, the promise of becoming, even becoming yourself. Our mind is not our own. The mind is like a crystal taking on the colors of its surroundings, made up of the sights and sounds of the environment, the society, the culture in which we live, the attitudes of the company we keep. Through yoga practices, the yogi stimulates the release of mind-altering chemicals and is able to access their own pharmaceutical laboratory and in so doing gains control of the mind, enabling them to go beyond thought and perhaps even become free of societal and cultural conformity that put pressure upon their identity. *Kyphi* is a type of incense that was burned in ancient Egypt at dusk to steady the mind and aid contemplation. When the mind is like a still pool you can look into it like a mirror.

99. *1986 Subject: Mysticism*

Moving Things

You cannot hold a moving object
You cannot hold a living thing

Not with the fingers of touch
Hearing, or smelling
Not with the fingers of taste or of vision

A truly moving object is no object at all
A truly living being cannot be touched

There is no love in sight
You must venture beyond seeing to love

No nouns only verbs only dance
Drop it quickly and keep going through
Jump in the ocean
Ride the wing, sing and so become
Nothing more or less
Than everything,
in motion

99. *Notes:* Talking about that which can't be talked about, for in the talking it dissolves. To know something really worth knowing, you have to dance with it and with every moment that you think you know it, drop it quickly and keep moving — going through. This is worth remembering in life as well as in death.

100. *1986 Subject: Perception, Time*

Rules of Conduct

This choosing one from the other
Draws a wall creates two sides
You know that the divider is not real
The cat is both dead and alive
See your situation as a map

Take it from there
For once you take the journey and arrive
You come back
You know who and where you are
You remember
Where you were and where you are next
When you know these places
You will have the time of your life
You will see through flimsy walls
You reach your hand right through
It comes to you that things
Exist in their own time and
If you were to mix up times in the
Perception of a thing
It would only lead to confusion
Because the key won't always fit
But this will matter only
If you are trying to unlock a door

Why do some-things like this and not like that,
cross the right leg under the left or
look both ways and avoid theft?

In order to follow through — follow through.
To know one way all the way to perfection,
is to come to know that you always knew all ways, perfectly.
From words to wordlessness and back again
But only if you go can you get there
The best place to start is at the beginning
So begin...
Immersed so completely in each step
So that the next is coming from the other and then the next
As long as there is vision there will be division
of everything from everything right from wrong

knowing things to be this or that
but never climbing over those walls
Is this true?
Well yes and no
So what to do?
Better, better, best
As long as you see yourself apart from the rest
strive for the good
as if it really existed as better than the rest
then you will be blessed

100. Notes: Duality exists because of time, and time continues because of duality. To be locked in the third dimension is to be bound by time and to perceive things as other or separate from themselves and from you. In order to break through the limits imposed by duality one must follow goodness as the rule of conduct. In an absolute sense, good and evil, right and left, do not exist, but if you want to come to that absolute realization then you must embrace certain ways of being. You must be on the side of the good in order to go past or beyond good and bad. The poem contains a reference to "Schrodinger's Cat," a famous scientific thought experiment done in 1935 that contributed to the development of quantum mechanics.

101. 1987 Subject: Mysticism, Perception, Yoga

The Best Is Yet to Come

Searching for the suspension
The ever-pending truth almost in reach
Fortunately for fortune's sake
You do just what needs to be done
Until there is no more need until
The voice of a hundred colors speaks
Until there is no more need to hear
Sound that has been sounding all along

Then is when you might happen upon
The orchestra of your own experience
This is where the fun begins
The making of your mind into your own
Caution now
Do not think you are in control
Manipulating all else around you
When you get there it is no place other
Than where you have been all along
Prepare yourself and be prepared
Purify remove by lifting ignorance
By its veils
Watch out for if you stumble
You fall as you have been falling all along
Into the source pool the natural beginning
Of the sound of it all
If you have not prepared
Yourself will run you over and you will surely
Lose your mind
You will discover yes that you are God
But here is a tip
Just in case you happen to trip and fall
Finding that you are Jesus, Krishna and all
The son of God the savior of the world
Remember that there is no need to run
Out and tell everyone else of your divinity
If you allow a moment to look a little closer
You may see that everyone else also is none
Other than Jesus, Krishna and all
To know yourself as God is but the first
Step of a long and winding stairway to the sun
Keep climbing the best is yet to come

101. Notes: When climbing the spiritual ladder it is best to stay humble. There are many pitfalls. When we think we have made some progress, our pride may trick us into believing that we alone have discovered something that no one else has found before. We get puffed up and think we are special. All the great masters of yoga tell us that if you're going to take one thing with you on your journey, take humility, because it will keep you going for as long as you need to go and it will deliver you to your destination. Usually those who say they know don't know, while those who know don't say.

102. 1987 Subject: Perception, Time

Keeping Places

Grave yards and other keeping places
Push out and up through
Everything I knew I tried with you
Once upon a time to see if it was true
Time can't be quiet it lives to tell
I would not could not be here to dwell
Could not have created my life
This dream of falling into a well
Each day and night
Softly I whisper
And serenely I shout
Is it that yearning that craving
That it's all about?
All and forever long will it take
It will still appear to be
As moving by means of
Minutes and degrees perpetually
The life of events is what you'll see
Test me test me I taunt
Give me something to live for to want
Awhile in the waiting tank until it is
Seen that there is no waiting for there

Is no other place to be
The room is your own making
The beginning with its middle its end
Then let us go again
Just one more time
You see I am still pretending to be
And loving every moment
We got in the illusion we are got
We are got we are forgotten
Never ever and around that too
Stars for eyes and a mouth
That cries
Drops of water hang on real long hairs
Called lashes
I was there too for the crashes
Am still in that keeping place
Up and up and around and through my vision
Caught the heavenly hue
The eyes are the portholes to the liver
The giver arrives to deliver
Who else could that be but our dear glycogen!
Consciousness is chemical
The first drug was oxygen
It is all the same as it ever was or not at all that way
All things pass away but never cease to exist
But for how long?
We all know the answer
It is forever as long as it takes
Nothing ever really goes away
Even if it seems to be dead and buried
It cannot be kept in place forever
Graveyards and other keeping places
Never seem to succeed in keeping
Anything in place for very long

102. *Notes:* Time goes on with or without our understanding of it or our accepting of it. Many things are like this in our lives, including how our bodies work. There is a reference in the poem to glycogen, which is a chemical found in the liver that allows carbohydrates to be converted into energy without a person consciously having to do anything. I am poetically referring to glycogen as a keeping place. As I was writing this poem, phrases from previous poems I had written came to me unsolicited. I believe this happened because the ideas encapsulated in those lines had not been fully understood before and begged for deeper investigation. They were like old memories arising like ghosts from their graves. The analogy of graveyards as keeping places is a way to describe how memories once long dead and forgotten can resurface at the oddest times because once done, everything continues to exist — stored in keeping places.

103. *1987 Subject: Time*

Should We Mention the Time and Space Dimension?

Time taking on dimension will get to see its space
When it is that time will be no longer
That is when time has moved into and thus become space
All seeing will be blinded by all being
Time will have assumed a body
Time expresses itself by extending itself
Time expressed is extension
Without expressional extension time will be no longer
Time will have become space
Without extension there is no need for measure
Within the reign of quantity
Measure is the foundation of geometry
Quantities of everything are expressed in number
Time though no less continuous than space
Can only be measured indirectly by attaching it to space
This attachment of time and space is called movement
Through this intermediary of movement
Time and space have their relationship

103. *Notes:* Time and Space are referenced throughout human history. In the biblical story of Cain and Abel, for example, who as René Guénon suggests in his book *The Reign of Quantity & the Signs of the Times*, provide two prototypes. Those who are fixed in space, sedentary farmers like Cain, who project into time and those who wander through space, nomads like Abel, who project into space. Sedentary people create visual art solidified as objects, fixed in space (architecture, sculpture, painting). While nomadic people create phonetic art that can be heard (music, poetry). Time is running out for nomadic people who no longer have much free space before them — time for them is moving into space.

104. *1987 Subject: Culture*

Diggers and Planters

Diggers and Planters
Along the shore
Diggers and planters
For ever more
How long is forever?
And when is it lost?
How long is forever?
And how much does it cost?
And where can we spend
Our days and our moments
Together on end?
Our days and our moments
Will never end
As long as it takes
To plant and to eat
As long as we contribute
Our souls to the sleep

104. *Notes:* Lyrics for a song dealing with the short-sighted origins of our present day, agricultural society. We have become the takers and have

forgotten how to be the givers — only giving if there is a good bargain in it for us. We have become bound in selfishness and unable to be other-centered. Our innate compassionate and ability to love has become compromised. Having distanced ourselves from God, others and the natural world — we have dug ourselves to sleep, miring ourselves deeper into ignorance. We dig, plant, keep, eat and sleep. We are right next to the shore of the ocean of possibilities, and yet we settle for so little in our miserliness. We can become so caught up in our dire, petty, impoverished existence and never look up to see the blue sky or hear the song of birds or feel the mist from the ocean waves nearby.

105. 1988 Subject: Life, Portrait

From the Children's Chronicles Vol. I

I was but one of four
close as any we stayed from day to day
We were deprived and neglected, they would say
but never battered,
We were free
Gypsy children we were called by some
"Stay away from them, there in that house
do you hear what I say?
I don't care if you're all having fun, you'll get a disease"
The cats enter through a rotted-out hole
in the bathroom floor to drape around our necks
like winter mufflers
Be sure to give the roaches a chance to retreat
switch on the light as you step off your bed of sleep
I only regret how serious a child I was in those days
sitting alone in the unfinished room
reading books, studying maps and
scrubbing the dirty purple carpet with a hairbrush
My sister was the lighthearted one
loved by my grandmother who named her 'Dolly'

Her name is Ivy she has blond hair and green eyes
and sits in a sand box singing soundtracks from
movies like Porgy and Bess and West Side Story
Her long thin arms drawing a piece of sugar bread
close to her laughing mouth of crooked teeth
My mother was a child like us only younger
she sold us to a traveling circus sideshow for a summer,
while she lived in the trailer with the Ferris Wheel operator
My brother, throwing kitchen knives and switchblades — aiming
at the painted halo slightly above my head
His ten-year-old self so sure
and why not? we had been practicing this act for a whole year
after watching the Circus Show on TV every Friday night
I am glad he never missed and my sister and I are alive today
I guess our talent was that we could stay still
We had such unwavering faith in his ability not to kill
He always seemed so fearless, my little brother,
jumping off the roof with a towel tied around his neck
as a Zorro cape
He could jump from a standing position into a midair somersault,
land on his feet, without a flinch on a chalked sidewalk
My mother adored him and called upon his
talents often to entertain her friends
He could be reduced to tears though, while in front
of the giant turtles in the aquarium at the zoo,
crouching behind my mother's tight black skirt and
faux leopard heels as she stroked his
crew-cut head with her bitten to the quick fingernails
laughing and telling him over and over again,
"Bubba you are so silly to be afraid of turtles who can't get to you."
We worshiped our mother as did many of the kids
Well after all she did drive a hot pink corvette convertible and wore
sunglasses to match
All the neighborhood teenage boys

hung out at our house
She gave them cigarettes and had the newest
Chubby Checker and Everly Brothers' records
She had actually been to the Peppermint Lounge
and had gone out with Joey Dee
But all of this was still way before President Kennedy
was shot and way before the mafia hit man took his
place as our jailer and tormentor and
my mother's live-in hypnotist,
but that's another story altogether

105. *Notes:* I wanted to write about my childhood, which was lived during the fifties and early sixties. I wanted to write about my mother, my sister and my brother in such a way as to tell about their magical qualities and the wonder that was my life as a child with them. It wasn't until I was into my adult years that I realized that I had had an unusual childhood. Until that time I figured my life had been a fairly normal American life. This poem is the first of a series that I hoped to continue to write but never did, or at least haven't yet.

106. *1988 Subject: Life, Perception*

Air Ventures

Paint these concrete walls hot pink
Potted palms stuffed toucans
It's so hot in this hangar meant for airplanes

Put on this grass skirt
Push your breasts into coconut shells
Trying so hard to make something happen

I remember the sound of the film projector
Like a fan flipping round through images
Spitting out beaches, jungles, waves, and sand

Blue Hawaiian Caribbean cosmopolitan
Margarita mai-tai piña colada
Lava ecstasy rum and coke grenadine delight

Air Ventures gonna fly you high
Right out of your mind so fine
See the world for a dime

I remember running alongside the Cessna
Feeling so alone in this fight
Please jump out I'm sure a storm is brewing

We're gonna take you on a flight tonight
Stumble down don't frown
If we die, we all die together

Hanging on a wing pulled down a plane
Punched, hit, spit upon
Cursed and thrown in jail

Days later pointing to the map
Into a car we all and my cat packed
Don't you ever open your mouth

Your name is mud you are despicable
Who do you think you are to call the police?
Dooming us to live in poverty

We were destined to fly
Venture into the blue sky of limitless delights
While you a stupid kid cut our bird like wings

The cat will die and serve you right
Paralyzed perhaps you will realize things
For it was you who destroyed your family's life

Deep immovable catatonia starts with a twitch
Pushed to the deep end nowhere else to go but here
Alone alone again again again.

106. *Notes:* It was August in Tucson, Arizona, 1967. I had turned 16 a month before. My stepfather had been working on a business plan named Air Ventures — a vacation club. He would talk people into paying money to join the club, their membership ensuring that he would fly them, in a small plane, to a different exotic location to be determined every month. To this day, I am not sure if he intended to actually carry this out or whether he had planned to collect the initial money and then skip town. He was a seasoned con man, very skilled in persuasion. He had swindled a woman, who ran the local dog grooming business, into lending him the capital. He rented a hangar at the airport and enlisted me, my mom, brother and sister as decorators. Unbelievably he somehow had procured three small Cessna planes. At the opening party it was a full house, all the wealthy of Tucson sitting at rented tables being served tropical drinks by kids dressed up: my sister and I in hula outfits with coconut shell bras, my brother in a gorilla costume, that must have been stifling. We took the orders to my sarong-clad mother behind the bar who mixed the drinks. My stepfather showed 8-mm travel films of faraway places like Tahiti and Bora Bora, with a glib sales pitch that no one seemed to be able to resist. At the end of the night every guest offered up their support in the form of a personal check, making Air Ventures an overnight success with a hundred plus members. My stepfather, who had been imbibing many Mai Tai cocktails, as well other brightly colored parasol-garnished drinks throughout the evening, was noticeably intoxicated. So when the last of the happy new Air Ventures members departed, and he announced to us, "C'mon, let's celebrate, get in the plane we're going for a ride!" I defiantly said, "No way, you're drunk."

He coerced my mom and brother to get in the plane as he readied it for takeoff. I became very worried, sure that they were heading for a crash. I began threatening him, "I'm going to call the tower and tell them you're drunk and they will deny you clearance." My mom intervened, "Don't talk to your father like that. Can't you at least be kind, this is his big night. Don't argue with him now — come on, Sherry, lighten-up. Let's have some fun, you're always so serious." Seeing my brother Marty, cowering beside her in his ridiculous gorilla outfit, I argued, "Mom this is crazy, he's going to kill us all." She laughed, "You're so pessimistic! Look at it this way — if we die, we will all die together. Sherry, just get in!"

My sister, Ivy, was scared and decided to stay with me as I went back into the hangar to call the airport tower. Afterwards I ran to the plane, which was already taxiing down the runway. It was very windy, not only due to the propeller, but also due to a summer storm that I realized was coming on fast, contributing to the drama of the situation. "Please stop!" I cried, "Mom, Marty, jump out!" It only took a few minutes for the airport cops to circle the plane and cause it to come to a halt. Using megaphones, they commanded my stepfather to deplane. He did and ran immediately to me, grabbing me by the neck and really laying into me with his fists, calling me quite ugly names. The police intervened to pull him away from me, but he reacted by attacking them, which caused my mom to attack the police officers, hitting and biting whomever she could. More police showed up and broke up the fight. My parents were forced into a police car, while my brother, sister and I were put in the back of another police car. We were sitting scared and silent, when my stepfather managed to break free of the police and ran over to the car where we were. He poked his head through the open window and spit on me and cursed me more, but as he was about to hit me, he was restrained and handcuffed and lead back to the car. A policeman who was sitting in the front seat of the squad car that we were in, turned around and said reassuringly, "Don't worry, when he sobers up, he will be thankful that you saved his life as well as his family's." I just hung my head and turned to look at Marty and Ivy. Marty said sarcastically, "Yeah, sure." So we were taken to the Youth Center, and my Mom and stepfather were taken to jail.

The next morning there was a picture on the front page of the *Tucson Daily Star* of the Cessna with my stepfather in the pilot's seat. The story was a sensationalized version of what happened, saying something like: "Frantic teen-age daughter hangs on tail of plane trying to save her family." Of course all of the people who had written checks to become members of the new Air Ventures Club cancelled their checks after seeing the paper. A kind neighbor put up some bail and my parents were released from jail, and we were also released from the youth center. As soon as my stepfather saw me, he sniggered, "So, are you happy now that you succeeded in ruining your family's life? We could have been rich. You stupid, stupid girl, how could you have called the cops on your own family? What kind of a monster are you? Do me and everyone else a favor, shut up. Don't open your ugly mouth again. Get out of my sight." Of course I felt mortified and without protest went to my room. When I asked my mother if she hated me, she replied, "No I don't hate you, but I am mad at you. You shouldn't have done that. We are really in trouble now." At home the curtains were all drawn and the shades pulled down. For several days we had to pretend that no one was home, while the bill collectors and curiosity seekers rang the doorbell and phone non-stop.

One night my stepfather placed a map of the United States on the floor and exasperatedly asked my mother, "So Evlyn, where do you want to go now?" She closed her eyes, pointed her finger on the map and giddily said, "How about here?" As she opened her eyes, we all saw that her finger had landed about halfway between Tacoma and Seattle, Washington. "Okay," he said, "We'll go to Seattle — no one knows me there. We'll drive out of here tomorrow morning, each one of you kids can take one shoebox filled with your stuff, that's all. We're leaving everything else here." My cat Taffy, who had traveled with me from West Virginia, fit perfectly into the box. We took off, my Mom driving, but about thirty minutes into the exodus Taffy started howling. It was really hot in the car with no air-conditioning. The windows had to be open and he was desperate to get out no matter how much I tried to console and calm him down. As we reached the outskirts of town, my stepfather told my Mom to pull off the highway. "We're are we going?" I asked. "You shut up." When we arrived at the animal shelter, he pulled Taffy out of my arms and threatened me, saying, "Don't open your mouth. You have no rights. Shut up or I'll kill you." I watched him go through the door with Taffy. My mom turned to me and said, "We're just going to leave him here, honey, until we find a new home, then we'll send for him, don't worry." I was so desperate and miserable that I actually believed her at that moment.

A few days later we were all staying in a roadside motel somewhere in Oregon. It was late at night and I couldn't sleep. I was feeling lonely and worried about Taffy. My stepfather had gone out. I had worked myself into a dark place full of regret and grief. I asked my mom when we were going to get Taffy back. She told me the truth that he wasn't coming back. She added though that he was a good-looking cat and maybe someone had already come in and adopted him by now. The truth hit me hard. I knew that Taffy had received a death sentence. I realized that I had lied to myself. I had convinced myself to believe what my mother had told me, but all the while I knew the truth. I had betrayed Taffy. I fell into deep despair, knowing that there was nothing I could do to change the situation that I myself had created. The finality of the realization of all that had occurred flooded into my mind: Losing Taffy, being alienated from my family, the Air Ventures folly, then back further reviewing other times I had instigated a catastrophe which affected the lives of others. My stepfather had gone out earlier, and now my mother said to us kids, "Let's watch some TV." We were all in a motel room that had two large beds, one of which — the one that we kids slept in — was pushed up against a wall. As they sat around the TV, I went and lay down on the bed as close to the wall as possible. My hand began to twitch, triggering a catatonic state. I knew that I would become very still soon. My mom, brother and sister, engaged in what they were watching, were unaware of what was happening to me. This was not the first time I became catatonic. It had happened before as a result of the realization that I had been the cause of some traumatic experience that had affected others, even though my initial intention had not been to cause them harm. I had come to recognize the symptoms, which would lead to complete rigidity of my body. It would begin with me feeling sad, then I would try to find a place to be alone. I felt trapped with no way out. I would try not to cry or make any noise. My body would start some involuntary repetitive movement, like touching two fingers together, then eventually something would click and paralysis would set in, my body becoming rigid. I would be motionless for minutes or hours.

In that motel room on a bed by myself I felt like I had years before when my grandmother would remind me that I had destroyed my mother's life. My mother had trained to become a professional musician but had become pregnant with me when she was 17 and had dropped her aspirations in order to raise a family. Her husband, the father of my brother and sister, had abandoned us shortly afterwards, and she was left as a single mom. My grandmother, (actually my great grandmother — she was my mother's grandmother) moved in with us when I was 7 to help. Whenever we would fall into some difficulty, financial usually, my grandmother reminded me that I was the cause of our family's predicament because I had destroyed my mother's life.

Now, in this motel room en route to a new city, I was facing the fact that not only had I destroyed my mother's chance for a career as a musician, but my family's chance of success as well. I had also destroyed the life of my cat, my only real friend, and now there was no one I could talk anything over with, there was nowhere to go, all options closed. I was a very troubled young girl. We did settle in Seattle, and my stepfather tried a few more get-rich-quick schemes, though nothing as grand as the Air Ventures venture.

Through the exercise of writing these notes — the story that accompanies this poem I was provided with the opportunity to see the emptiness in the experience. At the time I felt extreme self-loathing and saw my stepfather as an adversary coming at me. The hard fact that I faced when writing the story was the karmic truth that I *had* been the cause of the demise of the Air Ventures venture, as my stepfather had said — but not exactly as I had understood his accusatory words then. Now through distance and time, my perception is colored by compassion for all the characters involved, including myself. I have continued to work on letting go of blaming my stepfather and the perception of myself as a victim of his unfairness, my own self-loathing and the anger and confusion that I directed towards my stepfather. I try to see it all as a karmic play, the program for which I must have set in motion a long time before the events of the story — most likely before I was born. It is said, we choose our parents, or rather our past actions (karmas) do the choosing for us.

107. *1988 Subject: Perception, Yoga*

The Key

Remember that the key
which unlocks the door
to happiness in this world
is to let go
of finding fault with others
With the key
open the gate and
walk through
The way out is
always the way through
Let go
This moment
is forever new

107. Notes: This poem deals with a way to move forward — toward happiness, toward enlightenment, toward overcoming otherness — to get unstuck. Where most of us get stuck is finding fault with others and in blaming others for our unhappiness. The best way to open to the possibility of happiness is to let go of focusing on the shortcomings of others and blaming others. Don't even blame yourself — let go of blaming, let go of guilt. Negative emotions like blame, guilt, regret, anger etc. will only slow you down. The key is to start moving forward and keep going.

My Dear Friend

My dear friend
Take the time to develop a method
Employ a clever team
Stop your crying and stumble not
On the rags of your own sorrow
Build your home in the mouth of the tiger
Make it comfortable
Hang beautiful curtains
Burn incense brew some tea
Close your eyes, exude your own electricity
Breathing air under the soles of your feet
Suck the space into the forehead
Smile silently and heat the heart from inside
Color the lotus there with smoky pastels
Think for a moment through the mesh
See the back behind the front
And with the space in-between
Turn your hell into a living room heaven
Others may appear in the shadows
Do not forget to remember
That the story is of your making
And that you are only seeing something
Because you have allowed yourself
To forget that you are it already

108. Notes: Written to a friend of mine who was going through a difficult romantic relationship, this poem suggests a new perspective.

Appearances

It is hard to keep things in their keeping places
appearances are this way or that
depending on where you choose to be
My heart seems like a place of oozing mud
which as anyone could know,
if they just gave it some thought,
is very much like the continuous tumbling of clouds,
or the endless possibilities of a seashell
The appearance of the universe
is infinite and finite,
depending on who is doing the looking
Grace and Beauty,
at least hold on to those two
First let your eyes do the seeing,
this is a first step
Then let go of all the seeing and
be the being
So you see, this is not at all that easy
Try then, after the seeing, to let go
of what you think you know
Even this could prove difficult
because, after all, the eyes like to keep things imprisoned you know
Sight is good with differences
Touching likes same-nesses
Some would say let the heart be the steering wheel
I might say that too, but nonetheless
may I also ask, where does the heart,
this place of oozing mud, fit in?
The mind is movement and
like mercury cannot be trusted
Creation always occurs, that is, it happens,

with the assistance of time
Creation needs events,
just as movement is dependent upon time,
events are to time as heat is to fire —
they are qualities of it

It is hard to keep things in their keeping places
because things just don't keep —
they change they move
Their nature is time they are defined by events
Eyes ears nose tongue skin — time's very own creation
Grace and beauty will keep you here for a while —
they are to be your helpers, keeping you grounded
Don't worry they won't pull you under —
they can't, they are not heavy enough
Their very essence is light, you see
The sun the moon the stars, heat and cold
where have you all come from,
and are you going anywhere other
then where you have been?
You can only see the appearance
of coming and going in a good light
With light time begins — but the heart knows for sure
with being there is no end.

109. *Notes:* This poem is about the changeful nature of things, including one's own mind, which can be fickle, motivated by preferences and lacking true discernment. Looks can be deceiving but so can smell, taste and all the rest. Only being proves to be real. Even so, beauty and grace can be very helpful, even essential, in the quest for realness and the overcoming of the bondage of preferences. I am no doubt relying on what poet John Keats said, "Truth is beauty and beauty is truth". Even so, I throw in a metaphor describing my heart as an oozing place of mud and relate it to tumbling clouds, perhaps to add a bit of surrealism, shaking me out of judging things by their appearances.

PART 3 1990s FLOWERS — Reorientation: Attraction, Drama, Romance, Uncertainty, Musing, Memories

For me, the 1990s were permeated with death and loss and with this came trepidation for the future and a deep nostalgia and grieving for the past. The first death was the loss of my daily art discipline, which I had practiced since the 1970s. I was used to spending my days sitting at my art table writing and painting or practicing music and dance. Between the increasing duties involved with teaching yoga and administrating the Jivamukti Yoga School, I had less and less time for these pursuits. David and I were also becoming public personalities, so we had to spend time answering questions from the press as well as from other well-meaning people about yoga. David didn't seem to mind his transition from artist to public figure yogi; in fact, he seemed to be thriving. I remember our friend, musician/composer Bill Laswell, commenting at the time in regard to David's past, "...and he gave it all up for yoga!" But I found it difficult to accept that my creativity was being channeled into something I hadn't planned on doing. I missed my daily routine of artistic pursuits. My daily yoga practice was fulfilling, but I was unsure of my new identity as a yoga teacher and felt perhaps this was just a phase and I would be able to get back to my "real work" soon.

While I was experiencing this re-orientation, there were a lot of people dying around me, people who meant a lot to me. In June 1992, my brother Marty died. At the very end, while holding my sister's hand and mine, he said, "watch this," winked his left eye and pulled his consciousness out of his body. Marty's death for me was both traumatic and transformational. Two of my fellow Audio Letter band members, master musicians Don Cherry and Denis Charles, also died during this time. Two of our beloved cat companions, Gezar of Ling and Mr. Mouse, died during the first two years of the decade. Our guru Shri Brahmananda Sarasvati, whom we met in May of 1993 died that September. My alchemy teacher, Randy Hall, was found dead in his Seattle apartment of a heart attack in December 1993. My stepfather, Don Gannon, suffered a heart attack and died in 1996. Another important guru to us, Swami Nirmalananda died a willful death (*pryopravesha*) in December of 1997. Several friends who had been "regulars" at the Life Café died of AIDS, Billy Sleeze and Tex among them. One of my friends, Jesse Bernstein, a prolific Seattle writer, committed suicide in 1991 by cutting his own throat with a kitchen knife. An old boyfriend, Perry Phillips, came close to suicide but survived. With all the turmoil I again courted suicidal musings myself.

Incredibly, in the midst of all of this death there was intense life and creative construction going on. In 1990, David and I took a big step and opened the Jivamukti Yoga Center on 2nd Avenue and 9th Street in New York City, which required us to become a corporation, hire lawyers, open a bank account, buy insurance, and get a phone as well as a computer. Prior to this I had kept my money in a box in a dresser drawer in my bedroom. I had no need for a car as I rode my bike or walked everywhere, I needed to go.

During this decade David and I went on to open two more major yoga centers in New York City, doing most of the renovation work ourselves. We were quite overwhelmed with the administrative duties until a spunky decisive young woman, Elizabeth Tobier, who I would name Viveka (meaning discrimination) and affectionately call V.V., announced that we needed a manager. She nominated herself for the job and we enthusiastically accepted. Besides busily opening and renovating yoga centers, we completely gutted and rebuilt our apartment in the city and bought a house in Woodstock, New York. All the while we took many trips to India. Traveling to Mysore in the south to study Ashtanga Yoga with Sri K. Pattabhi Jois and to Vraja in North India to immerse ourselves in the Krishna Bhakti tradition of the Pusthi Marg under the tutelage of Shri Shyamdas. During this decade we continued to develop and refine an original style of yoga called "Jivamukti" and created a high-standard teacher training program to establish it as a codified method.

In 1993 we were invited to present at the first major yoga conference in America, Unity in Yoga, which was a celebration of 100 years of yoga in America. It was at the conference that we met our guru Shri Brahmananda Sarasvati; this would be the beginning of a long and fruitful association with his Ananda Ashram in upstate New York.

Presenting at the conference catapulted us into a yoga world community of conferences and brought a great deal of media attention. Seemingly overnight we became "known" and listened to by many people. We appeared on the Today Show, we were interviewed, filmed and quoted weekly in national and international magazines and newspapers. Jivamukti Yoga became a New York City phenomenon, attracting celebrity students as well as celebrity spiritual teachers like Swami Shankarananda, Swami Satchidananda, Alice Coltrane (Swami Turiyananda) and Professor Robert Thurman, all of whom became our close friends and spiritual advisors.

Music and bhakti were essential components of our teaching method, so we also found ourselves at the center of the kirtan explosion in the Western yoga world with the help of Shyamdas, Jai Uttal, Krishna Das and Bhagavan Das, all of whom held kirtans regularly at Jivamukti.

We made deep and lasting friendships with many high-profile people, not only from the spiritual and yoga world but also from the music, entertainment and fashion industries. Diane Keaton, Willem Dafoe, Donna Karan, Christy Turlington, Joan Jett, Beastie Boy Mike D., along with his wife, film maker Tamra Davis, and Sting and his multi-talented wife Trudie Styler, were all regular students at our 2nd Avenue and Lafayette Street schools.

On January 23rd, 1998 we held a grand opening party to celebrate the move of the Jivamukti Yoga School to a large space on Lafayette Street. Sting and his band provided music. David and I even performed an asana dance with live music by Sting. Bill Laswel, Ravi Coltrane as well as Bhagavan Das and Krishna Das performed. This event drew a lot of media coverage. Shortly afterwards more celebrities including Madonna started coming to class.

This was an intensely busy and creative time for David and me. We produced two films. *What is Yoga*, a documentary conceived and directed by our student Mary Bosakowski. It featured actor Willem Dafoe and a soundtrack put together by Janet Rienstra of Meta Records. Then in *Asana, Sacred Dance of the Yogis*, filmed by James Carman, David and I performed my choreography, which incorporated yoga asanas, to music by Sting, Jah Wobble and others.

Collaborating with Janet Rienstra, we made a spoken word/music CD titled *Chakra, the Seven Centers*, with music by Bill Laswell, Pharoah Sanders, DJ Cheb I Sabbah and others. We also produced four yoga instructional CDs with a lot of help from Janet Rienstra and Bill Laswell, who contributed music and also took care of all the studio recording and engineering. We manufactured and distributed these ourselves, with David providing all of the graphics and creating booklets to accompany each CD that included detailed photos of hundreds of asanas, which we had taken of each other.

We began a rich collaboration with photographer Martin Brading, creating a yoga asana calendar each year from 1997-2000. The photos taken for our calendar project would evolve into the book, *The Art of Yoga*. In 1999 I wrote and, with help from Barbara Boris and Gail Berrigan, self-published the book *Cats and Dogs are People, Too!* in order to shed light on the use of the rendered bodies of cats and dogs in commercial pet food and offer healthy, home-cooked recipes as an alternative.

Also in 1999, along with Janet Rienstra, David and I put on a Gala Fashion Show at our new Lafayette Street location and raised enough money to establish, within the Humane Society of New York City, The Animal-Mukti Clinic. This was New York City's first free spay and neuter clinic. The clinic, still operating, has reduced the number of dogs and cats euthanized in New York City by forty percent to date.

During this wonderfully productive time, I nonetheless doubted myself. I was passionately committed to practicing and teaching yoga but could not commit to viewing myself as a spiritual teacher and wanted to run away from my administrative duties as well as creative projects associated with the yoga school. I yearned for a "normal life". My personal life was falling apart; it was very high drama and quite unsettling.

In 1991, David took initiation from Swami Nirmalananda and became Swami Bodhananda. Taking the vows of a monk, he shaved his head and dressed in orange robes, leaving quite an impression when he walked down the streets of the Lower East Side. We lived in separate apartments during most of the decade.

After my brother died, I reunited with my old boyfriend Perry Phillips from Seattle and took a trip to India with him, but the culture shock he experienced in India actually ended our romantic relationship for good, (although we have remained friends.) I tried unsuccessfully to make other romantic relationships work. I suppose I was trying to escape my destiny. Despite many attempts to create, or fashion, or merely hold on to a "normal" life, I found myself constantly propelled into my "destiny." At that time, I remember Shyamdas saying to me, "Padma, you have to come to realize that God is your only true love." But due to my lack of spiritual maturity it was hard for me to understand what that meant. I felt conflicted and wasn't 100% convinced that living a renounced celibate life was for me. Perhaps secretly I still harbored dreams of a so-called "normal" life — one day getting married to someone who loved me and dedicating my life to family. But as I was getting older and the journey continued, it was becoming more and more apparent that that was not in the stars for me. I may have gone kicking and screaming, and tried to redirect fate, but no matter what I did, my former hopes and dreams seemed to be dissolving on their own as I found myself catapulted into a world, I didn't recollect planning for.

I didn't write much poetry during this time, compared to the decade of the eighties, as I was too involved with the administrative responsibilities and creative projects related to the yoga school. Most of the poems I did write during the nineties express intense yearning for what I thought was a lost life, some imagined age of innocence.

Limitless

When I called out it was you who were there
but where was that,
and how could I have known it was you?
I knew and I could tell
by the feel of your slow breath
on the palm of my hand.
You are there and I am here close as skin
It is one of life's precious things
this pretending to be two different people
This joy can outdo itself
when it is known for what it is:
the play of love
Because I am a limitless being
I am none other than you
and that is love itself.

110. *Notes:* Love is not dependent upon a physical experience with two people.
Love is our nature.

111. *1990 Subject: Love, Mysticism, Perception*

Fairy Story

So this is a fairy story
A trip between the three worlds for green children
To hear all the words you must press open your heart
Like a flower against a book page
And even so you must close your eyes
And drift like the sound of fluttering wings
And other such things
It goes like this

Up above the wet forest floor
The winds were laughing in delight
Body of bliss sat as a smile under a tree
Within a blanket of mist and breath
They swooned these creatures locked in
Each other riding the waves
On the ocean of everlastingness
As they kiss the lips of eternity
They float through doors of a wide-awake dream
Light and lightness itself

111. Notes: When the pressures of life become overwhelming, I try to remember to use my imagination and call upon the fairies, asking them to kindly invite me into their world of green. They clear my heart and lift me into a sweet space of recollection and give me a second chance, a second grace, in only a few seconds.

112. 1990 Subject: Poetry

A Most Pleasant Experience

It is amazing to me how I can write a poem
I know for sure that I can't —
it is too difficult for me to do
and yet —
it is the most pleasant experience to try
And after a while of typing there it is:
a poem
Not anything profound or great —
just something that gave
a most pleasant experience

112. Notes: The time spent writing a poem or painting a picture is a very joyful time for me. I feel happy in the midst of it. I learn things. I feel stretched and optimistic. It is not a chore; it is something done for delight.

All of It

To keep the company of saints
Is to walk in the world happy
Is to feel caressed by the smells of the trees
And the softness of grass under feet
It is to find compassion in the sight of
Garbage on the street
And the death of an innocent bird by poisoned water
All is none other than you
And you are it, all of it

113. *Notes:* Chanting God's name keeps us in good company, wherever we go. Mantras — the names of God — help us perceive everything as holy, and when we can see the world in that way we walk with saints. Trying to change the world outside of ourselves without first purifying our minds — which provide us with the perception of the world — will not bring positive results. We must change our perception of the world and in doing so we change the world. Chanting God's name can help us purify our perception, enabling us eventually to transcend the misperception that causes us to see ourselves as separate from the world and from God. This shift in perception is magical.

114. 1991 *Subject: Love, Mysticism, Perception*

The Face of an Angel

We're caught once again
    Way up here this time
    There is a terrible sweetness in misery
    Embarrassingly so:
A false illusion of doing something important
    When we come to our problems
    And try to figure out a way

This happens on and on doesn't it?
> But wait a minute to remember
> The look of the divine
> That beautiful glimpse towards light

That only angels have
> Because angels are none other but the face of God
> God can never be seen
> But angels appear from time to time
> To those who are humble and sincere
> And so we wait a minute
> To remember the face of an angel
> We need the faces of angels

It is called inspiration
> But really it is illusion
> Because when you know, you know that
> The face of an angel is hardly anything
> Like the divine
> The divine is black and terrible, it is all things
> It is the greed and suffering of a small grey mouse
> And the waste of a city
> To one who is light, all is the radiant body of God
> Angels are indeed the friends of those
> Who have given up
> To those who have surrendered their tiny wills
> To those who are simple and sincere
> Give up and angels are sure to come
> Their bodies are formed from the very stuff of surrender
> And their faces are breathtakingly beautiful

Pure and simple
> And what does it matter to one who is
> Humble and sincere, whether or not they
> Are being deluded by a beautiful face?

---

114. *Notes:* Superimposing the face of an angel upon the one you love is a practice that can lead to clearer perception of self and other.

Love Has No Body

The stars and the wind please carry me back
Which is really only a little away from here
Although it seems like thousands of miles
The stars and the wind take their time
As it was given to them for that reason
And so they should

We have come down, solidified here
In appearance only within this eye of time
So that we can just take the time
To think about it all
All of it, that is

We find that the world of sights and smells
Is just a lot of different songs
All made of sound

In these shapes and sighs
There are continuous whispers about it all
All of it, that is

Your silken skin softens to the touch
Which is drawn from my hand
Drawn from your own heart's desire
As you glide this hand of mind all over
The skin that is growing out of you

The sun and all of the stars make it appear
As trees and sky, calm lakes and your eyes
There is a way to become invisible
Only true lovers are given this power

It is none other than the power
Of complete being-ness all of it
Nothing hidden
But because it is all,
All of it, that is
It has no appearance and appears as nothing at all

115. *Notes:* The love has nobody idea creates a riddle of sorts, a semantic
puzzle. On one hand, the poem suggests that love is too large to be contained
in a material body, its source is eternal. It also implies that true love is not
possessive. When we fall in love, we may think we fall in love with a person,
but the poem insists that we fall through a crack in our conditioned world
into another realm — a love land, that is ever present and beyond the laws of
this material one.

116. *1991 Subject: Culture, Nature, Speciesism*

Who Speaks?

What is the simple religion of insects
What does their language say
To whom are they talking, with
Their clicking and clacking dialects?

Is it possible to talk to the wind?
Or is it the wind that is
Speaking through us?
To consider that we'd be so chagrined

But perhaps it is that
the elemental forces, the spirits of air
are the animators singing
through all things.

Most of the perceivable world
Is just a big puppet show
Put on by the invisible
Spirits of the air unfurled

The insects, fishes and birds
Have an undisputed pact
With the elementals
And perform in the ballet dance

Trees, rocks and fungi
pulsate and speak by means of
enveloping and digesting
mushrooming and leafing

While we humankind
Have convinced ourselves
That we are speaking from
Our own heart and mind

We deluded souls are under
The impression that air is
For the birds and fire
Only comes when we light a match

Those devas of ether
Of air and fire do not exist
Because superstitious people believe
Through a spell they can conjure

It is us who exist as
Their created musical instruments
In the grand symphony of life
It is we, who are being sung through

116. *Notes:* Most human beings regard nature as lacking intelligence and think that we are the only beings who have language or anything meaningful to say. To the contrary, all of nature is alive and communicates in its own way, including trees, rocks, fungi, oceans and insects, as well as the elemental forms of fire, water air and ether.

117. *1991 Subject: Time*

Scaling the Octaves

I don't know really, perhaps it's in the traveling
From dream to dream in and out of sleep
That time thing is sure playing an interesting part
Is it a part or is it actually the whole?
The whole thing appearing as parts of things
and also things themselves
So the thing is probably there in-between
the then and there
But we all know that in between there and then
is nothing
So the thing must be nothing
The very beginning of things themselves
Any and all of them
They will all prove eventually to have their beginnings
in that flow which is known
as nothing
But when we think about it we know
That in-between, that seemingly nothing
is indeed something
Because nothing is something, before or after all
But listen, it is only a little something
not much at all
A small thing hardly noticeable
to the big roving eyes of the slow machine

Crafted by love *Cthulhu* the fishy fiend
The one submerged in his watery deep dream
floating within our collective languid liquid sleep
That scaly snake that sees all but
pretends most of the time to be asleep
We must not underestimate
The love that that snake feels for us
For in its pretending it lets us think
we can get away with murder
It knows we must go, go, go through it all
To know all the spaces both up and under
Traveling the fish's scales teetering to fall
Scaling octaves licking the tongue
Music is the symbol for everyone
And when we or anyone else dies
we are held so tight by that noose
that we explode free for a moment
like the birth of baby worms
from a tight small hole
Those many legs and arms appear
Wiggling like so many
experiences dredged up from memory
to never drop off never atrophy
If you care to look you can see all of those
countless arms and legs undulating fingers and toes
floating and grasping
in the space of waves, the lap of time
In between nothing at all

117. *Notes:* An invitation to one of the sleeping "Deep Ones," the fictional mythical cosmic sea monster *Cthulhu*, to step out of a weird tale by H.P. Lovecraft and scale some octaves with us in a musical dream of giving birth to worms who may be able to worm hole their way into the future and bring some light into the darkness through the holes they make. Although, according to Lovecraft, a human tongue should not be able to pronounce the name of Cthulhu. You can try by saying: "Ka-laa-lōō".

Shut Up and Listen

Only these few words to describe all of this
Hardly does it seem fair
More likely it appears arrogant for one person
To speak so many millions of words in a lifetime
Saying this or that about this and that
It hardly seems fair
To say anything
To describe what can be seen with even the
Most enchanting schemes of words
Is barely enough
And yet
We think we have seen it all and can tell it
Like it is or was
But all we are doing is showing a small corner
Of a shadow of it and even that is a lie
Truth is immense
It is larger than the universe
Words wiggle out of minds filled with images
Linked together as a sequence of events in time
We cannot know what we are talking about
Until we are willing to stop talking
And break out of our small corner to reach
For possibilities that cannot be described
How to do that is to enter the mystical land of
Shut up and listen

118. *Notes:* The mystical experience cannot be described because it is coming from a place outside of time — the realm of the spirit, where words don't hold much importance. Every mystic knows that to quiet the mind is the only way to find a way through the whirlings (*vrittis*) of the mind. The word *mystic*, like the word *mystery*, refers to that which cannot be disclosed or talked about. The

Sanskrit equivalent words *mauni* and *mauna*, to which the English words mystic and mystery are related, mean "to shut up, be quiet, stop talking" and instead tune in — to listening. This is basically what meditation entails. The *Yoga Sutra* says, "*yogash chitta vritti nirodhah*", which means that when you stop identifying with your thoughts — the whirlings, the fluctuations of your mind, the images, sensations, feelings, etc. — then there is yoga — the realization of Truth, your connection to God. So yoga is for those who can meditate, those who are willing to stop talking long enough to be able to shut up and listen — those mystics who allow the wordless mystery to enfold them by being quiet and still in order to let go of what they think they know.

119. *1991 Subject: Perception*

At That Time

Then there is that smooth evening out time
when you are lying in your bed
The skin all over your body feeling the same
It's all smoothed out and the temperature
is even throughout
The body is calm and serene
You really don't need anything, or anyone
It is the beginning time of wild quiet titillation
Take time to witness it as it erupts,
softly pouring out of itself liquid fire
This is chemical, bio-chemical
and so — what, isn't in this great world of ours?
It comes in the morning as a reminder of the first rhyme — when
there was a separation, a birthing into time
Slow undulations of one morphing into two
giving birth to countless thoughts; the inexplicable courageous,
adventurous act of being a pretend individual
and so — what, isn't in this great world of ours, a pretension?
It is all appearing, pretending to be so many things

When we are together long fingered hands
take their time gliding along some smoothness
until it seems like too much, which signals the hardness
and determination to go somewhere
This is what it must be about
and so — what, why try to divert our attention away
from the simple fact of it?
In the same way we must not look
at a solar eclipse without special glasses
Apocalypse uncovers to reveal glory at that time
If you have planted the right seeds in the wild forest
you need only go to sleep and then wake up at that right time
to meet someone who is not afraid to reveal the world itself — to you.

119. *Notes:* An apocalyptic event need not be Earth shattering in an external material way. It can be an internal event, a inner journey into the core of one's own soul to reveal the hidden agenda for the evolution of the self.

120. *1991 Subject: Love*

Winter Roses

I'm so glad
Seeing the side of your face on my pillow
How much does a feather weigh in a quiet place?
I'll throw these arms around you like a garland
The smell of you is the smell of winter roses
Red and green

120. *Notes:* Savoring an experience.

Wiggly Little Things

Thoughts can be wiggly little things
Coming home and sitting down to it
So what does it really matter if one two or three get out today?
Tapping into it is the good part
Like a swallow bird gliding into a cave filled with worms and worms
Take what you like
Which one to pull out and which one to leave wiggling?
Take that one and slice it open
With a razor-sharp beak
Aim at some point, any mole will do
Let yourself go right into it
But remember you must tell it as you go
And that can take a lot of fast-talking
Putting all those words together, making pictures out of feelings
There is a sack of wonder in the smallest part of anything around
Whole stories can be built
Out of what happened in an hour's time
Just start talking, it doesn't matter if there is no one to hear you
And what you will have is a head with some stuff cleared out of it
But don't be getting your hopes up for
Some austere minimalism of the mind, no way
It will just keep right on making and making
Just look at your world, isn't it evidence of that?
You think you had nothing to do with it?
Take a moment and look at those worms in your head
Oozing out of your eyes and wherever
And they don't have to go out
They can go in too
Look around inside or out it doesn't matter
It came from you and you are where it's all going

You make it up as you go along and you can't stop
those wormy wiggling little things
Try it — think about it

121. *Notes:* Talking about the process of writing a poem and questioning the
worth of the endeavor.

122. *1992 Subject: Love*

There Is Love Here

It is late tonight and I remember these things
Hearing Penta's songs as she so perfectly sings
About the same people that I also knew and loved
Maybe they also loved me too
maybe they still do

I think of you as I so often do
rubbing my fingernails while we were sitting in a movie chair
For a long time you did that
You used to wear a thick leather watchband on your wrist
It made your hands look like a gladiator's
They were strong I remember I loved them so

When you allowed yourself to remember
that you were in love with me
your face changed and your eyes would
Roll up and back into your head like a saint's in samadhi
Your lips would become a deeper color of lavender and
They would quiver when you put them real close against my face
You wouldn't talk very much then
but you would make nice little sounds
Although I do remember you would say some things sometimes over

and over
Like the word "yes" and "there is love here,
there is love here"

As I am typing this, I look at the keys and see my fingernails
They are painted a bright shiny orchid color
I know you would have liked to see this color
It reminds me of that earring you used to sometimes wear
Oh well, all these things, what do they mean
We come and we go
That little thing life-less behind the rose bushes
Then little Eva lying dead
on the cold polished cement floor of my basement room
while you and I are arguing, miles away

Remembrances snapshot scenes
Jesse is singing on a tape
somehow it all reminds me of you
how to explain what it means?
I felt like I knew about some things and
wanted to share it all
With you back then and also now
At least you did get to spend some time with
Marty-man, didn't you?
I am so glad for that I can't really tell you why so clearly
It's all just feelings snapshot scenes
Hard to describe what I mean without
sounding like clichés

But hey, you know something?
Just to hear your voice is so wonderful to me
I have come to realize that you don't believe that I see a miracle in you
So what, anyway

There is summer and water, which you love,
I see you there and smell the sun on your skin

122. *Notes:* The title is something that my lover from many years before often would say to me. Those words would visit me, sometimes instigating a flood of memories, which I tried to capture in this poem.

123. *1992 Subject: Love*

In a Room There under the Ground

It was many a many a year ago
In a room there under the ground
A girl in a box warm with orange glow
Rough wooden rafters set down low

Several collected mirrors lined the wall
Silently catching glistening beads
The sweat of yearning and surprise
Sad sweet tears of knowing
What was to be coming and all

Muffled shuffling from upstairs
Where the amateur spell-casters worked
Frightened never these two
Locked together as silent mushrooms
Smooth, damp and still

Sometimes the flesh of roses heavy with wet
Soft skins shared their bed
Petals pressing between heart and thigh
Like a book where flowers lie

Furry and black little ears pick up
Outside by the window sounds
Of a beautiful hand tapping on the glass
Around its wrist a heavy band did bound

Even now when so much has passed
From those nights of deep even seclusion
One wonders why they are not
Still forever there

Things change you know
It unrolls right in front of you
The great fairy's tail unfolds
Flapping splashing in the bathtub water
To the horror of the night's gaze

Time is like a serpent's tail
With wondrous side effects
Under every scale
Offering up the richness of a poet's pen
What is now, remember, is due to what was then

123. *Notes:* The rented basement room in Seattle where I lived had an orange carpet on the floor. It was small, dark, cold and damp but would become transformed into a warm. luminous paradise when my beloved came to visit me.

124. *1992 Subject: Portrait*

We Shave Our Eyebrows in Mourning

Cats live in a cat world of audio delight
Big ears hear the secret conversation of mice

We sit at the breakfast table sipping tea
Our eyebrows shaved in mourning we

Beloved black and white cat died last night
Sweet Eva poisoned it cannot be right

Who is to blame what can be done, she is free
An electric thunderbolt over her heart did you see

She was our high-brow elegant higher sight
Egyptian whiskered goddess shines eyes bright

124. *Notes:* In ancient Egypt, most families lived with a cat, including perhaps the cat's extended family. The cat was viewed as an essential part of the household. When the beloved elder cat of the home died it was the custom for every human in the household to shave his or her eyebrows in mourning. Humans at that time revered cats as teachers of the subtleties of sound and vibration. With this knowledge, they believed the essence of life could be revealed to one's sight. Eva, a black and white cat with a white thunderbolt across her chest, had been my beloved cat companion for nine years, when she was cruelly poisoned and died. I wrote this poem almost ten years after her death, which is perhaps why it is able to have a lightness to it, which would not have been possible if I had tried to write it at the time of her death.

125. *1992 Subject: Portrait*

Fan Dance

They are holding secrets in outstretched hands
Here begins the dance of the fans

Oh the brave smell of a stone
Can move, or cannot can, there a cannot be

This whorl is a passion of smells
The wind is the strongest among us
Causing the waves to rise and the flames to fly

There is never stillness where there is fragrance
Here begins the dance of the fans

It is said that all forms of life generate from fire
But is not fire the compressed concentration of air?
They say all forms of life are born from the sea
But is not water split as liquidation of sound?

Oh the courage of a fluttering fan
Can move, or cannot can, there a cannot be
Reviving the spirits of the deed
Awake and go there once again
Fan shapes in a funnel then

Become so dense you are transparent
The far sounding whisper says.

This is a journey of countless lives
A sound barely heard; a sight nowhere seen
Remember within smells memory dwells
Courageous and brave as the wind
Blowing breezes between fingers of unfolded fans
Here begins the dance of the fans

125. *Notes:* My beloved friend Kathleen Hunt is a dancer. She is a genius of gesture and movement, as well as being expert in the use of essential oils and perfumes. This poem was written for her. It glorifies the air element, which is personified through Kathleen's ethereal dances and her way of looking at the comings and goings of the world from an expanded more all-encompassing elevated place.

Sum-time

when you see something so wrong
you know it needs changing

what is easy to forget is that
we are the ones who need the changing

gather up a whole bunch of moments
and make a sum-time

126. Notes: An encouragement to make the best of the time you have.

Bluebird

You had traveled meticulously way past each dissolving moment
Knowing you in the small way that I do I know that you savored
Every moment intoxicated with the taste of all that had transpired

Last night you saw the mirage in the distance
Your feet went walking toward it in your sleep

Now it is morning but we are not yet mourning
We are confused, you are not
But nonetheless we awake and rush through the dawn
to be by your side
The Ivy wants so much to help you to twine around and uplift you
But you remain motionless as if asleep not needing
anything from her or me

We do not know what to do
It is as if we have not received training for this

Often times I do remember a certain look you had on your face
I could not decipher it then but now I am almost able
to grasp its meaning
It was a look of incredulousness
As if to say, "Hey you know what to do, don't act so dumb."

Oh my Mr. Bluebird
My high lama of way-be-gone please forgive me as I know you will
Cause I realize now you have been so patient with me all along

Hey Noble one
I am in the presence of greatness and have been all along
What was wrong with me, how come I could not see until now?

They say we are in our own world when we die
Well what world is that really?
Is there any other world but our own anyway at any other time?

I was lost for a long time, you were so patient

At your funeral wake there were so many people
some in bodies some not, still so many
The air was dense with being
The air was dense with sound and sense

I must admit for if I don't I will most likely
fall into eternal stupidity for another several lifetimes
I must admit that you knew what you were doing all along

I did not know that until now
you have taught me so much

In a moment at the time of death
A secret revealed my secret love
My heart teacher
But who would understand that and so what if they do or don't?

They have many others to help them through the night
why should I bother
Why did it take me so long to recognize the time
the circumstances of the place
Why did you take so long to get there, I had to be a little girl
for almost three years
Before you came

For so many years you tried to tell me something but I could not listen
Until the moment of your death

You called us to your bedside
Each of your hands holding our hands close to you as you opened your
eyes and showed us the universe beyond words and things
We saw into your eyes as you suspended time for us

It must have taken so much strength for you to do that then
Where did that come from?
Where did you come from?

But that was nothing compared to what you managed next
You said to us, "Watch this," and winked your eye, then contracting
all your muscles and scrunching up your face
you pulled out of your body
up and out through the top of your head

You were gone out of that body
They all ran out of the room wailing in disbelief, in grief, in relief
I do not know, who knows?
We saw a bluebird fly past the window today.

127. *Notes:* This poem was written shortly after my brother's death while I was still entangled in grief. The notes were written more than 15 years later.

My brother, Marty, died on June 17, 1992, in a hospice in Seattle, Washington. He was 38 years old. I was honored to be present at his death. It was a most important experience. Everything I had innocently, but arrogantly, thought I knew about everything was shattered completely. I realized I knew nothing and that at best I had only been glimpsing a hint of the surface of something and mistaking that for reality...or spirituality, for that matter.

Marty's death was very unusual, as he died consciously. "There is a Tibetan term, *phowa*, for this kind of death," my friend Bob Thurman told me many years later when I recounted the story of my brother's death to him. Basically, he said that all lamas try for this type of auspicious death but very few accomplish it, as it takes lifetimes of practice and a huge storehouse of good karma.

Clinically, the cause of death was AIDS. Marty had been an IV drug user. He was an adventurer and had been a user of all sorts of drugs. He was an accomplished musician, guitarist, harmonica player and singer. His charisma, what he could convey through the sound of his voice when he performed, caused people to swoon. He was the only truly totally "feeling" person I have ever met. He would sometimes boast that he had only read three books in his life: *Bound for Glory, Catch a Fire* and the *Autobiography of Lenny Bruce*. He said that reading was not good for him as it affected his memory and compromised his ability to feel things directly. He was endowed with an almost supernatural photographic and auditory memory, as well as perfect pitch. He could hear a song once and be able to play and sing it. He could hear someone's voice and imitate it, not only mimicking the words that the person had said but somehow capturing and articulating the underlying motivation or emotion behind the words. This is a rare skill developed by *nada* yogis who understand the depth and meaning of sound. He lived what most people would call a hard life. He was sent to a reform institution when he was sixteen years old by my stepfather. Marty lived there with other under-age boys who had committed serious crimes like murder. His crime was that he ran away from an oppressive home life. Even so, when he had to appear at Juvenile Court, he would not disclose the physical and mental abuse that our stepfather had put him through, which was actually what had pushed him out of the house. There was something very unusual in the way that Marty never would put blame on others, gossip or speak badly about someone else. This purity of speech he retained throughout his whole life.

It sounds like I am making him out to be a saint, which by most people's standards he would not have been recognized as, while he was alive. He lived a very irresponsible life by society's values. He had become a father when he was eighteen, just out of the reformatory. His wife was a major drug user as well as dealer, who would be sent to prison when their baby boy was just six months old, leaving Marty a single dad. Shortly after, he met a thirteen-year-old girl with whom he started a relationship and who became the baby's new mom. He would try to get normal jobs to support his family but couldn't seem to hold down anything for very long. His real passion was music and he was always playing. He was the type of person who walked around the house wearing and playing his guitar, even when it wasn't plugged in. Several other musicians recognized his talent and recruited him for their bands. When blues or reggae bands would come through Seattle he was always asked to sit in; his harmonica playing was really great. Two professional touring bands, *Third World* and *The Shuggie Otis Band*, both asked him to join them on tour. Rather than show up at the hotel or airport to catch a plane or bus he would be passed out somewhere from a late-night party.

He was a steady member of two popular blues/reggae/funk Seattle bands, *Orpheus* and *Vizzion*, but he was high maintenance, not only due to his heavy drinking and drug use but also his charming and flirtatious way with girls. His charisma on stage would often outshine the bandleader, which resulted in some tension. But besides being a good musician, he was a real crowd pleaser and attracted many people to come and hear the music. He often brought his little baby boy with him to gigs, putting him to sleep in a box covered up with a coat or just on the floor in a dirty backstage area. Many women wanted to mother him and take care of him as they fell under his charm, but the burden quickly consumed them and he was unable to stay in relationships for long. His steady girlfriend, Dee Dee, the thirteen-year-old, endured a lot of neglect and abuse, as he expected her to be a mother not only to his son, but to himself as well. He was in and out of many relationships and the baby got bounced around a lot. He was also in and out of hospital emergency rooms and jails often, adding to the strain on him and on his various family and romantic relationships.

During the late 1980s he moved to New York City to be closer to me. At the time he said he wanted to move to the city, I welcomed him. I naïvely had no idea of the terrible danger that awaited him in my neighborhood. The Lower East Side was the cocaine/heroin capital of NYC. Most of the streets were unpaved, many of the buildings were bombed out and inhabited only by squatters and drug addicts and there were no lights to provide illumination on the city streets at night. The local drug lords had pay-off agreements with the police. It was normal for me to come home to my apartment on East 7th Street and have to walk around a line of twenty people waiting to buy drugs from the hole-in-the wall laundromat next to my building. The heart of the area was Tomkins Square Park. On the gate there was a sign, "Park closes at sundown and opens at sunrise," but no one was enforcing this curfew. The Park covered a two-block square bordered on the west by Avenue A, on the east by Avenue B, on the north by 10th Street and on the south by 7th Street, and it was home for many drug addicts. Many nights Marty could be found sleeping in the park on the stage in the band shell. Others pitched tents and made cardboard houses under the old large trees. Open fires at night provided warmth. The playground area was littered with hypodermic needles.

The Life Café, which bordered the park on the 10th Street side, was the major hangout for Marty. David and I both worked there and the three of us spent most of our hours there; it was like our home. Marty found lots of camaraderie amongst the café regulars. He quickly fell into heavy heroin use, sharing needles and living a very reckless existence. For a time he lived across the street in David's apartment, which was really a stinking, rat infested back room of a falling down junk shop. It did have a toilet and sink but no hot water.

I remember early one morning waking up to hear Marty yelling my name up to the 6th floor where I lived, and I ignored him. Later on that night he showed up at the café showing me a six-inch gash in his abdomen all stitched up. He said that he was on his way to my house and some guys mugged him and stabbed him; he made his way to the apartment and had tried to call up to me but I didn't answer. He went to the park, and one of his friends took him to the emergency room. When winter came, he often slept in the backseat of cars. This lifestyle took its toll, after a year he became very ill. We sent him back to Seattle, thinking his health would improve, but instead he quickly began to deteriorate. In a couple of months we learned that he had AIDS. He received medical help at that point and moved into a friend's house, which he shared with our sister, Ivy who became his caregiver. I visited Seattle several times during his illness. In June, I received a call from my sister saying that I needed to come immediately because the doctor said that he would be dead in less than a week. When he heard I was coming, he asked my friend Kat, who was going to pick me up at the airport, if he could come with her to surprise me. Even in his condition he had dressed himself and showed up to meet me. He looked very ill; his weight had dropped drastically, and he really looked like a living skeleton, with big sores on his body. But he was miraculously cheerful and upbeat.

Thinking about me, Kat took us to the café that she and her husband had recently opened. Thinking back on it, I feel now that I was very insensitive to Marty's condition and the terrible strain all this must have been for him, traveling to the airport, waiting for me, then sitting in a café with a latte in front of him which he couldn't drink. But he was there for me and for Kat.

We made our way back to the hospice where he was staying. Because of his condition, he occupied the best room in the house, which was reserved for those who were expected to die any minute. He shared the house with about ten other residents at the time all of whom had AIDS. Compared to the others, he was the sickest, yet he was the one patient in the house who was up and about meeting his sister at the airport and then even over the next four or five days making his daily rounds to visit the rooms of the other guys, doing his best to cheer them up.

On the sixth day he went into a coma-like condition and was unresponsive. Early on the morning of the seventh day my sister and I received a call from a nurse at the hospice, saying that we had to come immediately, that he would be dead in a very short time.

We stayed near him all morning and into the afternoon. In the late afternoon, my mother and I were sitting with him and he started to try to say something. He was very groggy, mumbling, and he didn't open his eyes. We had a very difficult time understanding him. The nurse came in and propped him up with some pillows. He quickly became more and more alert. I finally understood that he was saying, "Get Ivy." At that time my sister was sitting on the porch. My mother left the room to get my sister. When my sister came into the room, my brother opened his eyes wide and reached out his hands to hold our hands; his right holding mine, his left holding my sister's. He told us, using very clear language by this time, to get closer together and in front of him so that he could see us. As he held our hands, we leaned in, with our heads close together near to his face. He then looked at us without speaking — a look which I cannot begin to describe, but about which I can say only that what was coming through his eyes was devoid of any fear, sadness, regret, anger, pity or judgment. It was the look of total unconditional love. He was gazing at us with this look, enveloping us with this radiance. After about three minutes of this *darshan* he then said, "Watch this," smiled and winked his eye, summoned up his energy by inhaling, and on an exhaled breath, pulled up and out of his body through the top of his head!

As I froze in amazement, my sister ran wailing out of the room and outside on to the porch. As she stood there, in shock, she saw a little bluebird fly past the window of his room, landing on a branch of a nearby tree for just a moment before he flew into the sky.

Marty had consciously left his body and he did it with a touch of humor! The nurse and doctor who were present said that they had never witnessed a death like that. It was extraordinary. Most people, they confirmed, either die restlessly fighting or in a comatose state.

In that moment, my whole reality structure collapsed. I realized that I had been duped by my own conditioned projections about who I thought my brother was. Nothing that I had thought I knew about my brother was anywhere near the truth. Beginning to realize that humbled me; it stripped away any confidence I had; thinking that I knew anything at all about anyone or anything. Marty's skill at dying proved that he was a far superior spiritual being than any of us had ever encountered. He had been living with me as my brother for thirty-eight years, yet I had been blind to who he really was. This blindness, and the self-righteous pity I had been carrying for a man who turned out to be an illuminated soul, overwhelmed my ego. Who did I think I was to assume that I knew who he was? The strength that it must have taken him to accomplish that final act of love and reach out to us was beyond my comprehension, but it gave me a glimmer of what is possible in love.

Years after his death, through deeper investigation I have come to understand something of the logistics involved that could enable him to accomplish such a graceful, elegant and willful death. Patanjali describes a siddhi that arises when a yogi has mastered the ability to direct *udana vayu*, the prana that moves upward from the throat through the top of the head: *udanajayaj jala panka kantakadisua asamga utkrantishcha* PYS III. 40 The sutra translates as: Through mastery of udana one obtains the power to walk on water, thorns, mud or anything dangerous without being hurt, and can also levitate and leave the body at will at the time of death. In reflection, Marty, through his singing skills as well as restraint of speech — never engaging in blame, gossip or speaking negatively about other people had consciously practiced the purification of the *vishuddha* (throat) *chakra* and gained mastery of udana vayu. He always saw the bright side of things and was able to move through dark and dangerous places and not be tainted — at least spiritually.

My brother loved bluebirds. They symbolized joy, optimism and happiness — qualities to try to emulate, he would say. He had a beautiful bluebird tattooed on his arm. This poem is titled Bluebird, for him.

PART 4 2000s FRUITS — Manifestation: Something Useful

It took me until the new millennium to settle in and accept my path as a yoga practitioner, teacher and animal-rights/environmental activist. My heart was at peace; having let go of romantic longings that had underlain many of the poems of the last decade, I discovered a new freedom. Many of the poems written during this new period reflect a passionate desire to contribute something of value to others. This would take the form of poems as portraiture, although most of the poems in this decade directly reflect a call to activism. I wanted to lend my voice, through poetry, to a cause that could help alleviate suffering and the rapid destruction of our planet. Seeing *The Animals Film* in 1982 planted seeds which had been carefully nurtured year after year, and as the new millennium dawned I felt not only an urgency to speak out for the animals and the environment but the strength to do it. I could only hope that the teachings of yoga had penetrated into the hard shell of my ego and would allow me to begin to embrace a way of living that might actually enhance the lives of others.

Through the practice of yoga, especially with the cultivation of Krishna bhakti, a level of mental serenity had arisen, coupled with intense focus, enabling me to find more and more insightful, skillful and effective means — devoid of anger, blame and cynicism — to fulfill the vow I had made back in the 1980s to do all I could to take positive steps to stop the cruel exploitation of animals, which forms the foundation of our present global culture. During this decade David and I created a 125-acre wild forest sanctuary in Woodstock, New York, providing a safe home for many species of wild animals, trees and plants. We divided our time between running the school in New York City, which in 2006 would include a vegan cafe, and taking care of the sanctuary. During this decade, besides poems, I also found time to write and publish books, essays, teaching manuals and many written interviews. We traveled extensively worldwide spreading the message of yoga as a path to enlightenment through joyful compassion for all beings. Our tours incorporated a strong vegan message. Because pictures can sometimes speak a thousand words, and because my own initial wake-up call had been through seeing images of animals being abused, we showed similar films to people who were ready to look and listen. We sometimes attracted condemnation from others when we showed these films or even when we spoke or wrote about these issues, but we remained steadfast.

What has become more and more clear to me is that there is a war going on inside of us as well as outside of us, and that war is a war against all the animal nations as well as the planet, Nature herself. A war fueled by a deep spiritual disconnection within ourselves. I continue to receive many opportunities to speak about yoga and each time I try to use that opportunity to speak out for the animals and the Earth, because to me, these are the only worthwhile issues to put yourself on the line for these days. I have come to realize that although I practice yoga to get closer to God, I became a yoga teacher primarily because it gave me the opportunity to speak up for animals and to advocate veganism. I strongly feel that the way we are relating to and treating non-human animals (after all, we are animals too) is preventing our consciousness from evolving. If we are to survive as a species, if this planet is to survive, we human beings must find a way to live with the other animals and other forms of life that is harmonious and mutually beneficial.

If my poetry is to have any relevance to the world, if it is to have any relevance to me, I strongly feel that it must address the many ways in which we are exploiting and enslaving others without any regard for their happiness and well-being. We exploit with the false hope that we will gain for ourselves some kind of happiness and well-being. What I came to see during this decade was that I could utilize poetry to address these issues, and also offer a better, more feeling way to live.

Spiritual activism/activation has become a primary focus, and my writing has become a means to express the connection between yoga practices and animal rights, veganism, and environmentalism. The teachings and practices of yoga provide us with the means to dismantle our present culture, a culture founded upon the exploitation of animals, a culture whose "mission statement" could read: The Earth Belongs to Us. Basic to the yogic practices are the teachings of *asana*, which means "relationship to the Earth," *ahimsa*, which means "non-violence," and *karma*, which means "action." When referring to *asana* in the *Yoga Sutra*, the author Patanjali says that if one desires yoga, then their relationship to the Earth should come from a place of joy; it should be a mutually beneficial relationship. This concept challenges our cultural indoctrination that permits us to exploit others for our own gain, without concern for their well-being.

The aim of yoga is enlightenment. What is realized in the enlightened state is the oneness of being: how everyone and everything is connected and interdependent. Through the lens of enlightenment we see the atman, the eternal soul within each being, regardless of their outer material form —

whether they appear as a human, dog, cow, bird or tree. The enlightened ones walk through this world in a state of *sarvatma bhava* — the divine mood of love which allows outer differences to give way, revealing the atman, the divine identity within. They see God everywhere — in all things and beings. In order to move towards that state of awareness one starts by developing kindness, respect and compassion for others.

Our thoughts, our words and our deeds — all of our actions — create the world we live in. Nothing just appears without a cause; everything is connected. Everything we do will eventually but inevitably come back to us. The law of karma is self-evident, because it is according to the natural laws of the universe. Space is curved, so whatever is thrown "out-there" eventually finds its way back to its origin. When we are kind to others, that kindness will return to us. When you throw a pebble into a pond, ripples begin to form and move outward toward the banks of the pond. When those ripples reach the opposite shore, they reverse their direction and begin to ripple back toward the place where the pebble was thrown.

How we treat others will determine how others treat us; how others treat us will have a bearing on how we see ourselves; and how we see ourselves will determine who we are. The practices of yoga purify our perception, enabling us to see ourselves in others, all others, and then to go beyond seeing — to *be* yourself in the other, until otherness disappears. When otherness disappears only love remains, that love is the nature of the eternal atman — the divine spark of God within each being. Life is a series of relationships, and how we relate to the others in our lives is the most important factor determining our happiness or unhappiness. Ultimately there are no "others"; all is one. The yogic teachings suggest that if through our disconnection, we are still seeing others and not the one, then we should refrain from harming them, and through that practice (ahimsa) compassion will arise, and through compassion we will be transformed. This magical transformation instigates a shift in perception, allowing you to begin to perceive the interconnectedness of all beings and things. As poet T.S. Eliot said, "Heaven is that place where everything connects." So hell might be that place where nothing seems to connect. Through our own actions we can make our lives a heaven or hell depending on how we treat others.

I am still yearning to become a better yogi, poet, teacher, activist, and lover of God, as I feel I haven't even begun to incorporate the lessons I learned from my brother at the time of his death. He was trying to teach me about feeling, the place of deep feeling where self-righteousness, judgment and condemnation have no place, being swallowed up by the elixir of compassion.

Through the practice of writing, perhaps I will be able not only to share some useful information about animal and environmental activism, but also express something of the shared joyful soul space where all of us are connected. As Woody Guthrie said, if we see something about the world that we want to change, we could write a song about it, but the song has to be joyful, if we really do want to change the world. Joy and happiness are more powerful weapons than bitterness and anger. The poems in this chapter are the fruit of this investigation and hopefully you will taste the sweetness of our place in the natural world. I offer these fruits to you.

128. 2003 *Subject: Culture, Speciesism*

Show Mercy Show Grace

Don't leave them suffering in a dark place
why not let them out?
Let them out of the hole, to run and to roll
in the dust, yeah you
They could smell the breeze see the sights
Can you remember how that feels?
Or have you been so hypnotized by the fear
of not being liked?

When you have a choice,
come on, you always have a choice
who do you think is going to do it?
We can't wait for a better place
We are the ones
who make this space a place

Show mercy Show grace
Let us meditate
go to that space into the place
where time can be no longer

Sit down, going down
getting up by going down
getting out by going in
You only must go to get there...
Hear there and everywhere
Listen, when you have a choice
and you <u>do</u> have a choice

Show mercy Show grace
Let us meditate
go to that space into the place
where time can be no longer

There are many miracles here
Can you hear?
Can you be here?
Not bound by fear?

Be bold, walk in peace, let peace surround you
Let it be where you go, take it with you
Let no one tremble from the sight of you
Let no one run from the smell of you

Do they tremble at the thought of you?
And when they see you, do they run?
If they can that is —
and the ones that are forced to stay
do you have to make them pay?
for your lack of confidence?

Show mercy Show grace
Let us meditate
go to that space into the place
where time can be no longer

When you have a choice and you <u>do</u> have a choice
Set them free from your greed
Set them free from your fear
Set them free from your confusion
Set them free from your need
There has been too much killing
Here there and everywhere

Yes you, me and all the wees, we have a choice
Our own happiness depends on how
well we treat others now
spit it out and chew on that

Show mercy Show grace
Let us meditate
go to that space into the place
where time can be no longer

What you do will come back —
come back to you
It's the same for me
It's the same for you

Stop drinking milk
reduce your chances —
for coming back as a cow,
next time around
Oh come on now, don't frown
Let's have some fun before it is too late
Kindness always opens the gate
You can be the one who
shows mercy shows grace
Become a hero in your own time —
you don't even have to rhyme

128. *Notes:* It is always better to be kind than to be cruel. Most human beings justify the cruel exploitation of other animals by saying, "Yes it's evil, but it's a necessary evil." This poem challenges that and makes us aware that evil is never really necessary. Our "might is right" attitude betrays our own smallness, our low self-esteem. We inflate our egos and grasp for power by causing others pain and suffering, which will only ensure our own pain and suffering in the near or distant future. Violence only brings more violence, whereas happiness brings more happiness.

129. *2003 Subject: Love, Perception*

This Heaven

I have seen heaven
The heaven of look upon this

I have noticed when the veil lifts
Because I have walked under this

It is there, this heaven is behind the veil
Always happening, it is always there

There from the beginning
Eternity is already happening

How does it happen that we choose?
Sorrow over joy?

Disbelief in this heaven
Loving suffering more than any other pleasure

The veil is lifted it is a gift this lifting
What can we do but participate in the shifting?

At a wedding, children carrying a train
Laughing and tripping while lifting

You and your beloved have fallen
Down and rolled under

Now finding yourself behind the veil
How long can you remain in this heaven?

Beware it only takes a shift
A crooked look a turned down lip

You are out —
cast out

There can be no un-divine suffering
Behind this veil in this heaven

You are the lifter
Heaven comes from behind your own eyes

Birds with palm fronds flying past
Building a love nest over your head

Flower petals cascade down
The windowpane

The air is perfumed
Mangos taste like roses smell

Discovering how to love this suffering
Seeing opportunity in this hell

It will last for only an instant
Enough time to rearrange the molecules

Knowing this joy this suffering
In the timeless turning of it to itself

Don't wait for the perfect love
You will miss it and lifetimes without a kiss

Be this love
Love the day from the moment of awakening

Make this the heaven
Of look upon this

129. *Notes:* The world appears according to how we see it. Developing the ability to see heaven, to see that you live in heaven, that you are heaven-ly and so is everyone else, takes hard work. It is a psycho-kinetic skill — meaning that it takes a full integration of all aspects of your being — physical, energetic, emotional, intellectual and spiritual; in other words you can't just sit back and wish it were so. The medicine needed is Love, the magic elixir that enables one to see oneself in the other. But without kindness and compassion the medicine can't be found.

130. *2003 Subject: Culture*

Away

Did you ever go a day without throwing something away?
Can you tell me where is this place you call "away"?
Making garbage

We are throwing away our world
Indigenous people have no word for garbage
If we don't want to be treated like garbage
Then we should not make garbage out of the world
What we do to the world
We do to ourselves
Sooner or later
But it is certain
What you do always comes back to you
There is always a solution
Bring your own bag
Bring your own cup too
When the world gets filled up to the limit with trash
When all the landfills are filled with garbage
When all the lakes are filled to the brim
Then what next?
What new frontier can we turn into a dump?
How about the moon?
Let's take our garbage and dump it on the moon
It's the perfect way to clean up the environment!
We can just keep cutting away chunks of Mother's body,
Form it into stuff, use it for a while
And then when it wears out or becomes out of style
Take it to the big garbage dump on the moon
After a few centuries of this there won't be anything
Left of Mother's body
She would have been hacked into clumps
Reformed into stuff and
Sent to the moon
There would be nothing left of her
We'd have to go to the moon to sort through
All the trash to find pieces of what she once was
But that would be difficult because there is no gravity
On the moon so the trash might very well float off

And into other backyards of Venus and Mars
Or float in space and obscure the twinkling of the stars
Could we find a better solution?
Something preventative perhaps
— Like stop making trash
Stop turning ourselves and our planet into
Trash we want to throw away
There is no such a place as this place
We call "away"

130. *Notes:* On January 1, 2000, I was having a conversation with a man who was excited to share with me his idea for how to dispose of all of the trash we are making on the planet. "We should take it to the moon," he said. "That way we can save our environment." As he was talking to me, I saw a picture in my mind of rocket ships leaving the Earth on the hour filled with trash, headed for the big garbage dump that was now the moon. I also saw all the tons of fuel it would take to power these rockets. I saw in my imagination this scene fast forwarded to where the Earth keeps shrinking, as we turn her resources into garbage, while the moon gets heavier with all of this. I said to my friend, "Why not just simply stop making so much trash? Why not compost and recycle? All of the trash was once a part of the Earth, we should render it back to her." He didn't get me and I didn't get him either. My dear friend, the activist, Julia Butterfly talks often about our thoughtless way of throwing things away and how if we are to figure out a sustainable way to live with this planet then we have to stop throwing it and ourselves away, because once it's gone it's gone, and there really is no place called "away."

131. *2004 Subject: Perception*

In the Dream

In the dream you were good to me
You wanted me to be near to you
And this wanting allowed me to feel
So elated hopeful to awake with excitement
For the unfolding of the day

What does it mean to feel
That way?
As I walk, I share it all with you
As I talk, I share it all with you
And I remember that I never have to
Actually meet with you.

131. Notes: We don't have to actually meet face to face with someone in order to work things out. Dreams can sometimes provide us with ways to resolve lingering issues with others. The experience in a pleasant dream can last throughout a waking day, providing strength and optimism that can last a lifetime.

132. 2004 Subject: Culture, Speciesism

The Silence of Us All

There are 7 billion human beings on the planet they say
Each one going about their business
While 150 million land animals are put to death every day
Making 56 billion a year can you spin it?
6 million dead every hour
100,000 die in a minute
27 billion slaughtered each year
Just in our Land of the Free - Home of the Brave
As we go about the important business of the day

Why should we bother?
Animals are animals you might say
They slaughter and eat each other every day

No way! ...wait!
The animals who we eat, the cows, goats, and sheep,

Are vegetarians who do not eat meat
Unless it is forced down their throats
Which is quite an easy feat
These creatures are docile by nature
But we human beings
Trying our best to make a buck
We don't even give a flying f**k
After all it is only some poor slob
Chained in a stall who cannot speak after all
Besides isn't that what God put them here for?

If we want to reduce the fear in our own lives
In our country, city, town, neighborhood, home
In our nervous systems, then why not start with something
Nearby, close to home
Most of us interact with animals three times a day
When we sit down to eat them
Couldn't we try to improve this relationship?
Instead of exploiting all the mothers
Who give milk, eggs and birth to babies,
Only to live lives of mourning.

Babies taken from their mothers
Mother dripping tears and milk
While we capitalize on their loss
And harvest the white liquid from the nipple
As we dribble and talk "conversation"
Meeting in restaurants and cafes
When are we going to be kind?
How many rhymes will it take?
To cause us to pause before we order that
Burger and Shake?

Speak out.

What better way?
If you won't speak,
What are you busy saying?
Whatever else you had to say,
It's not worth that much today

132. *Notes:* The title was inspired by an interview I heard with Dr. Martin Luther King. When he was asked why it took so long to make progress in the civil rights movement, was it really the case that so many people in the United States opposed treating black people as equal to white people, Dr. King responded that in fact, there wasn't that much opposition voiced, but the reason that progress was so long in coming was due to "the silence of so many good people." I also heard an interview with the Dalai Lama in which he said something to the effect of "if we don't have a spirituality that embraces the present environmental devastation of our planet, then it won't be an effective spiritual practice." Our horrific treatment of non-human animals is the leading cause of global warming, as well as the water, soil and air pollution of our planet. Raising animals for food not only contributes to environmental disease, but human diseases as well. Heart disease, cancer and diabetes can all be linked to a meat/dairy-based diet. We treat animals as if they belonged to us, exploiting them for any and all purposes as if we had the right to do so. This behavior is so sanctioned in our culture that to speak out against it or to speak up for the animals is thought of as radical, strange and certainly not normal. Americans alone slaughter 27 billion animals a year (this figure includes 10 billion land animals and 17 billion sea creatures, approximately). This number is many more times the human population globally. If we human beings are to survive, if this planet is to survive, we must stop our exploitation of these other animals, other peoples, other nations. It is the most important political issue facing us, yet most of us don't want to face it much less talk about it.

133. *2004 Subject: Yoga*

This Makes That

It is great when we decide to go
Toward the light and drop the strife

Greeting the day in a special way
What will you do, with what will you pay?

A tomato seed planted
Never can bring an apple tree

How do you become what you wish
When you grow up who will you be?

Our beginning so one say-eth
Shows what our end will be

133. *Notes*: Whatever is happening to us now is a result of things we have done in the past. This is how karma works. To know what your past was, or what your future will be, look at what you are doing now.

134. *2004 Subject: Culture*

I Am That

Ka
Tat Twam Asi
While the Gods Play
An Act of State
Stupid White Man
How it All Vegan

Shadows of Forgotten Ancestors
Angels
Thieves in High Places
Transcend
Media Control
The Psychology of Man's Possible Evolution
The Physics of Angels
A People's History of the United States
Prometheus Rising
The Chalice and the Blade
I-Me-Mine
The Story of B
The Third Chimpanzee
Beyond Culture
In Search of the Cradle of Civilization
Dominion
The Empty Ocean
Luna
Up from Eden
The Transformative Vision
Food of the Gods
The Holy
Flesh of the Gods
Diet for a New America
Fairy Gold
The Gods of the Egyptians
Beauty, Power and Grace
The Beatles in Rishikesh
God and Huxley
God and the American writer
Surprised by Joy
The Lover's Life
The Inner Revolution
The Textbook of Yoga Psychology

The Turning Point
The Time Falling Bodies Take To Light
Cats and Dogs Are People, Too!
Gaia a Way of Knowing
The Cat Who Came for Christmas
The Principal Teaching of Buddhism
The Alchemical Body
God
I am That

134. Notes: A "found" poem made of titles from some of the books in my library at home at the time.

135. 2004 Subject: Culture, Nature

The Brave Smell of a Stone

It cannot be that only we can smell
It cannot be that only we can taste
It cannot be that only we can see
It cannot be that only we can feel
It cannot be that only we can hear
It cannot be that only we can talk
It cannot be that only we can know

We are of it and yet we can't seem to acknowledge it
We are of it and yet we seem to despise it
We are of it but can't bring ourselves to care for it
We are of it but can't seem to love it
We destroy it in hopes of gaining some of it
We destroy it in hopes of owning some of it
We destroy it in hopes of happiness

Who is it that we think we are?
Who is it that we think they are?
Who is it that we think it is?
What is love but knowing that connection is possible?
What is love but wanting that possible connection?
What is it that sits waiting for us to connect?
What is it that mourns us, our disconnect?

Oh land of the free, oh home of the slave
Oh heart of the bird, oh moan of the tree
Oh sigh of the air, oh smile of the frog
Oh shudder of the horse, oh sway of the log
Oh flight of the snake, oh tone of the bee
The brave smell of a stone makes me cry out,
It cannot belong to you or me

135. *Notes:* The Earth herself is living. All living beings together make up this one body of the Earth. We human beings have spent an awfully long time trying to make ourselves out to be a separate case. We have given ourselves the right to use, pillage, abuse and destroy the Earth and all other Earthly beings, in the vain hope of progress. The sad truth is that as we destroy the Earth, we destroy ourselves. If we are to survive as a species, we must have the consciousness to see ourselves as an interconnected part of the whole of life.

136. *2004 Subject: Portrait*

Stripey Boy

There was this little boy today, who followed me into the garden to play
We went out together in the drizzling rain
He helped me plant seeds
sunflowers, zinnias, cosmos, and sweet peas
Then he jumped in a box, mischief in mind,

Scratching in the damp, airy dirt with his furry hands
He managed to cover his body up to his chest, in just a sec
His green eyes asked imploringly, "will you help me?"
So I took the shovel and covered this flirt with dirt
Only leaving his face and a bit of tail exposed
What a miracle this little boy is, I had to suppose
He stayed like that not moving about,
then with a blink and a meow, he sprouted himself,
Shot up like a weed out of the ground
shaking off dirt, he came running around,
jumped into my arms, we walked back to the house, in the rain with the
hoe, shovel and spade
What a charming muddy little fellow he made

136. *Notes*: As a mischievous kitten, Stripey Boy loved to play with me in the garden. We had rescued him, his mom, and his two sisters, from a "kill" shelter. The cat family appreciated their new home with us in the country.

137. *2004 Subject: Portrait*

For Julie

You owe it to the world
She wants you to succeed
Do not sell yourself cheap
You have a greater destiny
You can't afford to weep
Clear your house
There are those who
Will not understand
Do not expect them to
You have no time
To wait until they do

They will in time
Do not worry
They will be fine
Beauty fades with
The dusking of the day
They are doing their best
You say
But is their best the best
For you today?

137. *Notes:* A dear friend was going through some challenging times. I wrote this to cheer her up and to help support her in her decision to move away from a challenging relationship.

138. *2004 Subject: Portrait*

For Alex

Looking into the lake so deep
A young man hesitates
He holds in his two hands
A crystal, a wand, a mirror
And a flower

As he steps into the water
His hands open like falling stars
Releasing his hold on time

The crystal catches a rainbow
The wand is picked up swiftly
By a bluebird which sweeps
Across the mirror surface
Of the lake so deep
Never uttering a peep

The flower floats so effortlessly
And whispers
I will be gone with the summer
Wind but am ever new
I will be born again and again in you

138. Notes: I wrote this as a birthday gift for my nephew when he turned 14.

139. 2004 Subject: Perception, Yoga

No Victims Here (Hear)

All the way to Heaven is heaven
it has to be or we will never get there
We cannot help but to be political
for it means the one body
And come on,
you know as well as I do
that we are the world
There are no good guys and bad guys
there is only disguise
The one blue sky
appears as many
How to know the One
Listen, Hear, Look.
The way is easy for those
who have no preferences
There can be no victims here
And no one to blame for your tears
The world is empty and appears
according to how you see it
with your ears!

139. *Notes: Karma* means "action." The world appears according to how we see it. How we see it comes from our past actions. No one is a victim of circumstance; everything that happens to us is a result of how we have treated others. There is a play on the word *here*: If you see yourself as a victim it is difficult to hear the truth.

140. *2004 Subject: Culture, Speciesism*

What Did He Do to Make Them So Mad?

What did he do to make them so mad
that they had to nail him to a cross for being so bad!
What was his crime against the state —
which moved them all to such hate?

Have you seen a movie or read a book —
that tells you how he went too far —
The Passion, The Last Temptation, The Super Star?
But what was it that he did,
That they would fear their own annihilation —
from his tempestuous, tantrum, tempting temptation?

I have seen it
In this Essene
It is no watered-down story of a victim's distress
Or of a pilgrim's quest
It is the story of an activist —
I and my father are one
There is no difference between god and the creation
What you do to one you do to the whole
The story's old been told and told

Jerusalem at the time

Taxes had to be paid
Sacrifices had to be made
Money had to be changed
This Israel, see it if you will
The great Temple on the Hill
Even then the walls did wail
With the lust for money
Tainted with the cries of the kill
Gentle mourning doves,
Baby goats, and sheep
No fruits, no flowers accepted here
Only a bloody corpse will do
Life desecrated for a holy price
The law said you had to pay in blood
And buy an animal for the sacrifice

To get the temple priests to kill your feast
You must pay in Holy-City currency
No foreign coins or bills accepted
Money was exchanged, animals
Bought and then brought up the hill
Wailing to the temple door
Inside their throats were cut
Canals flowing with innocent blood
Jerusalem the city of the red flood
Rivers and tributaries, gutters of gore
Flow from the famous Temple of Lore

I have seen it
In this Essene
A vegetarian honoring life
As the way to the Divine
Thou shalt not kill no man no ram
No more killing no need to

The temple is within you
Do not defile it with death
Those who wield the sword
Shall perish by the sword
Love thy neighbor as thyself

But even with his words thus spoke
there was much money to be made
From the sale of these gentle folk
The economy of the society has grown
Profited from their exploitation and pain
The Nazarene turned the tables and said enough!
Violence only brings more of the same
You cannot plant an olive seed and
Expect to harvest wheat
To know become like the one you seek
So He upset their plans
Cut the tethering ropes
Opened the cages while
They watched their profits fly
Their anger rose their voices high
"We are the chosen,
Killing is the sanctioned, lawful way,
Who are you to say?"
So he stood there mute and frozen
And they took him away
And frozen he is to this day
This animal activist
Liberator of the oppressed
But alive is he today inside each one of us who cares
He is the sacred heart of the Passion
And the best passion, as everybody knows,
Is com-passion

140. *Notes:* The New Testament Bible relates that Jesus became angry and turned over some tables outside the Jewish temple in Jerusalem a few days before Passover. The intriguing question for me has always been: Why did he do that? What were those tables set up for? Matthew tells us in verse 21:12 that "Jesus entered the temple courtyard and began to drive out all the people buying and selling animals for sacrifice. He knocked over the tables of the moneychangers and the benches of those selling doves." And John 2.14-16 relates that "Jesus found those in the temple who were selling oxen, sheep, pigeons and doves, and the moneychangers. He made a whip of cords and drove them all out of the temple, he opened the cages, poured out the money and overturned the tables and instructed, Do not make God's house a house of trade."

I have often pondered these scriptures. When I was a young Catholic schoolgirl, this incident was used to justify anger: "There are times when it is good to be bad," our parish priest would say, "even Jesus got mad."

That answer was not satisfying to me, I wanted to understand the "why" part of his anger. So I went to Israel on a quest, visiting many sacred sites and from the research and experience gained, came to understand something of the huge status, politically and commercially, that the ritualized killing of animals had for the religion at the time that Jesus lived. The large temple in Jerusalem operated pretty much as a slaughterhouse, where animals were killed routinely by temple priests, then offered to God. Most temples in the ancient world (including Vedic India) engaged in the ritualistic slaughter of animals. They became the precursors of our modern day slaughterhouses where the killing continues, but the worship stopped.

Outside the temple of Jerusalem, there was a live market where animals were for sale as well as moneychangers who facilitated, for out of state foreigners, a currency exchange for the purchase of those animals intended to be killed. It is generally known that Jesus was a member of the Essenes, a Jewish sect who engaged in yogic-like practices including vegetarianism. The Essene philosophy did not support killing or eating animals.

It was the sale and slaughter of animals in a live market a few days before Passover that led Jesus to the only aggressive confrontation reported in his ministry and ultimately gave the religious authorities reason to demand his crucifixion a few days later. It is ironic that with the crucifixion on Good Friday, Jesus himself became the sacrificial lamb. Jesus offered a radical message that love should be extended to all of creation, including animals — a message just as threatening then as it is now to the economic, religious and political establishments.

It is believed by many biblical scholars that animal sacrifice replaced human sacrifice. In the Old Testament book of Genesis, God first tells Abraham to kill his son Isaac as an offering, then later when the knife is at Isaac's throat, God sends an angel to stop the murder, and suggests he kill a goat instead. With the growth of farming and animal agriculture the use of human beings as victims of religious sacrifice became outdated, looked upon as barbaric and to kill an animal more civilized. Special priests were entrusted with the job and relegated to positions of mediators. But they were really just executioners and butchers skilled at the dirty work of killing.

By definition, a religious sacrifice involves the intentional offering of some item of importance (a human being, animal, grain, fruit etc.), to a higher purpose, most often to propitiate divine beings to ensure a favor from them. Fire was essential for the sacrifice. The ancients viewed fire as a demigod himself who assisted the deliverance of the offering upwards to the gods by the means of flames and smoke. Since the discovery of fire trends can be observed over the centuries, where specific objects used in the sacrifice gained or waned in popularity. Humans, goats, sheep, horses, buffalos, and other animals have all had their time and place on the bloody altars (and many still do). Also plants, trees, fruits, vegetables, and grains have gone in and out of popularity. Such sacrifices usually involved the recitation of prayers, mantras or magical spells, before, and during the killing, cooking and eating of the victim. But sometimes the sacrificial victim was not eaten. Such sacrifices where referred to as "burnt sacrifices" — where the fire was allowed to consume the body of the victim rendering it burnt and uneatable. Hence, we have the modern meaning of sacrifice as depriving oneself of the enjoyment of consumption.

Early first century Christian missionaries used the allegory of Jesus as the sacrificial lamb as a central teaching point in their attempts to convert pagans. For example, when Saint Patrick, a Christian missionary, arrived in Ireland in 432AD, the Druids were still engaged in religious human sacrifice. Patrick convinced them that Jesus died for their sins so nobody else ever has to. History tells us that Patrick's mission was accomplished and shortly after human sacrifice disappeared from Ireland. Although I don't think they went overnight from eating humans to a vegan diet! Most likely mutton shanks, or the like, replaced crispy human thighs. Although they dropped the cannibalism, Christians in Ireland or other countries then and now would most likely not think to extend this message to mean that animals should not die and be eaten on holidays or on any day.

Perhaps we human beings are a bit hard of hearing, it takes us along time for a message to sink in. Two thousand years ago, Jesus challenged the old testament dictates that proscribed the hiring of a priest, as a go-between to perform an animal sacrifice in order to win God's love. He came with the message of love — no being has to be sacrificed on God's altar. Everyone is welcomed into the kingdom of Heaven.

141. 2005 Subject: Portrait

Happy Birthday Poem for David

Hands grown strong from a loving heart
On your day the warm summer will start

David dear today life is here
Longest day of the year

Feeding cats salad corn and peas
Then sitting in the sunroom to study Patanjali

Floating from a mountain to a dog
Swimming in the pond with the fishes and a frog

Being with flowers, trees and bees
Gathering mushrooms, smelling the breeze

Digging the ground on our knees
Dirty hands planting seeds

Sharing with bears, foxes, birds and deer
Food, which can lift from the soul all fear

Visiting Oak Tree making wishes to bury inside
Looking up into the sky so blue and so wide

Silently walking through the forest with a trail of cats
As evening drapes the porch and wakes the bats

Boca burgers, mashed potatoes, spinach and rice
Makes a birthday dinner yummy and nice

Light the candles and shake the plastic jar
Calling all fur-ees from near and afar

Yes there are three angels who hover over thee
When night comes with dreams you will see

As you sleep with kit-kats around and above
That it was always you that I love

141. *Notes:* David and I have made a promise not to give material gifts to each other on birthdays. But we do give each other cards and sometimes poems. On June 21, 2005 I wrote this poem in honor of his 55th birthday. The hyphenated word "fur-ees" that appears in the tenth stanza is a word I made up to describe cats, those that have fur. The reference to three angels comes from a time that David had a Kirlian photograph of himself made, revealing three globes of light above his head (see #177 Notes).

142. *2005 Subject: Poetry*

Whatcha Doin'?

Whatcha doin', writing down a recipe?
"Yep," I answered and went away
Sitting down feeling free

The rice is on low simmering
With spinach, tomatoes
Red beans and hijiki

Darkness has come
Descended they say
But to me it is the ascending
Time of the day

Alone but together am I
Now
The day was spent in
Absorption... of gathering
Preparation for this eve
This time of potentiality

Possibilities are impossible
To see unless there is
A crack in the egg
Of a mind conditioned

Strive to find a way
Each and every day
Fiqure it out
Don't worry about
What they say

Write your poems
Fragments, whatever
Succinct notations
Design them graciously
To send into the future

You will become very large
In the presence of hopefulness
Cultivate it courageously
Under all circumstances

Let your egg crack
Every so often
Then take a step
Back and get on track

Feel life through feeling
Joined your body being
It will be over
Before you know it
Every moment is an opportunity

142. *Notes:* A poet spends every moment in either preparation for writing poems or in actually writing them. There comes a time when there is no difference felt between the two. Everything that happens seems to be an opportunity filled with possibilities.

143. *2005 Subject: Perception, Poetry*

Past an Open Window

After the first line appears the poem unfolds
like when a bird flies past an open window
and you happen to be standing there

You see it as significant, that is the first miracle,
the second is you have the good sense to write it down
capturing the sound

But in order for the whole thing to manifest you first and foremost
have to possess within you, beyond a shadow of a doubt,
faith in the possibility of possibilities

Here are a few first lines that flew by like birds past an open window:

"Barrabás came to us by the sea, the child Clara wrote
in her delicate calligraphy"
First words from Isabel Allende's, *House of Spirits*

Then there is this one:
"It was many and many a year ago in a kingdom by the sea that a
maiden there lived whom you may know by the name of Annabel lee."
That is Edgar Allen Poe however could it not be?

"To see a world in a grain of sand and a heaven in a wildflower, hold
infinity in the palm of your hand and eternity in an hour."
No arguing Mr. William Blake's "Auguries..."

A good first line is an invocation — the words act as a spell
causing a shift in your perception,
allowing you to see what you had not thought possible

The words beckon and if the poet follows will lead them
into places of mystery that they
never could get to on their own before

With a good first line, the poem writes itself unfolding
as simple and profound as seeing a bird fly
past an open window

143. *Notes:* This poem is an appreciation of the magic involved in creativity.

144. *2005 Subject: Yoga*

Sailing

You only must go to get **there**
How much fuel is measured by **care**

Having set your sight on the **true**
Then you know the getting is never up to **you**

You cannot commit a **mistake**
Nor a wrong turn can you **make**

First tie yourself to the **source**
Now relax to enable yourself to stay on **course**

By recalling what you **yearn**
You will know when to **turn**

Being at the right place at the right **time**
Allows you to know yourself as the **rhyme**

It has taken forever up until **now**
Count your blessings come on... **wow!**

If you don't forget where you want to **go**
No obstacles will arise to stub your **toe**

No matter how far you may **float**
Drifting from shore you **won't**

Align with your heart not with your **head**
Be sure to let go of all that's been **said**

Like rabbits who zig-zag running to **find**
Climbing a mountain in 'round about **time**

But if you insist on trying to find the **fix**
For something that never was wrong in the **mix**

Pollution will arise and cloud the **eyes**
Of those who see others as out there not **wise**

Never go for the direct **route**
Even if you are tempted by pockets of **loot**

As a baby learning to walk crashes to a **crawl**
Thousands of times without one blush in the **fall**

Forever will there be problems **appearing**
Don't get caught tripping the **steering**

With ticking not tacking we trade joy for what's **right**
Up all night lest we fall into dreams of almighty **flight**

Tacking is an art that stretches and **pulls**
What is true from deception not diminishing the **full**

Correction of errors kills the worm on the **corn**
While the soil and the air walk crippled to the **morn**

Correction of course is something you **do**
With every breath, word and sigh coming gracefully **through**

If not sooner than later in all of our **heads**
For sure we will all appear to be stopped **dead**

144. *Notes:* We will never get where we want to go if we constantly allow ourselves to be directed by whim, nor will get where we truly want to go if we attempt to get there by following a straight line. Space is curved. If we can employ the tacking skills that are involved in sailing a boat, we will be able to stay on course and arrive at our destination. If you have had experience sailing, or riding a bike up a steep hill, then you know that navigation is not always linear; it sometimes requires the sailor or cyclist to go "off course," veering to the right or left and back again, and in the end the destination is reached. If we don't know how to change our course along the way, we will not end up at our intended destination. In other words, if we let our karmas drive us then we repeat patterns and tendencies that we have set in motion through unconscious actions long ago. But if we want to be free of those

tendencies and alter our course, then we may have to pull back into reflection and decide if where we are going is truly where we want to go. We must stay on track by keeping in sight where we want to go, then allowing ourselves to get there. This poem addresses our preoccupation with trying to fix symptoms and neglecting causes. The **bolded** words at the end of each line, taken together, form a poem within a poem.

145. 2005 *Subject: Culture, Speciesism*

Slavery

To force someone to work not for their sake
To force someone to live in bondage for your take
To exploit and subjugate is to eradicate another's face
We who dominate
Chain children to looms,
Tie women to brooms,
Calves to doom
Women, babies, puppies,
Milk, eggs, legs, thighs, meat
Carpets, sex, and golden geese
What you do to somebody
You do to yourself guaranteed
The full telling will be revealed but first
Ask, who really belongs to you
You don't even belong to you
Every*body* is borrowed from Mother Earth

145. *Notes:* We humans are animals too, that is a biological fact. Enslaving others, including other animals perpetuates prejudice and exploitation. If we ourselves want to be free then we should not enslave others — as it doesn't serve our aim.

Brave Mr. Bird

Flies at our window at night
Feathers intact
Hops along the sill
Screaming at the cat
"Why did you kill
Tell me what I am going to do
Now
Without her?"

146. *Notes:* One of the cats killed a bird and for days after, the bird's mate, in grief and despair, would fly bravely at the window demanding an explanation.

Roses

Satyam shivam sundaram
Fifty five rose bushes delivered to my door
Little sprouting seedlings
to celebrate my birthday with best wishes ever more
Teasing Yellow Georgia befriends
pink Generous Gardener
Both climb the fence with red Courageous,
Crème de la crème, and the Impressionist
Such varied inclinations to right up, climb, and ramble over the door
William Morris is a shrub, good for hedges
it has been said

While Jude the Obscure with perfume so sweet
offers kisses to cool the most blistering summer heat
Blue Star is sure to spread across a night sky
Lady in Waiting and Jane Grey are blushing pink in quite fragrant ways
Frilly Falstaff seems he'll be bold
We dug him a hole next to Welsh Gold

There were the four delicate pinks
from three years past
Poor things, I did not know they needed
a two by two-foot hole to grow
We dug them up showered their roots
Pruned and put them to bed in hopes they'll shoot

Upright Mr. Lincoln doesn't seem to have a smell
We tucked him in any way, too soon now to tell
There was one from the bunch we hadn't a clue
As to height, fragrance or hue
I dug a deep hole and she got that one as hers
All clean and cozy with many horse turds

Besides the mentioned above
There were five more of these delightful shrubs
Destined to arrive late next week
Alec bright red with Kept Secret and Velvet Plume
Blue Compassion and Cameo Perfume
All add up to a garden of fifty-five roses
safe behind wire
I think this is a message that it is time to retire

147. Notes: On my fifty-fifth birthday some very dear friends sent me fifty-five baby rose bushes, each with a beguiling name — a very poetic and thoughtful gift. But for the remainder of the summer we certainly had our work cut out for us, creating "The Maha Laxmi Rose Garden." First of all a fence had to be made, and a retaining wall, then beds laid, and filled with rich soil. Each rose had to be planted in a hole two feet wide and two feet deep. It takes about four to six hours to dig one hole. When it came time to put each rose into its newly dug hole, as a christening, I chanted a Sanskrit mantra taught to me by my teacher, Shri Brahmananda Sarasvati: *satyam shivam sundaram*, which bestows a birthday wish for truth, bliss and beauty. And with that, I hoped for the best for each baby rose.

148. *2006 Subject: Perception, Portrait*

Singing

You smelled the coming of the sun
Laughing at puzzles riddles dissolve
Tongue tasting watery due
The green of the grass was only for you

Singing releases fire into air
Children master the sequence
Of letters that make up a word
Not the tones that make a melody
They grow up not knowing how to sing

Touched, you quiver like a shuddering deer
Phrases fall out of your mouth like tears

Whole symphonies whirl in delight
As syllables measure the black from the white
Of notes that make up a song
Not the rhythm that would rather
The rhyme never be gone

You can learn you have only to listen
Hearing brings eye opening clarity
Dissolve riddles by laughing at puzzles

148. *Notes*: Singing is like talking only it demands better listening. Talking could learn something from singing and then words perhaps would mean more. A singer friend of mine, who is also good at crossword puzzles, inspired this poem as did a radio show I heard about a study of Chinese-speaking children who have perfect pitch. The study correlated musical ability to those who speak tonal languages like Chinese, Thai and Vietnamese.

149. *2007 Subject: Culture, Speciesism*

Unbecoming Human

It seems to me that if you yourself want to be free
Then you would not make a slave of anyone

It seems to me that if you wanted to live in peace
You would not terrorize others

It seems to me that if you always wanted to have enough
You would not impoverish anyone

It seems to me that if you wanted a chance to live
You would not deprive anyone else of life

It seems to me that if you never wanted anyone to eat you
You would not be so hungry to eat others

You say that it's okay to hurt, rape and exploit as long
As the other is another

You say that it has always been this way
It is part of being human

I would like to try then to un-become human
Because it seems so unbecoming to be a human

To be human seems to be someone who never
Really says what they mean or means what they say

To be a human seems to be someone who
Never has time to listen because they are too busy talking

To be human seems to be disconnected from all that is
All the while yearning to connect to all that is

A human seems to be someone who says they want
Need and desire but are not willing to provide that for others

You say that it has always been this way
It is part of being human

I want to un-become a human being and become
A someone who you may not be able to see or recognize
Yet...

149. *Notes*: I was inspired to write this poem, after reading a paper by Jessica C. Patterson, a student at Colorado State University entitled, "(Un)Becoming Human." Most human beings are meat, milk and blood drinkers. In the world today vegans are rare and viewed as not normal — perhaps by some as not even human. Most people profess to want peace on Earth. Many see themselves as caring, conscious, intelligent human beings. But the fact is that the majority of human beings, because they eat other animals, are suffering from major disconnect and seem not to be able to see the impact of their actions on themselves and our greater world. Low self-esteem causes one to feel a need to exert, or to terrorize or to derive pleasure from exerting, power over others.

We take pride in saying we are superior to other animals because we have language and can communicate. But like Humpty Dumpty from Lewis Carroll's *Through the Looking Glass*, we use words to say whatever it is we want to say at the time we say it. "When I use a word," Humpty Dumpty said to Alice, "it means just what I choose it to mean." The animal-user industries regularly use words like *welfare* and *humane,* just like Humpty Dumpty might use these words to mean whatever he wants them to mean. The word *humane,* according to Webster, is defined as "marked by compassion, sympathy or consideration for other human beings or animals," and the American College Dictionary defines *humane* as "characterized by kindness, mercy or compassion." So when we read on a cellophane package of lamb chops in the supermarket a label that says, "Humanely slaughtered," what does that mean? We are defiling our ability to speak through misusing language. Originally the word *human* came from the Latin word *humus,* meaning close to the earth, soil, dirt, it is also related to the word *humble* meaning not proud, not haughty or arrogant. In this poem I am questioning whether or not I want to continue to be a member of the club that calls itself human, because the popular definition of *human* seems to have veered away from anything close to resembling humility.

150. 2007 *Subject: Culture, Speciesism, Yoga*

Spiritual Activation

Angry thoughts disarray the heart
      Pierce through the deformity with breath as your start
Shatter with a blow or a throw
      You could do it inside a wishing well
      where your feelings once fell
If all else fails, embrace it with your holiness
Wrapping your everything around
Using the sound
      Of the breath, what else could be better?
Yes that's it...the face of look upon you
Praying and Om-ing alone cannot do
Sitting at a lotus altar
      while babies stumble to their slaughter
Nervous laughter holds you back from
      doing what you ought to

This Armageddon of look upon you
Is not going to stop, even in the forest, even in the shop
        hear the bodies going chop chop
It has only just begun
Birth is bloody — so many shades of red, she said
        You don't know what it's like to be dead
You heard them plotting to do disturbing things —
        what stopped you from intervening?
You are reeling in your obedience to ineffectualness
Afraid of being humiliated? Stepping out of line?
Oh look at that face of look upon you!
Guilt paralyzes your mouth —
        you cannot speak
Lies fill your ears —
        snuffing out the cries
Feet rooted in cement forgetfulness of who you are

So what to do?
Remember anyway and say something —
        anything
Pierce through the deformity
        With a voice from the farm and the killing floor
And when your own death is closing in
        You will realize that the only thing
You ever really had in life was your effect —
        upon others
Your end will come as a rattling snake slithering in
And as you leave you will see
        that look upon you
You never ever had time, certainly no time to lose
Your body will stretch towards that last breath —
        so do your best
To see that all that you see is coming
        from inside of you

Nothing and no one has not been born
      from inside of you
Pierce through the deformity by means of breathing
Absorb into your rainbow body the pixelation of these phantoms
With the embrace of recognition —
      allow black and white to collide into colors wondrous fair
And go on into the future of not knowing where.

150. *Notes:* Poems are often cryptic, intentionally written in code with deeper meaning embedded. This poem appears in a book I wrote titled, *Yoga and Vegetarianism*. The book has been translated into several languages. During the translation into Russian the translator felt quite challenged and wrote me detailed questions, asking me to explain many of the passages. The poem is esoteric to English speakers, I can only imagine how difficult it might appear to a Russian speaker. The notes that follow came out of my dialogue with the Russian translator, whom I have so such respect for.

Angry thoughts
Angry thoughts deform a person — distort their heart — turn them into a distortion of their True Self. Yoga practice starts with breathing. To be aware of each breath you take — every word you speak. To breathe is to be alive. The precious opportunity of having a body — of being alive allows us to resolve our karmas — to let go of negative thoughts like anger, which cause our bodies and minds to become monstrous and deformed. With such a deformed body and mind it is difficult for the contents of the heart to shine through. To allow the heart to open and love to flow from it we must start with purifying our thoughts. Thoughts are made of words and words are created from breath. We start the purification process with breathing, then we can speak true, sweet and effectual words and not be embarrassed, afraid or nervous to speak up when we see a person abusing an animal.

You could do it inside a wishing well where your feelings once fell.
In this line I am asking us to go back to that deep well inside of us and remember goodness. We all want to be good people. It is our deepest wish. At times when we are feeling deep emotions this desire to be good wells up inside of us.

If all else fails, embrace it with your holiness
I am being encouraging here and saying that you are holy — you are whole

and complete already. You don't have to struggle to be good — it is your true nature — you only need to remember the goodness of your eternal soul.

Wrapping your everything around it
"It" refers to the true Self — your core — your true heart — the Divine Self — the atman, the eternal soul, beyond the body and mind.

Wrapping your everything around — means: put your whole life into this project of discovering the truth of who you really are and for that you have to let go of seeing yourself as separate from others. You have to see it all in a (w)holy way.

Look upon you
Everyone and everything you see is you. The whole world and all that you see is a mirror. When you see others — you see yourself.

Nervous laughter holds you back from
Doing what you ought to
Often times when we see another person hurting an animal who is helpless, it distresses us, we know it is wrong, and yet we are afraid and lack the confidence to speak out or to reach out and stop the violence and so we react with nervous laughter. This laughter is an ugly distortion of the emotion of anger. Which links back to the first line of the poem about how angry thoughts can cause distortion of our true (good, kind, compassionate) nature. We start the purification process with breathing, then we can speak true, sweet and effectual words and not be embarrassed, afraid or nervous to speak up when we see a person abusing an animal.

This Armageddon of look upon you
Armageddon is a biblical reference found in the Book of Revelation of the New Testament. The Greek word "Armageddon" means the place where the apocalypse will happen — the end of the world, the Day of Judgment. The Greek word apocalypse means to uncover or to reveal. Armageddon is the place of revelation. So, what I am saying in the poem is that the revelation will be that everyone you see, you will see them as your own self — not as separate from you. But that doesn't mean that the world will stop, just because your perception of it has changed. *This Armageddon of look upon you is not going to stop, even in the forest, even in the shop...*

Oh, look at that face of look upon you!
Can you face the truth — that everyone you see is your own face?

Pierce through the deformity
With a voice from the farm and the killing floor
If we could recognize that the animals enslaved on the farms and the ones on the killing floor of the slaughterhouses are our own selves, then we would realize that when we enslave, torture and murder them — we are hurting ourselves. Only a closed heart covered over with the deformity of ignorance (negative thoughts — anger, greed, selfishness, cruel words, etc.) would be able to do such a horrid perverted thing. So when you speak up for the ones who are being abused you are actually speaking up for yourself — and are piercing through your deformity.

As you leave you will see that look upon you
The phrase here: *as you leave* — means as you die — as you leave your life — your body. It is said that at the time of death you will see your whole life pass before you and also that you will see the truth of your real existence — if only for a moment you will get a look at your true self.

...the pixelation of these phantoms
Why do I use the word pixelation? We live our life as actors starring in films about ourselves. In the art of movie making — as the camera rolls, the movements of people appear smooth, but are actually made up of small individual stop actions. When a picture on a computer screen is being built — it is built from tiny pixelations — parts of the whole. Often times when you are watching a film on a computer, the timing will become slowed down revealing the digital forms of the images on the screen. These digital forms are made of pixels. So the picture instead of appearing as smooth looks jerky and made of puzzle pieces either grouping together or dissolving. I purposely used the word pixelation to describe what happens to the images of the forms that we see when we are dying. The images are people who we have known in our lives. Those people are phantoms, which have been projected out of our own karmas. Meaning they do not really exist outside of our own minds. When our breath is leaving our body at the time of death, our body dissolves and those phantoms also dissolve. Visually what that looks like to a dying person is that a person's world — including all the people that have populated it, dissolves as pixelations — the puzzle of our life breaks down into tiny black and white particles. The word pixie is related to the word pixelation. A pixie is a mischievous fairy who is known for causing trouble by breaking things up and scattering all the pieces causing our vision of the world and ourselves to become disorganized and chaotic — so we have to work hard to put some

order back. At the time of death — there are enzymes in our cells that act like pixies of entropy decomposing our physical bodies and scattering its elemental parts to become absorbed back into the Earth.

allow black and white to collide into colors wonderous fair
And go into the future of not knowing where

Black and white is a reference to your old way of seeing, a way that was cloaked in ignorance and saw the world made up of this and that, black and white you and them etc. (a world of duality). By saying, *go into the future of not knowing where* — I am saying that when you break through this illusion of duality and realize the oneness of being, this is going to be a totally new world, and you must be brave in this new world of the future as you will have no past to reference. This is the ending of the poem and I wanted it to be optimistic and to convey a sense of wonder and adventure — going somewhere where you have never been and having no expectations. But I do say that it will be *wondrous* and *fair*. I am using the world *fair* here to mean beautiful — lovely, harmonious etc., and also because it will rhyme with the last world of the poem, *where*.

In summary, the poem is presenting activism from a spiritual, or yogic point of view rather than just a social/materialistic one. I am asking the reader to look deeper into what it means to be an activist. In particular in this case, an animal rights activist. To merely position yourself in a black and white world where there are good guys and bad guys and you are going to be a super-hero avenging the evildoers and defending the weak is to miss the deeper significance; the opportunity for spiritual evolution through spiritual activation. I am not calling for humans to act in a charitable way towards abused animals. To be charitable towards others is to miss the point. Charity puts you in a false superior position and only elicits pity towards the unfortunate other. Humans are not superior over the animals. The yogic teachings tell us that there are no others — everyone is our own self. To realize this is to become enlightened. This is what all the practices are aimed to bring about. Yogic enlightenment is often termed, "Self-realization". The Enlightened Mind experiences the Oneness of being where otherness disappears and only oneness remains — only love — only God. To see the true Self in others you start by seeing the self in the other as your own self — this takes great kindness and compassion. Treating others as you would want to be treated is the key to cutting through the illusion of separateness. Through God's mercy and grace, that compassion and kindness will then blossom into a deeper realization that there is nothing but God. The practitioner can then move to the loving worship of God. God is the ultimate source of all Love. God alone exists.

All that we see is empty; it comes from our own past actions, and because of that each situation we encounter provides us with a preparation for our own death, when our whole life will pass before us. With kindness and compassion, not anger and judgment, we change others, the world and ourselves, which ultimately are not different entities. But nonetheless, we do have to speak up when we have the opportunity to make a difference.

151. 2007 Subject: Perception

Through Listening

Through Listening
Hearing is possible
Through hearing
Knowing arises
Through knowing
Becoming occurs
Through becoming
Being
By means of being
All is possible

151. Notes: This poem offers a radical approach to how we construct our sense of who we are. In our culture, we tend to favor the sense of sight over other senses. The *Hatha Yoga Pradipika*, an ancient yogic scripture, gives high importance to listening as a means of Self-realization. And in fact, even modern-day physics tells us that all of material existence is comprised of sound. Thus, whatever we "see," we are in a sense hearing. In that way, listening is the key.

Widening Lanes

They've cut the living tree people
with sharp machine powered blades
Those saws don't know what they're doing

As if that wasn't enough
Big metal claws ripped and
Pulled the roots from the ground

Silencing their exuberance for life
Never will they rise again
To buckle the pavement

Delicate pink and purple wildflowers
Mowed over easily making way to pour
Hot asphalt over what is moist and fertile

Poisoning the ground water underneath
For now —
And for the future

All because so many people
Want a smooth and expedient ride
To and from New York City

Who cares about who,
may be living in-between

152. *Notes:* I wrote this while driving into New York City, as a passenger in a car, one day. Looking out the window I saw so much highway construction and destruction of the wild forest to make the freeway wider to accommodate more people driving. I saw so much death along the highway, so many deer,

raccoons and squirrels, as well as the giant silent ones, the trees, who don't have a chance, as they could not possibly run away, and even if they could, where could they really find safety from our weapons of destruction? As we widen our highway lanes, we shrink our forests, and perhaps our hearts.

Throughout our history, we human beings have not recognized trees as the people they are. We have seen them as inanimate objects, cutting them down to clear land so we could pave roads, plant crops, build houses or for any number of reasons, without any remorse or thought of the suffering of the trees.

There is a story found in an ancient Hindu Sanskrit text, the *Srimad Bhagavatam* that tells about a time in another yuga when the pracetas, the sons of King Pracinabarhi, decided to do intense yogic austerities underwater for ten thousand years. After they emerged from their sadhana in the ocean they saw that the Earth was covered in billions of trees. To see the planet gone wild with trees caused them to become very angry. During their intense sadhana they had developed *siddhis*, yogic powers and could breathe fire. They directed their dragon mouths cruelly towards the trees, burning as many as they could to ashes. Soma, the god of the moon intervened on behalf of the trees and stopped their cruel massacre, saying:

> *antar dehesu bhutanam atmaste harir isvarah*
> *sarvam tad-dhisnyam iksadhvam evam vas*
> *tosito hy asau* — *Srimad Bhagavatam* 6. 4.13

"God lives in the hearts of every living being, whether moving or unmoving, including animals, rocks, and trees. Try to see that everybody is actually a residence of the Lord, for this reason, stop killing these trees."

153. *2007 Subject: Culture, Speciesism*

Period Pieces

Period pieces
Dramatic romantic
Horses pulling carriages
Chickens in barnyards
Duck feet nailed to the

Kitchen floor
Empire waisted gowns
Bonnets and boots
Suits made of loot
One doesn't have to look
Too deeply in order to see
The silent slaves
Always in the picture
But never acknowledged
The visible yet invisible
What of their lives?
Unrequited love castrated
Lonely orphans growing old
Who is ever interested?
In the ambitions
Of a succulent pig
Or the shiny black horse
That the handsome
Aristocrat yanks at the mouth
And dismounts?
Hopes and wonders
Mere background
Blended with the architecture
The close-ups are always
Of the love-torn principals
Never the furry or feathered extras

153. *Notes*: When I watch a movie or TV series set in another era, I am always aware of the animals, silent slaves never acknowledged in the film, who appear and disappear like so many extras. I watch these animals — other people, other nations, building civilization through their toil and suffering. I have never had a conversation with anyone who ever saw these films the way I have seen them, and this not only worries me but baffles me, that these other beings could go so unnoticed or at best be admired merely as part of the ornamentation of the period, like the details of costume or architecture in a period piece film.

Two Babies

Two babies waddling along
Little duck following puppy
Both are fluffy
Out alone on a street
Somewhere in China
We get a glimpse through YouTube
One minute sent on the electronic wire
To make you laugh
And email it to many friends
So cute this downy duck
So cute this big-eyed puppy
So alone these two orphans
Barely able to walk
We see the puppy sniffing for food
While little duck follows
What will they find?
Where can they go?
Last shot, tired puppy lays down
On a dirty sidewalk
Human feet many shoes walking by
In a hurry no one stops
His eyes look so tired and
Prematurely aged
Baby duck moves his big
Webbed feet trying to find the perfect
Spot to get close to puppy
Circling back and forth
Puppy rest his head on his paws
Baby duck pushes close to cuddle
Against a furry cheek

The camera's eye crops in close
To reveal that baby duck is not well
Eyes are watery, puss-filled and desperate
I am sure they must be hungry and thirsty
I am sure no one will stop to ask
Them if they are alright.
Why is the camera acting as
An innocent by-stander?
Why am I, the poet behaving
As a witness who does not
Interfere?
What will become of these two?
Their stress and disparate bond
Of friendship passes as cute
Who cares?
It's just entertainment
A momentary break while you are
Scrolling through.

154. *Notes:* Someone sent us a link to a video that was circulating online. It was supposed to be cute. It featured an orphaned duck and puppy abandoned on the streets of a bustling city who find each other in a sea of disinterested, busy human beings. I was very disturbed by what I saw.

155. *2007 Subject: Culture, Speciesism*

Right?

I would like to say that
slavery cannot be the way of the future —
nor is it permissible now!

Excuse me, oh my, what have I said?

don't throw me out of the house
I wish I was dead
please let me stay,
hey, I promise I can make myself
less offensive, let me apologize,
after all we *are* friends,
Right?

OK let me try that again:
What I meant to say is that
slavery is not the way of "my" future.
Yes, I am just speaking for myself —
me, myself and I.
It is my preference speaking and
slavery is just another preference
like chocolate or vanilla
like pork chops or tofu,
Right?

I am so sorry to have sounded so self-righteous
and fanatical to suggest the doing away
with such an unspeakable thing as slavery.
I take full responsibility for my opinions.
Forgive me if I am placing too much importance
upon my feelings and personal beliefs.
We should all be courteous and open-minded
when it comes to other people's preferences,
Right?

No one would want to be thought of as someone
who is judgmental and makes others feel uncomfortable,
while they are about to eat a piece of meat.
A Debbie-dower, miss prim and proper no fun, goody two-shoes,
who wants to be someone like that?
Right?

So serious, so boring with her personal views,
as if everyone should do what she wants them to do.
Or they are just not good enough,
Right?

But what *shall* we serve at the party?
We want everyone to have fun.
We don't want to offend anyone,
by making them eat things they
are not used to eating,
Right?

Most people do eat animals after-all,
it is the most normal thing in the world.
Eating animals could be called a national pastime,
but let's not go there right now,
Right?

I mean don't worry be happy, it's a party, let's relax
and have some fun, it is what we all want to do,
what we long to do.
I mean even the poorest person
wants a chicken in the pot every Sunday.
Well why not every day?
Right?

Whatever we want,
chicken, cow, goat or sheep,
a lobster, a frog,

Or depending on what part of the world,
we come from we might want to eat,
a deer or a buffalo, a cat or a dog
How about a wild pig?

Michael Pollan did it and liked it,
Or a little black bear, that might taste
gamey and good, why not? Ah, come on,
don't tell me you're squeamish?
Hey how about some fish?
Come on, be free, be wild,
don't be so conservative, so ordinary
After all we're at a party and they're serving
it for free
Right?

I must remember that what other people do
is none of my business.
Whatever they want to eat
is their decision, I have no
right to interfere,
Right?

I should be tolerant, of who they kill,
after all they are paying the bill
I should be quiet and polite, after all it is
their right,
Right?

Even if this flesh, milk and blood, insatiable greed
pollutes the planet and causes
fear, famine, war, poverty and disease,
I should keep my opinions to myself,
it is not right to interfere with the right
of others to pursue happiness,
Right?

But when will the time be right to question,
who should have the right to wrong others?

Shouldn't we look at how our unchecked
right to satisfy our greed
might be at the root cause of why
we never feel we have enough?
No one of us can live in a bubble anymore
as if we ever could before.
What anyone of us decides to do, does affect us all,
Right?

Just like you, I don't want to hear things
that are unpleasant or see suffering.
Why can't we talk about this?
I'm a guest at this party and so are you,
where platters of beef, shrimp and foie gras
are served as snacks to fuel our small talk.
I guess it is a party, after all,
the conversation should not get too heavy,
Right?

We are all kinds of people
just trying to shuffle along, like everybody else,
Right?

One hundred years from this day
what will the kind people say?
That they were like frogs in a pot of water
pretending not to notice, the flame underneath
slowly starting to heat up their cold feet,
Right?

155. *Notes:* Living in a society in which the exploitation and eating of animals goes unquestioned and seems normal, I often feel like a stranger in a strange land. This estranged way of life, this culture will come to an end; it will crash down. Maybe it will happen soon, I don't know, but I do know it will come to an end, and I am glad about this. In fact the knowledge that this way of living will cease gives

me hope and optimism. Love will triumph. Our present culture is based on the concept: "might is right," right? Meaning that if you have the power, the means and the money, it is your right to enslave and exploit others without any regard for their happiness or well-being. This way of living is not mutually beneficial to other animals or the planet and will come crashing down, because it can't sustain itself in its cruelty and disconnection. I want to be totally fine with this cultural entropy but it also means the entropy of my own egoic self-grasping. I pray to have the strength to be fearless as "I" dissolve with this culture, I pray to be open enough to learn how to live in a new way, that my own sense of what is right and what is wrong won't continue to enslave me and disconnect me from others. If I want to be part of the solution and not a continuation of the problem, then I have to let go of judging others. I have to free myself from self-righteousness and cultivate compassion. If I want to contribute to the dismantling of this culture of slavery, then I must dismantle the slave as well as the master within myself. In yogic terms, the concepts of *raga* and *dvesha* — the hankering after that which you like and running away from that which you don't like — must be overcome, if I am to develop clarity and be able to act from a place of deep compassion for all beings.

156. 2007 Subject: Portrait

Sea of Malachite

Your voice drops like pebbles
into a sea of malachite
Underneath exploding into sunlight
continuously all bright

156. Notes: A birthday poem for a friend of mine who is a singer, a musical vehicle for bringing brightness into the world.

Verlaine Verlaine

Only the marvelous nothing but the beautiful
One thing we happen to see is how it happens to be
Desire issues necessity
Verlaine Verlaine
Shooting gun in hand
And knife in heart
Grasping at the wind
Your head turned in the other direction
While your fingers clutch and open without much release
Moaning in your writhing emptiness
A thousand peacock eyes
To perfection battered and fried
Where do you think you are going with all of this?
You have relinquished your gift
The gift to say what you mean
And to mean what you say
Willingly placing a sack over your weary head
To say nothing of your sagging bed
All for who or rather for what
A young boy's green rotting teeth
Enclosed behind the prison of a smile-less face!
Verlaine, you stupid idiot I hope that with all the time
Which has passed you have come to your senses
And stepped out of your blood-soaked cloak of sweet meat
Whimpering at the dirty feet of blue-eyed deceit
How duped you were by the very machine you so smugly spit at
As if that wad were enough to dismantle it
How duped you were by ten long white fingernails flakey and fat
As if that pus were enough to dismantle it
How duped you were by one who could deftly hold a tit for a tat

As if that hand were enough to dismantle it
How duped you were by the mirror of your head in a hat
As if that possession were enough to dismantle it
In one hand and as well as tremble with a razor blade in another
Do you know by now that to be wild is not to be
Limping and grimacing with every step
Sending tremors to wounds sliced into the vulnerable skin
Of the upper inner reaches of your prized thighs.
The revolution has come but it is not in the smoky factories
And the right to eat chicken or to keep slaves
To walk light on a mantle of living grass with an exhale of free breath
Under each step of bare feet, soles of the wind
This will come to you in due time.
Only the Marvelous nothing but the beautiful
Will be allowed to remain as you awaken from the slumber of deceit
Forget about the age of enlightenment
Put it behind you as it was nothing of the sort
We are not hard and cold machines
Nor the Earth Herself is not
She is the delicate soft downy underside
Of a bird's body which barely but featherly covers
A pulsating heart pumping
Out a song of celebration
Continuously creating waves of meaning
With more depth of feeling than any line
From Rimbaud's pretentious musings
To walk light on a mantle of living grass with an exhale of free breath
Under each step of bare feet, soles of the wind
This will come to you in due time.
Only the marvelous nothing but the beautiful

157. *Notes:* Nineteenth century French poet Paul Verlaine was a leading symbolist poet who formed the Decadents with Charles Baudelaire. Verlaine's romantic affair with poet Arthur Rimbaud was part of his attempt to live a free, libertarian lifestyle based on decadent self-debauchery. Together with

Rimbaud, Verlaine set the course for the poet's life, which continued to manifest in the beat and punk rock movements, which also celebrated the strange aesthetic of addiction, sickness, razor blades and hopelessness. Although I acknowledge Verlaine's contribution to poetry and especially how he opened the doorway for free verse, I oppose the philosophy that he and his poet friends professed and expressed that with this scathing bit of verse.

158. 2007 *Subject: Nature*

Leave Me Alone

The Maple she speaks:
Why rake up all of my leaves?
Why not leave it to me?
How is it you think you know better than a tree?
I have worked diligently and wise
By means of the alchemy of photosynthesize
And managed to change sunlight,
Water and metals,
Into a cloak of green for myself, are you listening?
I never asked anything from you
Not even a crust of bread or a hand-me-down shoe
Instead I have stayed quite put,
Made my own way, lived longer than you and seen
Many seasons come and go
I have even managed to make my own soil in which
To stretch my growing feet
Who are you to think you know better than a tree?
When it comes to my care
Why not question yourself and seek —
The answer to why you rake up all the autumn leaves
And then think it better to put fertilizer all around me
This is not what I was intending to eat

Leave me with my leafs of red and gold
Leave my leafs alone
Please leave me alone

158. *Notes:* Every October I am reminded that I fail to understand the reason behind the silly tradition of raking leaves. These fallen leaves are perfect; the tree knows what she is doing. It seems to be another one of those many ways in which we fail to trust that nature knows what's best for her.

159. *2007 Subject: Nature, Time*

Eternity with you

Version #1

We are like the continuous tumbling of clouds
or the endless possibilities of a seashell
extending eternally
both coming from and going to

We are precious
In this spiral galaxy of stars
Whose graceful curvy arms sweep the dust of space
Like a Catherine wheel
Defining and illuminating what has already happened
Gesturing forward into the feel
Of the infinity of potential tastes

Locked in an everlastingness
Life evolves as she rolls out
Changed we shall rise again
forever the same forever changes

We have always been here

The evidence is mounting
The evidence is mounting
See it in numerical coherence
No accidental slips
No synchronistic side-effects

Seeds don't slip through fingers
by chance and fall as victims to the ground
Life is never that chaotic
And she is always on time
Waving us through

We have always been born
to love magic
To be surprised by joy
Continuously as it is never ever done
This magic is a shift in perception
Don't forget all the things
which make us happy

The wind whispers us to where
I will meet you there
And if time must come to an end
I will be happy to spend
....eternity with you

Version #2 (Which became the lyrics for the song *Pashupati* on the album *Sharanam*)

Seashell Seashell....
We are like the continuous tumbling of clouds
or the endless possibilities of a seashell
We are precious in this galaxy of stars
Graceful arms curve and sweep the dust of space
Sweep the dust of space — infinity of taste

Locked in everlastingness
Changed we shall change we shall rise again
Rise again each time a gain again a-gain
Over and over and over again
Over and over and over again
Forever the same forever change
We have always, always been here
Seeds don't slip through fingers by chance
Life is never that chaotic
Life is never that chaotic
And she is always on time
On time
And she is always on time
Magic is a shift in perception
In perception in perception
If time must come to an end
May I may I be happy to spend eternity with you
Eternity with you ...eternity...eternity with you
Eternity with you
With you

159. *Notes:* Nothing about nature is chaotic or random. We humans have projected a wrong idea that says to be wild is to be unorganized. This could not be further from the truth. Scientists who have had the opportunity to live with wild animals, for instance, or marine biologists who study sea creatures, can't help but to recognize the intricate organization and harmony with which those who are aligned with nature interact with their environment. It is curvy, cyclical, musical and magical, and it is always on time without needing an alarm clock.

Two versions appear here, the first is the original poem from which I improvised a song for the album *Sharanam*.

There are a couple of phrases in version #1 that I borrowed from other poets/songwriters: Verse 3: "forever changes" should be credited to Arthur Lee, from the Album *Forever Changes* by the band Love. Verse 6: "born to love magic" should be credited to Nick Drake's lyric: "I was made to love magic" from the album *Time of No reply*.

For Stephan

This is a
Loving adornment to be taken into a
Wild place and
Placed carefully on your favorite tree
The alpha and the omega
The living end is the beginning again and
Again...each time a-gaining over and over
Again
You are our dear friend
Visionary who has invited all of us
To be a part of a beautiful dream
You have dreamed us up
So happy to be your friends
You are the tree we are ornaments
On your limbs
Your endlessness your omega is
Our beginning-ness over and over
Again
We celebrate your appearance
Please stay in our lives
May you continuously be happy
And free

160. *Notes:* When my friend, Stephan Rechtschaffen, co-founder of Omega Institute, turned sixty we gave him a large ceramic bubble, meant to be hung on a tree and I included this poem in the birthday gift box.

A Flower Waits to Greet Me

When was the world new?
Oh my wizard of change, teach me the lessons
To enable me to go
You have gone from the land I know
But nonetheless
For your own good remember that
Water laughs and laughs anew
Do the children know
I don't really go
Into that answer — these days
These days
They have lips of skin
And hard beaks of need
Taken so much all these hands of greed
My beauty my cotton all
Soft and white dyed with the pink
Light of the land
The shifting of sand
The meaning of a fan
Perhaps one and the same
Don't you believe blindly for a second
For she is the mirror of the land
This world made anew
For me and for you
It is her the Is always So-This
The stars shine bright in the
Night and the day and in you and
All along the way
Where else will we go
For ever will we know

That sounds good — forever sounds good
If lace and light and the face
Of an open flower waits to greet me
On my way this day
I can make it
I can say that's okay,
But if not, I will be on my way

161. *Notes:* At some point, believe it or not, people in America didn't have so much stuff. It wasn't that long ago. You can go and visit some old historical houses even today and see how some people lived. They didn't have closets to hold all of their clothes. They had a few nails pounded in the back of their bedroom door on which they hung their clothes. Each person would have one or two changes of clothes...that's all. They lived a simpler life. These days, we have so much in America. Even a poor person usually has many clothes...full closets and dressers of drawers. Some people even rent storage spaces to store their stuff because it can't all fit in their apartments. We live in cities where there is so little land to be seen, as it is all covered over with asphalt and concrete or buildings. When you go from the city to the country where there are still some patches of land where grass, trees and flowers grow, if you are there long enough, the flowers and trees and grass will start to talk to you and tell you things that you realize you haven't thought of much before. And if you are very lucky, you might see a fish in a stream. If you could but have the good sense to lean down and listen to that fish, they might tell you something important, something very important, about how things really come about, and you will know that you can only live until you die and then you may not get another chance at this wondrous life. It is best to honor the beauty of life by being kind. It allows you to enter into a magical realm of sublime delight. Let yourself go into distant lands wondrous and fair. Stay as long as you like. But as soon as like turns to dislike, get out as quick as you can.

Patti Presses

Press Patti Press
The white against the black
For a long moment
Ever so firmly
Ever so much there
Every single word
Said with so much care

162. *Notes:* As an artist Patti Smith is so deliberate, so on purpose. She reminds me of a vision I once saw in a film of a Vedic priest preparing a yajna, placing each stone mindfully, on purpose. *Nyasa* is a Sanskrit word meaning to place on purpose (see Notes for poem #7). Patti Smith can appear simultaneously vulnerable and yet so durable. At a fundraising auction, David and I bought a photograph that she had taken of a statue of the Buddha. She signed it, "for David and Sharon." And as she wrote those words, she said them out loud so deliberately, her whole being pressing into us with equal emphasis on both the words as well as the spaces in between heard and seen.

163. 2009 *Subject: Portrait*

Penta

She comes to us as a star
Limbs spread wide
A red-haired skinny girl tries to run
Big hands grab and push her back
Like workers on a farm
Shoving imprisoned animals around
With a pole crushing to the ground

Once again once again, she sings for help
Tries to find the door — the stargate

Magic incantation diverts fate

Broadening into a song
Listen, it is so good it can shatter glass
While her palms implore why me why me?
Her fingers offer answers
Penta, Penta come and sit and stay
And let us see.

163. *Notes:* I have a friend whose name is Penta. She is like a five-pointed star. To the ancients a star always meant a doorway. Penta seems to be searching for the door — for the doorway to herself — and she does it gracefully, at times recklessly, but always beautifully. She is like a starfish. People like to collect her, but only when she keeps still. She is very full of life. She loves to eat the food she loves and does it with gusto. She is loving and inviting, never judgmental or condemning. She is very beautiful. She has red hair and white skin. She used to be very thin, but when she had her baby girl, whom she named Cazzamira, her body blossomed into voluptuous curves. She is a talented singer and performer. Her voice is so strong that it can forcefully alter molecules as it thunders out from her red painted lips. She also speaks French, and has a closet filled with hats, clothes and shoes.

164. *2009 Subject: Nature*

The Humility of a Leaf

Turned faceless to face the day
Open for the night
No rest while your preciousness is waiting large and bold
So innocent so huge who is unable to move
Cannot gather to themselves
Who pass the time like a baby overgrown and ever growing
mouth wide open
like a fat downy baby with an obstinate hold
The air is cold and can't help it

He shivers in the wind
Holding on he tries his best to continue working night and day
So frail so light who is so used
Cannot gather through themselves
Green turns into gold as veins dehydrate even thirst will cease
Desire curled inward
like striped old feet with nothing more to say

The leaf lets go
Surrendering to the air
A blessed time for the fair fairies who take delight
In cushioning the dying leaf's fragile flight
Can gather themselves
one by one caressing the floating see-through sheet
delivering precious goods
departed leaves to be left alone arriving after a fall
All the woodland celebrates
the arrival of one who has left
who now rests his weariness against the cool forest floor
Allowing time to dissolve all past boundaries of form
Can gather together
In the secret place where universes weave
through his body of fertile soil
to be reborn
Like all who die and leave behind discover the new as more

164. *Notes:* Most of us who suffer (even unknowingly) from the prevalent disease of our day, the disease of disconnect, can miss the subtlety involved in the relationship between a leaf, a tree and the soil. Most of us casually assume that the soil came first and then the tree, who then sprouts leaves to blow whimsically in the breeze. But the real truth is that it is the tree who creates the soil. The modest leaves do far more work than most of us realize, and they do their work in a devoted, tireless way, exemplifying the most exalted humility. They are the caretakers of the tree. Without them the tree would die. The leaves bring the nourishment of light into the dense hungry body of the tree through the complex alchemy of photosynthesis. When a leaf has worked

himself to a point of utter fatigue, he becomes frail and ceases to be able to hold on to the branch any longer. It is at this point that he leaves the beloved, large body of his tree and surrenders to the fall into the unknown — he becomes a *tyagi* — one who has renounced or let go of all attachments to doing. It is also at this time that all the elemental beings, especially the fairies of air, who seem to come out of nowhere to rescue the leaf, providing him safe passage as he descends toward death awaiting him on the forest floor. Much like the mythical stories of when a great mahatma or saint dies...all of heaven is awakened and the celestial nymphs and angels come to delightfully guide the holy being into the next heaven. Like the mahatma, the leaf is also greeted with a celestial entourage that gently delivers him to the heaven of the forest floor. As the body of the leaf disintegrates, it joins other dying leaves to become soil. The leaf is reborn as the vast, deep, fertile soil of the forest floor, able to renew a whole forest of trees, which will eventually sprout leaves, continuing the cycle of life.

The last line of verse two contains a reference to the witch of the west, who dies when Dorothy's house falls upon her from the sky. As viewers of the film, *The Wizard of Oz*, we don't actually see the witch — we only get a brief glimpse of her striped stocking feet curling backward, retreating under the house.

165. 2009 Subject: Culture, Speciesism

Slavery is Bad

Slavery is bad for humans and other living things
Slavery is bad for the future of planet Earth
I see a world where there is no Sea-World
I see a world where there are no farms or corrals
I see a world where all the cages are empty
No fences — no departments of defenses

Is your sister off to college and
there's no one to take care of the dog?
Jeff, go get my rifle and shoot the darn thing,
he's chained up by the wall.

Never before in the whole history of this planet has there been a species
With so much power to destroy and so little consciousness about it.

Oh who me?
How could what I do matter?
It's just my lunch — a small ham and cheese sandwich
between two slices of bread

Should we be pessimistic about the future?
Well if you aren't then you don't understand the figures and facts
Should we be optimistic about the future?
Well if you aren't then you are being lax
and aren't paying attention
To all the kookie freaky people that are moving to ensure that
we all have a future
While others are either working full time —
eating, complaining, or blaming
While they who dare to care about others
Are creating a momentum which will flood the unsuspecting
while they sleep
And when we all wake up and turn off the television,
unplug all of the appliances
Stop the newspaper and magazine presses
and step outside of our barricades
we will wake to a rich green world where
The wild ones who live in the remaining forests,
the finned ones who live in the waters
and the winged ones who still have reason to sing
are the famous people —
the ones that we all want to learn from and emulate

We will come to our senses and listen
We will remember that we do know how to talk
to a sparrow and understand the heart of a fox
we will remember that our fellow Earthlings are actually intelligent

because they know how to live harmoniously with nature
because they see themselves as not separate from Her
because they don't make trash and throw things away
and because perhaps they don't wear clothes
— they are less self-conscious

A couple of centuries back three out of four human beings
on this Earth were slaves
A few crazy people thought freedom was a good idea
and thought slavery was not — they were called abolitionists

The abolitionist movement was unusual because
it was other-centered
The abolitionists dared to care
about the happiness and freedom of others
most of whom they had never even met.

They focused on abolishing human slavery
But slavery is not over —
billions of animals are still slaves
Rivers are still slaves
Forests are still our slaves
Even the sky we think we own.

Only someone stupid would think it is cheaper to destroy the Earth
now rather than renew, restore and sustain it
Only someone stupid would poison their own water
Only someone stupid would not treat others like they oughta

Should we be pessimistic about the future?
Well if you aren't then you don't understand the figures and facts
Should we be optimistic about the future?
Well if you aren't then you are being lax
and aren't paying attention

165. *Notes:* On the same night, two different friends of mine emailed me essays. One was the commencement speech by Paul Hawkins given to the class of 2009 at the University of Portland, and the other was a pro-vegan article written by Ezra Klein for the Washington Post entitled, "The Meat of the Matter." I was inspired to know that there are more and more people speaking up for nature with optimism and the courage to say that how we are treating our fellow animals and the Earth is wrong and we need to stop it immediately and find a different way of living — a different way of relating to each other and the planet. The opening line is a takeoff of a slogan that appeared on many bumper stickers during the 1960s: "War is bad for children and other living things."

166. *2009 Subject: Portrait*

Zorn

Destroyed, murdered, his name denotes a
   catastrophe — How could this be?
The lapine citizens of Watership Down,
   the Rabbits tried to tell me —
   but only could wiggle their noses
I saw him with two wheels and a horn
nildro-hain the blackbird's song —
   my heart trembled, zorn!
one shoe orange one shoe blue
   She said forget it — so wrong are you
You could only be right if you were from Tokyo
So please come on, don't forget your bow —
   we gotta go!
Always a sense of safety floods over me
When I see him walking down the other side
   of the street and remember that
I am invisible and free with my soundless feet

166. Notes: I love John Zorn, the zany, prolific, genius composer, national treasure, and modern-day Mozart. We have lived in the same New York City apartment building since 1983, along with other musicians who were part of the progressive downtown music scene of the 1980s. I was reading the book *Watership Down,* and in it the author, Richard Adams, creates a "Lapine Glossary" at the end of the book to help the reader understand some of the more obscure words that are part of Adam's rabbit language. For example *nildro-hain* means the song of the blackbird. The word *zorn* appears in that glossary also, but I was confused to learn that to those rabbits *zorn* means "catastrophic." It is true that John's music is drawn out of the chaos of New York City. At the same time much of his music is rooted in the suffering and the zest for living expressed in the ancient Jewish musical, and mystical tradition. John Zorn's universality is also expressed as well, in a sensitivity to the suffering of the Japanese people at the tragic end of the second World War. Like all great composers he has an uncanny skill to turn catastrophe into wondrous triumph.

PART 5 2010s SEEDS — MYSTERIES:
To be unpacked and re-cycled

I had thought that I'd be done with this poetry book by 2010, but when the first decade of the millennium came and went, I found myself continuing to write poems, still engaged in the exploration of poetic formulas. The book had traveled in time from roots, shoots, flowers to fruits. Fruits are soft, sweet, voluptuous and juicy a perfect way to end a season and a poetry memoir — or so I thought. But then I realized that I had overlooked something important: Fruits contain seeds. Seeds are dark, and mysterious somewhat like black holes in the sense that they contain very condensed bits of information. When planted, the fertility inside a seed can instigate a new cycle of existence. One seed, one timeless singularity can birth a universe, but only if that seed is nurtured, cared for and given the right conditions will it unfold and release its potential. Otherwise a seed can stay contained in its death-defying darkness, dormant or imploding upon itself indefinitely. So I watered the seeds and many new poems showed themselves.

Why does the book stop at 2019? I like the mathematics of 1972-2019. The formula 1972 numerically adds up like this: 1+9+7+2+10=19, 1+9=10, 1+0=1 and 2019 adds up like this: 2+0+1+9= 30, 3+0=3. If you add the reduced sum of both years together: 1972 (1) plus 2019 (3), you arrive at the number 4. There are 229 poems in this book. If you add 2+2+9 you get 13. Reduce that number by adding 1+3 and you will arrive at 4. According to numerology the number four represents stability, order and completion, it is equated with the geometrical form of the square, the symbol for foundation. Like a seed it contains potential. Four is said to be the number that connects the spirit with the physical world of structure and form. I have an affinity with the number four as I was born on the fourth day of the month. I pay attention to numbers, because they provide me with maps or grids to contemplate possible meanings.

Although the years that the poems were written add up to the number four, and the number of poems in the book also add up to four, the book spans five decades. Five is a star-like number expansively radiating outward — I see these five decades and the poems written as stars, polka-dotting a black sky, which is one life — one view of the universe.

Yogis recognize that the primary pursuit in life is to establish a loving relationship with God. To serve God is to serve what is true and good, and to look for that in every being and situation. In the *Bhagavad Gita*, Krishna tells us to love others for the sake of God, who dwells within every being, as the atman, the eternal soul.

If a person serves only themselves, working for temporary material rewards, like money, recognition or self-expression, no true happiness can result. Physical relationships between, husbands, wives, friends, children etc. cannot be relied upon to bring lasting happiness because bodies, minds and personalities are all impermanent.

Like all of us, I was born in into this world with *samskaras*, predisposed inclinations, unresolved karmas hankering to be fulfilled. My particular samskaras where connected with the communicative arts. An artist's job is to uplift others, but without acknowledging the divine transcendental source of all upliftment, an artist runs the risk of mere self-expression. None of us, no matter how creative, is original. God is the original seed source of all creation. All art forms, to have any real value, must point back to the seed from which everything sprouts. Otherwise we continue to plant seeds that will sprout and bring us back to rebirth in the material world. Unless we devote ourselves to loving service to that supreme cause of all causes, we are doomed to *samsara* (the cycle of birth, growth, decay, death and rebirth) again and again.

Poems come in all shapes and sizes. Some poems are short and concise, others are musings and tend to ramble, some are musical and could be songs while others are clever and catch you by surprise, making you laugh or say *aha!* Even so, I think good poems are succinct, like seeds containing information with the potential for universal application. If our work can be offered to enhance the lives of others and increase God's bliss, without expectation of reward or even acknowledgement, but only for the joy of offering, then our work might move us to the transcendental realization of who the ultimate doer really is. God is the ultimate doer and the ultimate truth. No one can know the whole truth, but together we can begin to know.

Each of us sees reality through our own unique spyglass. Through the magic of communication, we share our discoveries and in doing so shifts in perception can arise. It is my hope that these final poems are taken as seeds — that they are planted, finding fertile ground in the hearts and minds of others, because without someone to listen, the words of a poet cannot be heard. For those who have ears to hear these poems are for you.

Chemistry vs. Alchemy

It happens *over* time but actually not really
More like *with* time... with the assistance of time
She, time that is, loves to lend a helping hand
Chemistry demands immediate results
Which is fine for Agni the hot head,
Who catches on quickly and can respond to the summons
      of anyone who calls
But there is more than one way to light a fire
Striking a match the flame catches... the burner turns blue
Transformation is imminent
The alchemist on the other hand enjoys a slow boil
Side by side hand in hand with time... a creative partnership
      to savor as well as cognize the
Separation of elements and the wonder of their reconfiguration

167. Notes: In our relative world, growth, transformation and the rearranging of elements occurs where there is time. Spiritual practice, *sadhana*, involves discipline, a process said to occur *over time* — a steady, repeated application in order to attain results. We can think of time as a person, as a goddess and call her Nature. But to use phrases like "it happens *over* time" seems not to give time her due credit for the part she plays. Instead we could say *with* rather than *over*. The term *over* can imply dominance — to get something over on somebody. As a species we have been determined to finding ways to dominate and exploit Nature. The practices of yoga as well as alchemy are magical practices that alter one's perception of the world and of time. Such an altered perception can help one to live in harmony with Nature, rather than viewing themselves as separate from Nature and lording over her. That harmonious relationship can lead to the arising of enlightenment — the transformation of the individual into someone more inclusive — one who knows themselves as part of the whole of creation rather than a self-centered, skin-encapsulated ego.

      The yogi as alchemist works with Nature to effect their own transformation from ignorance to enlightenment. This takes time. In fact without the part she plays, no transformation is possible. Nature gives us a vehicle, a body, enabling us to experience life. The experiences of life provide us with opportunities to resolve our past karmas. There is an alchemical precept that states: "through repetition the magic is forced to rise." I like this saying because it equates repetition, which can only occur with and by the agent of time, to the key ingredient necessary for magic to arise.

My definition of magic is a shift in perception — one comes to see themselves and the world of others as different than they once did. So when magic arises there is a change — transformation — which is what the practice of alchemy, as well as chemistry, aims to bring about. The difference between chemistry and alchemy lies in how each practice associates with time. With the art of chemistry, there is a desire for immediate results, whereas with the art of alchemy, the results are cumulative over time. But of course, alchemy does involve chemistry.

168. 2010 *Subject: Portrait*

Lange Lange

The doctor's calling
With his bright blue eyes
Like a robin free falling from
Cobbing webs of moss so high
Conic fingers emerge
From trembling hands star-shaped
We both bumped into each other
After our great escape
Two dancers on the floor of time
Waltzing to songs with or without rhyme
There is so much to talk about
As you fill me with laughter
All of your serious opinions drop
    from your heart like when a summer's breeze
    shakes the water from the tree

How can we not be delighted
>   to see the drops shatter on the grass
>   into rainbow pixelations of light?
Always you remind me not to fight
Let go breathe slow and deep
>   remember
>   it is all just right

168. Notes: This is a poem for my friend Dr. Andrew Lange, who is an alchemist and Homeopathic doctor. We met in Seattle while he was studying at the John Bastyr School of Natural Medicine and I was working part-time in an ice-cream parlor. He came in late one night near closing time and ordered an ice-cream cone. I tried to talk him out of it, as I didn't believe that anyone should be eating ice cream — certainly not someone who was studying to become a healer. He told me that he had been out drinking beer and that ice-cream was his remedy for over-indulgence. I asked him what he did and he replied, "I'm an alchemist." I said, "Oh that's interesting as I am also an alchemist." We then engaged in a friendly battle of wits — a verbal/energetic sparring. He was very clever and could throw out some quick-witted punches some of which I was able to catch and throw back at him, some of which I surrendered to and allowed to pierce deep into my heart. He and I have reminded steadfast friends for many years.

169. 2010 Subject: Mysticism, Yoga

That's It

It's gonna be alright
It's gonna be alright
Darling, it's gonna be alright

But who is *it*? — that you are talking about?
that's it — it's *that!*

And you can't name that any better than that
Any better than it, cause that's it — Tat Twam Asi

You are that, and that's that
You are it — that's it, I am that, you are that
It is that, and that's that

It's gonna be alright
It's gonna be alright
Darling, it's gonna be alright
It's just that — it's always alright

169. Notes: Often when we reach to comfort someone, we tell them, "It's going to be alright." We don't use the person's name, for instance: "John's going to be alright" or "Mary's going to be alright"; instead we say, "It's" going to be alright. Why do we say it like that? I think it is because "it" is the truth. "It" is "that" which is always alright — all right — no matter how sad, injured, afraid, lonely or confused. "You" on the other hand might be sad, injured, afraid, lonely or confused. But only because you, at that moment, have forgotten who you really are. You have forgotten that you are it — that which is eternal existence, knowledge and bliss (*satchidananda*). You have forgotten your atman, the eternal divine Self within.

When we encounter the suffering of another, that suffering is a momentary forgetting of Self. The true Self is eternal; it is boundless, limitless joy; it was never born and will never die, and because of that, "It's going to be alright" is the most reassuring and true statement that can be made. We suffer because at the time we are suffering, we are forgetting who we really are — we are identifying with a body or mind. This is called *avidya* in Sanskrit, and it means "ignorance — ignorance of our true identity." *Avidya* can also be defined as "misidentification — thinking that we are someone who we are not." We all do it. In fact, most of us spend our entire lives, even many lifetimes, mistakenly thinking that we are someone whom we are not. We identify ourselves as our personality — as the body and mind. We think we were born and we think that someday we will die and in-between we live our lives. We have resigned ourselves, or accepted, that those lives will have ups and downs — we will have good times and bad times. So when someone that we care about is going through one of those bad moments, we often show kindness towards them with the assurance that "it" will be alright, and as we do that, we remind them as well as ourselves that we really are "It," and that "it" is alright. "It" is always all right — it is not possible for "it" to be anything else but "that."

Tat Twam Asi is one of the mahavakyas, or great sayings from the Vedas (it is from the Chhandogya Upanishad of the Sama Veda). In essence, the summation of the Vedic philosophy, which underlies the yogic teachings, can be stated as: the supreme Self and the individual self are one. Tat Twam Asi is the final teaching of the Upanishads. Those three words, often translated as "That thou art" or "You are That," sum up the entire philosophical teachings of Vedanta. And since they are said by one person to another about that other, they can be used as a blessing: Tat Twam Asi — You are That, You are the Self, You are Divine. Yes, that's it! — and with that it's going to be alright.

170. 2010 Subject: Perception

Teeth Are Alive

Teeth are alive
I know this
    because
they can be coaxed
    into doing
        things
they themselves
    might not have
        thought
    of doing
        before

170. Notes: As I was flossing my teeth one night, I remembered having heard once that each individual tooth is not fixed. Teeth, like any other part of a living body, are alive, they change, they grow, they are also sensitive, responsive and can be talked to, communicated with. I also recalled that when I was around seven years old, I straightened my then crooked teeth by

looking at them in a mirror and talking to them — showing them with my fingers how I would like for them to grow. The project worked — my teeth became straight without the application of dental braces.

171. 2010 *Subject: Portrait*

Cat Breath

beige furry eyebrows
two
each underneath
a creamy colored chest
like stubby legs
holding up
a precious trunk
which contains
inside
the beating heart
of my
beloved

with eyes closed
he twitches
a whisker
I lean my face
closer
as he sneezes
I can smell
sweet putrid perfume
his hot breath
how can I resist?
I savor
his open mouth

— a distillation
of decomposing
parts
of leaves, roots, wings
and other
        things

171. *Notes:* One morning I was drinking tea and eating toast with my beloved cat Miten, who sat on the table in the sunshine in front of me, with his front legs tucked under his chest, as cats often like to sit. When I looked at him, those little beige colored feet curled under his creamy colored chest looked like furry eyebrows. He looked so beautiful and content sitting there, having just eaten his breakfast of toast. He also likes to eat lettuce, cucumbers, arugula or shredded raw carrots. His diet is mostly vegetables, for which he has a great appetite, but he also enjoys an occasional bird or small mammal. His breath often smells pretty rank — but my love for him is so great that somehow, I never feel repulsed by it.

172. *2010 Subject: Life*

So Sure

You find it is not so hard
You find it is not too far

Tumble tumble tumble
Tumble tumble tumble
Down down to the ground

Crawling on your belly
In your fears

So sure of the rising sun
So sure you will get to stay
Another day

Death comes quick
Like a thief in the night
Like a thief in the night
with a knife

172. *Notes:* Most of the time when we feel we are getting clear, making some spiritual progress, maybe even feeling the *kundalini* rising, instead of going with it, we quickly do something to subvert the process, to pull us downward again to what is familiar even if it is painful. And we might do this over and over again with the arrogant assumption that we will have another chance, another day to see the sun rise, another day to begin again. For example, in a yoga class we grab a bottle of water and start drinking. What this does is to deactivate the upward moving *prana* and call into motion *apana*, which grounds us energetically and brings us down. Or we stay out late at night drinking or taking drugs, come home and go to sleep with the assurance that we will wake up the next day and have another chance. This subverting of success can play out in many areas — like when you get a "lucky" break, but don't have the self-confidence to follow through so you make sure that you place enough handicaps on yourself to show the world you have a good excuse for not being successful.

173. *2010 Subject: Nature, Yoga*

Overhead

Cause when the trees start flying overhead
Overhead overhead

It's when those trees are flying overhead
Overhead overhead

And when the fish start swimming overhead
Overhead overhead

It's when those fish are flying overhead
Overhead overhead

Before the dogs take off overhead
Overhead overhead

Their noses smell the air overhead
Overhead overhead

Follow the smell to the farthest
Stillness in the north overhead
Goes on forever there overhead
Aurora Borealis northern lights
Falling in swirls like waterfalls
Lighting up the trees overhead
The snow does not seem so cold at all

While shimmering dazzling lights
Dance in the night sky overhead
Overhead overhead

173. Notes: This is a poem about going over the head — beyond thought, going
to the top, through smell, taste, sight, touch and hearing, to the rapture of
merger with the beloved in the north pole of the body — the crown chakra,
the place of heightened awareness. This poem is about meditation; it is about
yoga; it is about enlightenment, the dawning or awaking of consciousness/
awareness. Kundalini reunites with Shiva in the still, quiet, snowy
mountaintops of the Himalayas, beyond the borders, beyond the tree line.
The *sahasrara* chakra lights up in dazzling colors — the northern lights
shower over the tree, the *sushumna*, like a waterfall, and it all happens in the
cold stillness of the snow, in the midst of all the infinite crystals of pure
shape. The northern lights, or Aurora Borealis, are more visible near the
North Pole due to longer periods of darkness and the magnetic field. Aurora

is the name of the Greek goddess of dawn and Borealis, which is the Greek name for the north wind, is an appropriate analogy for enlightenment, which is, after all, a dawning of awareness where the winds, the *prana vayus*, flow freely in the central channel and light up the whole tree like at Christmas. Kundalini is much like Aurora, the sleeping beauty in the Brothers Grimm tale. Aurora, like kundalini, awakens with the kiss of eternity in the ecstatic stillness of prince Shiva's abode of joy in the top of the head after having made her way up through the tree to the top. The air/wind/pranic element of the *anahata* or heart chakra gives her the needed momentum to let go of thought, the divisive attribute of the mind, which separates you from me and allows "we". Unity triumphs over separation as her wings open to embrace surrender and she flies home, or *OM*, to the reality of love and unity, which is in the North Pole of the body.

Whatever astronomical phenomenon we can witness appears to us because it is a reflection of an inner reality inside of us, whether actual or potential. The Aurora Borealis, which is thought by most scientists to occur in the ionosphere, also occurs inside of us, in our physical body, and actually it can only occur in the ionosphere *because* it occurs inside of us. We project it from inside of us to what we perceive as "out there," but actually there is no out there out there, independent of what is "in here."

This poem came to me while I was riding my bike on the country roads near my home in Woodstock. The words and images flew to me in the form of a song. Previous to my bike ride, I had been listening to Daniel Lanois's CD *Black Dub*, and in a strange way, when I heard Trixie Whitely's vocals, something in the arrangement by Lanois reminded me of the Lilac Fairy from Tchaikovsky's orchestral work for the ballet *The Sleeping Beauty*. In that ballet, the Lilac Fairy has a leading role in the introduction of the first movement, bringing the message of light, hope and cohesion in the midst of darkness, despair and chaos, much like the Aurora Borealis.

174. *2010 Subject: Perception*

Mommy

Mommy Mommie Mommeeee
Really means Ma=me, Ma is me!

Wave good-by, wave to me
Wave to mommy, wave to me
I am your mother, can't you see,
It is me?
Ma is me!
Turn your little hand around
Wave to mommy, wave to me
I am your mother, can't you see,
Ma is me!

174. *Notes*: I had an insight about the word *mommy* — how it may have come to be the name that children (and some adults) calls their mother — and it occurred to me that it was related to how babies wave. Little kids are encouraged to wave to others. They have seen others wave to them, so when they wave back — they do so with the palm of their hand facing towards them — not to the person that they are waving at — and when the kid does this, everyone laughs, and of course the child gets confused and self-conscious, and thinks, "Why are they laughing, I thought I was supposed to do this with my hand, they told me to do it, they told me to wave, what am I doing so wrong, so stupid, to make them laugh at me?" But when the child sees others wave, what he sees is a palm turned to face him with fingers opening and closing, and he identifies that with the word, "wave." So it makes sense to him, when he is asked to wave, to do exactly what he has seen others do and what he has seen is that palm facing towards him/her with fingers opening and closing and so he does just that. Communication can be a funny thing. When a mother is trying to communicate to her child about herself, she tells the child that she is his/her mother. But she usually doesn't use the word mother because it is too formal. A mother likes to be called *mommy* by her small child. The word *mommy* comes from a mother trying to identify herself to her child: she says: Ma — Me! Which means: Ma is me or mother, your mother is me. I am your Ma, Ma is Me! The mother is saying that the word Ma indicates her, so she says to her child: Ma=me (mommie). So the child learns that and says back to his/her mother, "Mommy!"

I'll Meet You There

I longed for you then
While my body was young

I searched for you then
But you had not yet come

When all these days turn into night
With my heart in my soul I will take flight

Promise me this that you will wait
Because to be hasty again will seal our fate

Promise me you will come in winter, then
I can manage to be there by summer's gate

Through careful timing we'll
Accomplish this and tune our hearts to sing

All this feeling it can't be wrong
I know somewhere there's got to be a song

And if ever time itself will cease to be
I'll meet you there in eternity.

175. *Notes:* Relationships are often time bound. In our culture, if a woman is a lot older than a man, she only has a few limited choices for how that relationship could unfold. It may be true that we have all been each other's mothers, sons, lovers, etc., in past lifetimes, but as the poem proposes, if we could get the timing right, perhaps in the next life we could meet up again in bodies of a more compatible age, at least according to society's conventions.

Drink Tea

Drink tea be happy
Alchemically magically
The combination
Of leaf and water
Opens the window
To quietude and delight
Such simple beauty
Can put things right

176. *Notes:* A friend was getting married on Sunday. On Saturday night I wrapped up her wedding gift, which was an assortment of teas and a porcelain Chinese tea set, which included a teapot and small cups and this poem. The underlying implied message being that if she encountered difficult times in her marriage, a quiet moment of contemplation with a cup of tea might be just the thing to put things right again.

177. 2011 *Subject: Portrait*

Come and Gone

You have three angels
        living above your head
With nothing more to do
        than press your thoughts
Into the endless blue of the sky
Those winged ones remind me that
        You were never born
        and we have never met
We have been with each other all along
So what does it matter when another year
        Has come and gone

177. *Notes: I* wrote this poem for David on his 61st birthday. The reference to the three angels came from a time when he had his picture taken by means of Kirlian photography. The photographer explained that the three lights appearing above his head in the picture were protective angelic forms who always reside above his head. She also said that most people are attracted to David because they sense those angels and are actually drawn to the angels and not to David. I don't know about that, but that is what she said.

178. 2011 *Subject: Culture, Speciesism*

When I Wake Up

When will we stop shooting tigers and clubbing baby seals?
When will we stop this genocide of wild people?
This war on all the animal nations, this war against Mother Nature?

I must be sleeping, this must be a bad dream
and when I wake up from this nightmare of screams
The deer will see me and not run in fear
The rabbit's heart will not quicken when I'm near
The bears will roam
Coyotes will not silence their songs
The birds will not stumble with clipped wings
nor will the fish drown without their fins
The mink will not circle crazy in their cage
Horses forced to jump driven by men enraged
All of this will cease to be
When I wake up

The pigeons will not have to scavenge through vomit
The monkeys and beagles will not convulse in fits
as bathroom cleanser eats away their bones
Flesh cut open again and again
agonizing in a cold metal box alone

Waiting for the next cruel procedure
Which ultimately, they won't be able to endure
Then thrown away to be picked up by the garbage man
or sold to the renderers and packed in a cat food can
All of this will cease to be
When I wake up

With her fluid tongue the snake will talk to me and tell me
 of things I have forgotten
We will run through meadows the foxes and I
Falling and tumbling with delight
Our days will become bright
As our hearts open to the light
The darkness of the past swallowed as
I step naked into the apocalypse
Finally free of lies
in the summer night alight with fireflies
Perhaps my body will grow velvety fur and
I will let go of the cumbersome chore of racing
for planes dragging suitcases filled with clothes from place to place
All of this will come to be
When I wake up

But when will I wake up from this bad dream?
When will I do something to cause this violence to cease to be?
When will I wake up as a liberator for countless beings?
When will I burn down the labs, pull down the fences, open the cages
and set them free?

They say first free yourself, then you can free others
But what better way to spend our time, on our way to liberation then to
do all we can now to free others of their degradation?
Somewhere inside we know that freeing others *is* the way
to free ourselves.

This realization may take a dawning
So yes take your time, if you must, to finish your yawning
To finally become fully awake, out of bed off and running
We will need liberators, who are clear headed, well rested and cunning

But please don't wait too long,
the alarm has already sounded
You may not think you are ready, but the animals are —
Wolves are howling and the lynx are pacing
It is too late to press the snooze again and fall back
into a futureless dream
We're all here waiting for you, some trembling in cages,
some crouched in bushes, under a dark moon,
Hooded headed and armed with bolt cutters
Right over here under the gutters
Once and for all tired of ignoring the scream
You there, aren't you part of our team?

When will we wake up and do something to cause all this violence
to cease to be?
When will we wake up as liberators for countless beings who all want
to be free?

Only when I wake up then?
can this truly happen?
Yes, it is indeed up to me,
but I am you and you are me,
and so it all comes back around to us — you see.

178. *Notes:* I wrote this poem around the time of my birthday. Having been born on July 4th, I have always felt aligned with the cause of liberation. Every birthday feels like another wake-up call, reminding me to stay on point and to renew my commitment to doing all I can to free my own mind of speciesism, to help educate other human beings and ultimately to free the animals who are all victims of our prejudice. I want to be a liberator, not an enslaver, and I

believe that I am not alone. For those of us interested in freedom, there is no
better way to ensure our own freedom than to do all we can to ensure the
freedom of others. The majority of human beings seem to be intent on taking
away the freedom of other animals: imprisoning them in laboratories, race
tracks, kennels, fur ranches, farms, zoos, aquariums and circuses and other
horrible ways too numerous to list here, not realizing that ultimately what we
do to others we do to ourselves. This poem is a letter to myself as well as other
activists to wake up and join together to liberate our fellow animals from
cruel, man-made prisons and to put an end to the insane exploitation and
slaughter of defenseless animals — fellow Earthlings caught together with us
in the web of life. Animal liberation is our own liberation — lest we forget that
we are animals too.

179. *2011 Subject: Portrait*

I Love the Incredible String Band

I love tall robin who should have been the short
I love the short heron who should have been the tall robin
Listen to that Robin and a Heron as they sing of many things
Like whispering trees, black cherries for rings,
and mushroom type things
And wondrous light bound up tight in a painting box
while shadowy fingers tip a witch's hat to a fox
Lickety-licorice and the gently tender rose,
all blown away now smiling as dust be diamonds
while big buildings tower and fall
Mercy I cry, city — what'cha been doin'?
you look like a ruin to me!
I would rather fly with those incredible birds,
who just get brighter every day and every time,
I hear them — they scatter brightness in their way and they
taught me how to love them
Krishna colors on the wall — I know you belong to everybody but you

can't deny that I'm you
So true, so very true
Sleepers awake — let's
listen to their flutes and flowers
in a forest of moss
and wear green crowns, tattered gowns
and mad hatter hats and sit with
hedgehogs and pigs who eat acorns
This will be a very cellular song
this moment so light and lighter
we will give all our brightness away and it will only make us brighter
Oh for lifetimes how I have longed to follow them to
distant lands wondrous and fair
In the highlands of Scotland,
I heard they are there.

179. *Notes*: If there was a 1960s band that I would love to have joined it would have been the Incredible String Band. The music is magical, it lifts and shifts. I would also call the music auspicious because it resembles the flight of birds and the messages in the songs, appear to have come from birds — a robin and a heron specifically. Robin Williamson and Mike Heron were/are genius musicians, songwriters and shapeshifters, who certainly foretell a brighter future with their songs. Forgive me, but I also feel that their bird-like names should be reversed, because Robin Williamson, the taller and more elegantly aloof of the two, seems more like a heron, and Mike Heron, shorter, clever and quick of wit, seems more of a robin. Of the two charming girls in the band, Rose was the perfect rose and Licorice never a name more precise. This little poem is an homage to them and is made up of references to some of their mystical songs. I loved them in the 1960s and I still love them and listen to their music now and will continue, as it makes me feel brighter and brighter every time I hear them.

Let Us Be Remembering

What are we to do and how are we to do it?
Who to ask and who to listen to?
The air is dense with invisible pollution
Too much talking
Many words a jumbling topsy-turvy
A conundrum
Of what have-yous and what-nots
So much confusion — can't make much sense
Certainly can't assume anyone is saying
What they are meaning or meaning what they
Are saying
Let us be remembering
To be calm and gracious
Forgive them as they know not
What they say or where their
Words, thoughts and feelings come from
Let us be remembering
The most important thing is to
Never ever
Get snarled caught in the trap
Of seeing ourselves as a victim
Of a person or situation like that
Let us be remembering
Everything comes from us
Please do not look alarmed and play the innocent
You have created your oppressors
As well as all the people who
Are behaving badly around you
Pretending that they know not what you
Are talking about

Make it clear from the start
Lay out your plans,
Complete with expectations
And be forthcoming with your
Capacities — don't exaggerate
Or you may get yourself in trouble
Down the road more or less traveled
Let us be remembering that
This is a game
We do not make up the rules
Our job is to play
Let us be remembering
That tactics are different from strategy
We should arm ourselves with an
Abundance of both
And go forth joyfully with a sense of adventure

180. *Notes:* To see oneself as a victim prevents one from being able to see oneself as an enlightened being. We must be on our guard at all times not to fall into the alluring trap of blaming others and seeing ourselves as an innocent victim of unfair treatment or disregard. Each one of us is a master of our own reality. We have created our present situation according to how we have treated others in our past. To play the game of life takes not only a sense of adventure, but attention to detail — we need to strategically plot our course and use appropriate tactics to realize our goal — using strategy for long term and tactics for short term results. Don't get mired in idealism with expectations about how people should behave or how you wish things had turned out. Accept the game as it is, and don't demand it to be otherwise. When you can do this, daily life becomes much more fun. You discover the element of play as you discover the necessity for fluidity in your maneuvers. If you can remember to be kind and compassionate, then you will most likely be able to forgive yourself and others.

The fact is we are living at a time when it is very difficult for people to tell you the truth. It is not that they mean to lie, it is just that they are being bombarded with so many electrical impulses from cell phones, computers, radios, televisions, etc., that it is difficult for a person to actually know what they are thinking or feeling.

Everyone is so saturated with information that seems to be coming at them from invisible forces that it is challenging to maintain a connection to one's own heart, and that makes it difficult for anyone to say what they mean and mean what they say. The world has become a tower of Babel. How do we maneuver through it? First and foremost don't get angry. Remember to be kind to others and to never see yourself as a victim of another's shortcomings — no matter how short those comings may appear!

181. *2011 Subject: Portrait*

No Tail

No tail the dear deer wanders back into the forest
The forest is dark to me but home to her

She will come again tonight or tomorrow
Munch a lunch of oats, corn and seeds

She eats standing up ready to flee
Sparked by just the sound of me

And yet here she is, back again
Why after so many years is she still afraid?

Is it only hunger that moves her to visit me?
I'd like to think it is at least curiosity

181. Notes: One of the deer that visits us every day at our forest sanctuary has no tail, just a little pink stump of bone no bigger than a finger. We guessed that her tail was shot off by a hunter some years back or perhaps infected by some skin disease that caused all the fur and flesh to disintegrate until all that was left was the bone. At any rate she is a regular member of our family now. It is odd that even though we have become so familiar with each other, she is still very skittish and afraid every time she sees us. I wish this weren't so. I wish so much that I could comfort her more and help her to feel that she is beautiful regardless of her lack of a tail. I wish that she could see us as friends, but then again, I have to feel that her apprehension in the presence of human beings is necessary for her survival.

182. 2011 *Subject: Nature*

Whack the Weed Down

I couldn't get my breath
My throat was closing in, trapping me
in my skin
David went in search of wild nettles
to make me a soothing tea

He walked through the forest and fields
over three long years

Then one spring day in May
out by the kitchen door, among the roses
a tall green nettle man stood
his leaves shimmering in the
dappled light under the birch tree

All that summer I drank tea
that he provided for me
and was able to easily breath and to see
the more stinging leaves I picked
taller and stronger he grew
until his height — ten feet flew
His roots spreading so deep
they began to loosen
the blue stones in the wall

I loved the tall green man
who gave so generously
and would introduce him to
all who would visit me

Every morning we would come
and sit by him in the garden
drinking tea, Miten my cat and me

On a clear day in late September
I awoke alone in the house, made
tea and went with my cat
trotting after me to sit by
the man in the garden

My stomach grew tight
my heart dropped low
with my breath in a rasp
I cried, "Oh no!"

Some cruel fiend
had come in the morning
and cut my stinging man down to the ground
By the looks of the torn and ragged stalks
the weapon must have been
a whacking machine

How could he cut down so mercilessly,
such a gracious and willing guest
who only came beckoned,
at our request?

This sundown he will return
for his dinner waiting on the table

It is then that I must speak out,
he knows I will —
already he is bristling with defense

"Why, I simply want to know,
did you cut down the nettle plant?
Winter will be coming fast,
nature would have not allowed
those willowy branches
to last through the snow."

I had hoped the Green man would
have been pleased with our company
and returned again next spring...
"Oh please! it's only a weed!"

Weed or not he came to help
answered our call of need
"Oh please! it's only a weed!
that was getting way too tall
besides there are still the roots
the plant will grow back in the spring,
it's only a weed after all!"

This may be true, but nonetheless
Why return graciousness
With such callousness?

You have stripped him bare
rendered him to a mere few stumps
why would he risk another humiliation,
and attempt to sprout new leaves again,
after such ungrateful treatment?

"If the nettle doesn't grow back
fine — another is sure to take its place
anyway weeds should not be allowed
to grow so tall in a garden after all."

182. *Notes:* This poem tells the story of a wild nettle plant that appeared one day in our garden. I have asthma and drinking tea made of these leaves helped me to breathe better. One September day I went out to the garden to discover to my horror that the nettle plant had been cut down, leaving only a few torn and ragged stumps on the ground. I was filled with sadness and felt this to be a senseless act of cruelty — surely there could be no reasoning behind it. The nettle hadn't been hurting anyone. Besides that, with winter coming I was sure that the leaves and stalks would wither anyway on their own, so there would be no need to cut them. I don't know that much about botany, herbs or agriculture, but I do know that roots become strong by being nourished by the leaves and stems of a plant. The leaves draw nourishment from the sun and channel it through the stems into the roots. The roots hibernate throughout the winter and resurrect themselves in the spring when the stalks begin to sprout. By cutting down a plant in the early fall I thought it would deprive it of its ability to draw the last remaining nourishment needed to survive through the winter. My assumptions were correct and the nettle plants did not return the following spring. But the good news is some years later the green man did return again — this time in another location in the garden, where he has a designated sequestered plot all his own.

183. *2011 Subject: Yoga*

Wish-Fulfilling Tree

How did this happen to me?
I love you my Lord — please deliver me
What has happened to us all?
I know you alone can only see
There are moments you have given to me
When I can feel and remember to be kind

It is surely in the name — that magical spell
That takes me out of this human body
And into the realm of naked no clothes
Then I am alone
My gopi sari hangs on the wishing tree
Then you drape it over me and
All of my body becomes transformed into ecstasy
Beauty surrounds us and is within us
If we could only see
We have such a short time on Earth
In the limited vehicle we have
We become so attached to our body
But even so we don't really go deeply
Into our attachment for if we did we could
Free it — transforming our body into a magical wish fulfilling tree
able to transport us into eternity

183. *Notes:* My guru, Shri Brahmananda Sarasvati taught, "You are not the body although you have a body." The body is meant to be used as a vehicle to bring one closer to God. Through remembering God, the recitation of God's name and being kind to others, the body becomes an instrument — a wish-fulfilling tree, rooted in the Earth and reaching upward towards the heavens of limitless possibility.

184. *2011 Subject: Perception*

Eat Vegetables

When my stepfather was dying
I stayed by my mother's side
In the hospital day and night

He had been a heavy drinker
His liver and kidneys were

Dis-eased — he had exhausted
The benefits of dialysis
His body was decaying
and now fate was catching
Up to him

We had been living on
Vending machine food and coffee
On the fourth day, I suggested we
Take a break, go home, I would cook
Something for us to eat
She agreed

Arriving to a barren kitchen
In the trailer
where she lived,
I managed to find some
potatoes, canned peas, corn
and beans

"Will this be enough for you,
Mom?" I asked.
"Yes, I want to just eat vegetables,
I am so tired of death," she said.

184. *Notes:* Poems are not bound by time restraints. They can pop up at anytime, appearing as a tapestry woven from past memories. This is one such poem. It was in 1976 that my stepfather died an agonizing death. During his final week I spent a lot of time in the hospital with my mother. This poem recounts one such day where she let me cook dinner for her while she was taking a break from her vigil at the hospital by his side. My mother was not a vegetarian by any means, so for her to ask to eat only vegetables was unusual, but her reasoning was pretty sane.

Slave Trade

Such a craze this trading in slaves
Still not many notice
How could *they* when they are
so enslaved in the maze
Of this crazy slave trade
If you mention that slaves fuel
the world economy
They will for sure say,
"Slavery is over that's a shameful thing of the past."
And wave it off — dismissed as "oh that."
But show *them* a picture of a rabbit in a cage,
a dog chained, a tethered calf
Or a warehouse full of sheep and pigs,
all helpless in their grief and stench.
Then *their* eyes will surely open wide
But just for a moment until
They wave it off — dismissed as "oh that,"
and say, "They're just animals —
you *sure* fooled me for a crazy moment.
I thought you were talking about slaves."

185. Notes: The average person is appalled by the idea of slavery and yet they conveniently block out from their awareness and are in denial of the fact that the foundation of our culture, of our economy, is built upon billions of animals exploited as slaves. The financial crisis, the troubled stock market, cannot be fixed if we continue to insist upon trading in slaves. We have to think more radically if we want to get to the root of the money issue and find solutions. For that we have to start by examining how our economy and way of life is built upon the trading of livestock. I attended a forum recently in my neighborhood entitled, "The Future of Money," and one of the speakers suggested that the solution to the money crisis is in creating "local currency," which meant that small communities would print their own money and use this to buy stuff in their local communities. She went on to explain that eventually her dream would be that the local currency would actually be backed up with "real wealth." She described what she meant by real wealth: "Not in the form of gold or silver, but in the form of basic things that we could really use, like for instance chickens. So if someone was raising chickens, they could convert those chickens into local currency dollars. A hundred chickens could mean a hundred local currency dollars." She talked about chickens as if they were not included as members of the community, not worthy of respect and the right to pursue happiness, and certainly lacking any kind of recognizable feelings. She spoke about chickens as if they were there for the "pickin'." What she was actually suggesting is that we go back in time to when we bartered with each other for the things we felt we needed. The problem with this is that it isn't radical enough. The use of animals as currency is a really old idea and actually forms the basis of our present culture. Our current economic problems stem from this. If we want to solve our money problems and evolve, we must pull ourselves out of the mindset of viewing other animals and the rest of nature as slaves to be exploited as resources and currency.

186. 2011 *Subject: Nature*

Under a Sky of Stars

He would always find opportunities
to go to a park
Walk barefoot on the grass amidst the trees or
along the shore of a lake
Dig toes into the dark musky earth or
running along a beach in the sand
Swimming in the ocean waves holding hands

He was an outsider
Who liked camping and taking
week-long walks
through remote jungle areas in India and

cook potatoes in a fire pit near some temple
Watch a thousand bats fly into the night
as the moon went full

The others were insiders
with never even a thought of the pleasures
of sleeping under a sky of stars

186. *Notes:* Most friends that I have known didn't like to venture out much and preferred to stay indoors. Inside in controlled environments we tend to feel safe and comfortable. The exception was Shyamdas, who took every opportunity to be out and about. He seemed to thrive in wide open expansive environments where the next moment was unpredictable and totally out of his control. He was fearless and believed with all his heart that God protects His devotees. His trust and faith were exemplary while a bit unnerving for us — his more cautionary friends who had yet to discover Shri Krishna's refuge and sought shelter in our own indoor realities.

187. *2011 Subject: Culture, Nature, Speciesism*

The Bear

How can they live, these bears?
Certainly they must only be able barely
With his big bear belly so big to fill
So much he would have to find to eat
bear head, and bear feet
When he is too tired of the cold world
In his bear way he retreats into sleep
Clawing into the earth with his bare hands
He digs a hollow and covers with dirt
Sitting motionless with a mind withdrawn
A yogi-bear naked holed up in a cave
While the season passes nails grow long

Heart slows down, breath but a quiet song
Absorbed in cosmic unity until
The karmas awaken his will
To roam about as a wild one in the sun
They like the daytime as much as you or me
To warm their bear face in the afternoon
Better to pick berries when you can see
But often this is not allowed
They have to try to become invisible
And slink along blending into the dusk
With the trees and bushes
"You saw a bear? Impossible here,
it was only the moon playing
with a shadow — probably you saw a big dog."
This is 2012 in the United States of America
Shopping malls, freeways, clear cuts, fracking
Even the Canadian Geese have no place to land
Most of the foxes and beavers are dead
How could someone as big as a bear get fed?

187. Notes: Quite often we see bears in the forest where we live. Bears are always around our house in the summertime. They walk right up onto the porch. They are meditative creatures, able to lower their metabolism and reduce their need to interact with the "outer world" for long winter months. In fact they spend most of the year hibernating. What could that mean but a deep retreat — going inside to touch the source of all being? We humans often perceive the actions of other animals as just instinctual, lacking any higher level of conscious intention. But what if it turns out that the bears are actually meditating, withdrawing their consciousness from the world into a deeper, more expanded source? Our spiritual literature is filled with stories about great Indian and Tibetan yogis who have sat in caves lost to the world in deep absorption until their hair and nails grew long. We have great respect for their renunciation abilities. Perhaps other animals also engage in such practices? The truth is that we don't really know why other animals do what they do. It would be human-centric of us to say that other animals don't meditate and that only human beings yearn for spiritual knowledge.

I don't think that only human beings are intelligent or wise or spiritual. Perhaps we are the loudest in broadcasting to others how wise, intelligent or saintly we are, but that doesn't mean we are the only ones who may be. I think it is more likely that other animals, just like some of us, have spiritual aspirations, while some do not. I am sure we could learn a thing about connecting deeply to what is deep from bears if only we could get close enough to them to be able to hear and understand the wisdom, they might impart to us. But we have never attempted to learn their ways, much less their language. We barely know who these bear-people are! And at this time on the Earth, they are (and with good reason) extremely shy and easily frightened by human beings. I can't understand how they are able to get enough to eat to tide them over the winter months. I also can't figure out where they go to sleep or meditate. For all the times I've walked through the forest I have never seen a bear den. We have seen poor, skinny, mangy bears with little or no hair or fur. Whenever I see a naked bear like this, I am filled with pity. A bear with no fur looks pretty much like a human being. And to see a naked starving bare bear person in the yard like that is a sad sight and there is little I can do to help. There are not many places in the world where bears still roam free. To live in Woodstock, one hundred miles from New York City, and see bears often, wow it is indeed wonderful and amazing. But how long can it last— what is this world coming to? I can only barely imagine. Perhaps eventually they will gradually fade away and become mythical creatures, like unicorns or dragons that humans in the future will argue about whether or not they actually existed.

188. 2011 *Subject: Culture, Speciesism*

Human Rights

Human Rights you say?
Why don't I fight for Human Rights you say?
For the right to do what?
To consume more
To plunder more
To take more
To enslave more

To buy more stuff
For the right to humiliate and destroy
The wise and humble heart
Inside an elephant, a mustang,
Or a snow leopard?

No thank you.
Humans have way too many rights as it is,
I'll get behind animal rights, thank you
And get to the root of the problem
I want to learn how-to live-in harmony from
Those who have the know-how of how to live —
Those other animals
Who have no desire,
To increase their wages, buy a mortgage,
get the latest app, raise pigs for slaughter
Or dress in cheap clothes from China

I have to say no thank you.
I will not support any more human rights
we humans have far too many rights as it is
And still we don't know
How to live
More human rights
Will only lead to more human wrongs

If we could be truthful to our name —
we may be able to rearrange ourselves
Our name, "human" means
Of the Earth, low to the ground
Connected to the soil — like humus
So when Michael Franti
Says, "Stay Human"
He means stay humble —
Close and connected to the Earth

But for most to be human is
To be elevated above the Earth
To lord over all other beings
To change the language to suit
Our purposes is to invert
So as to exaggerate our worth

I'd rather be radical and stand with the Earth
And try my best to think bigger than thoughts
So that is why I am a spiritual activist
cause it encompasses more of us
We are all animals after all
Anima means soul it is the animating force
Within all of life
Why divide and myopically focus on one
Group of bodies and ignore the rest
While the atman, the pulsation of the universe
vibrates beyond the body and mind eternally
Forward and backward through time
Human rights is too marginal a cause
I stand with the soul forgivingly
within the circled "A" of anarchy

188. *Notes*: Several years back, I heard Ingrid Newkirk, founder of PETA, give a talk where she spoke about animal rights as not being the same as human rights. She explained, "When we talk about animal rights, we are not talking about giving animals the right to drive a car or vote. We are talking about simply treating another species with respect for who they are." I am often ridiculed for being an animal rights activist, attacked and condemned for loving animals more than human beings. I am repeatedly asked the question, "How can you work so hard for the rights of animals when there is so much human suffering in the world?" I often answer, "Because I am trying to get at the root of the suffering." I feel without a doubt, that to be an animal rights activist is a noble cause, because it gets closer to the root cause. So many of our human problems, like poverty, lack of clean water, disease and starvation, stem from how we are treating animals. Raising animals for food is very

destructive to the environment as well as the psychological atmosphere in which we all live. Besides, why view compassion as if it only existed in each one of us in a small finite amount and if we gave some to one being it would deplete us and if we gave it to many beings we would run out. Compassion cannot be measured; it is not something you can keep tied up in a miserly little bag and divvy it out when you feel some poor unfortunate is deserving. Compassion is limitless; it is the essential nature of your being. You can't run out of it.

Human rights can be such a sham, because in many cases, it only really means the right to shop — the promise of a lifetime of consumerism. We human beings have already taken too much and don't even know when enough is enough. Real needs are not wrong but wants on the other hand can lead to major problems. Our culture cultivates wants — the desire for material things — above all other ventures. Material things don't satisfy those who seek illumination, freedom and lasting happiness. I'm actually not so keen on the idea of rights anyway, human or animal, because it presumes there is someone in the position to give them, ensuring an automatic hierarchy. As my friend Jessica Patterson, author of Unbecoming Human, says, "The very notion of "rights" sets up an unequal — and therefore unbalanced and exploitive — dynamic between the ones in power (the ones who can "give" or grant rights) and the powerless recipient of the rights. And so, while it seems to be an equalizer, it reinforces the gap and subtly, insidiously, reinforces the inequality that allows for exploitation." When most people speak of human rights, they are talking about the right of the poor to have what the rich have. But this plan is all still on the level of ego/material gratification. It is all still bound by the cultural mindset that ensures us that the Earth and all other animals belong to us and that to exploit them — turn them into commodities — is our human right and will bring us happiness. You know the song, "This Land is your land this land is our land..." Rubbish — we have no right to own the Earth or to own anybody. The yogi wants to become free of the ego — the sense of self as separate from all other selves — and cultivate a desire to know the *atman*, the eternal essential Self that is the animator of all living beings. True anarchy means "Self-rule,"— Self with a capital "S." It is this Self that the yogi seeks to realize and to surrender to rather than allowing the insatiable ego to have free reign. To see the Self in others is the essential practice of yoga. Giving blessings to others and bowing to the Self in each being awakens the Self within you. Through this perceptual practice, eventually but inevitably otherness will disappear and only the One will remain — only God, only the Self. Perhaps it is in this spirit that people like Mother Teresa worked — seeing all the people she was feeding and cleaning, not as suffering souls but as God coming to her, giving her an opportunity to touch God. This type of anarchy is a radical practice that can bring one to enlightened realization. Many may feel uncomfortable with my use of anarchy as a spiritual term, because to many people anarchy means lawlessness, chaos, hedonism and the unbridled right to do whatever you want regardless of anybody else (actually sounds more like the popular conception of human rights). Many words in our culture have become inverted and their original meaning lost. My teacher Swami Nirmalananda, the anarchist swami, taught that anarchy means "Self-rule"— not to abide by laws outside of one's divine Self. So yes, you could say that it is all dependent on whether you are using an upper or lower case "s". Language can of course be turned around to suit anybody's purpose. For example, many of us forget that the word *human* actually comes from the root word *humus*, which means "close to or of the Earth" (interestingly, the word *humility* shares the same root), and the word *animal* comes from the root word *anima*, which means "soul" (interestingly — the word *animate* shares the same root). So even when most of us use words like *human, animal* or even *anarchy*, we don't know what we are really talking about. If we did, then to identify ourselves as human would mean that we would see ourselves as humble and one with the Earth and all beings. And every time we used the word *animal*, we would remember that it means to have a soul, to be alive, and with that remembrance we would recognize that all animals have souls. All living beings have souls; having a soul is what causes them to live, to be animated. If we practiced saying what we mean and meaning what we say, the world would be a different place.

I received a catalogue in the mail from the Heifer Foundation asking me to contribute money to their "human rights organization." It explained to me how I could choose to specify how my donation should be used by looking at the pictures in the catalogue of various animals — sheep, goats, pigs and chickens — and decide if I wanted to buy a couple of pigs for a poor family in Bolivia, so they could set up their own business and raise their standard of living, or arrange to have a baby goat sent to a poor family in Kenya so that they could exploit it as a slave for its whole life, selling and drinking its milk, selling its wool and babies, etc. I wrote them a letter expressing my disgust for their shortsighted support of animal slavery and exploitation as an solution for human poverty. Afterward I wrote this poem as an invitation to rethink what we mean by human rights and who we are calling an animal and perhaps even what the real meaning of anarchy is.

Looking Glass

Looking Glass tell me what you see
I can't tell you anything beyond what you already know
The whole world including the rising sun
Is there because you wish for it to be
Your eyes foretell the depth of your soul
The speckled flakes within your iris are clouds of anger
frustration ignorance sadness and greed
Everyone we behold tells us who we are
And the limits of what we can be
A billion mirrors plus the sun, shine back
Upon us everyone
Looking Glass tell me what you see
I am blind and empty it is you who make it come to be
Million-year old carbon a diamond body come to life
With snakes continuously conversing in entwining delight
Shining one this is all your making
Drop the blame embrace the name
Celestial lips kiss the flute and worlds spring to life
The luminous Christ is born in a cave
this very night by means of
pixelations and sound vibrations
Musical and measured
Even the evening star radiates Her song
And sings 'cause she has taken a shining to you
Mirrored delight in the black of illumined sight
there is nothing to tell and no one to free
The whole world including the rising sun
Is there because you wish it to be

189. *Notes:* I read a posting on a friend's Facebook page where he said that he was filing a lawsuit against the city of New York and the New York City

Police Department, because the police sprayed him with pepper spray while he was involved in a peaceful demonstration. In his posting he said, "See you in court, bitches!" His use of derogatory language was interesting to me, as it seemed to contradict his commitment towards creating a new world free of hierarchy. Perhaps this was only a momentary slip for him into the old paradigm. It can happen to the best of us. Anyway the fact is the word *bitch* refers to a female dog in heat. It is commonly used as a derogatory term to insult someone, and its power as an insult is rooted in the notion that female dogs that want to have sex are pitiful, lowly creatures without shame or any shred of dignity, driven by hormonal instinct. It is used as a way to insult another human being by equating them with not only a dog, but with a female dog. The use of the word *bitches* is speciesist as well as misogynistic and reveals a deep hatred for nature. After I read his Facebook posting, John Lennon's lyrics came to my mind, "If you want money for people with minds that hate, all I can tell you brother is you have to wait…" If we want to create a new world, perhaps we should be careful not to perpetuate the old one — where hatred of nature, animals and women is prevalent. The words we speak affect the soundscape in which we live: reality is created by sound. There is nothing outside of us that has not come from inside of us. Even the Sun is a projection of our own inner self. There are no others, only mirrors, reflections. The world appears according to how we see it. How we see it is determined by our thoughts, and our thoughts are made of words. The universe pulsates with music, the songs we sing and the words we say.

190. 2012 *Subject: Perception, Yoga*

Always Moving

Asana pulls *this* inward
Poetry draws *that* outward
Streaming through nadis
Pranic pulsation results
Available to hear
Sound feels
As moving always
Always moving

190. *Notes:* The practice of asana pulls our self (*this*: our personality) inward, then the writing of poetry draws our bigger Self (*that*: our divine core) outward. *Nadi* is a Sanskrit word meaning "sound stream." Sound streams through our physical bodies through *nadis* (subtle channels found in the astral body) and informs and connects us to the universe — to the cosmic world of which we are a part. The life force or *prana* moves through these subtle nadis. Our bodies are made of sound. We can even reconstruct our bodies, change the molecular condition of our physical forms, by means of sound — by the songs we sing, the words we speak and the thoughts we listen to. You cannot separate the sound of thoughts and words from physical material existence — it is what makes us physical. We are sound, always moving. Sarah Herrington wrote a book of poetry titled, *Always Moving*. I was sitting at my kitchen table one morning drinking tea and her book was on the table, and the title and beautiful black and white photo of the author inspired me to write this poem.

191. 2012 *Subject: Nature, Yoga*

Purr

When they purr
They are reciting mantra
I am sure
Happy or sad
Stressed or at rest
Keeping connected
To what is best

191. *Notes:* Many people say that cats purr when they are happy, that it is a sign that they are feeling good. But actually my observations (and the observations of others as well) suggest that this isn't always so. For example, cats kept isolated in cages in laboratories awaiting a surgical procedure purr, cats who are ill purr, cats who are experiencing pain purr, as well as cats who are contented sitting on a warm lap by a fire are also known to purr. My feeling is that purring for them may be like what chanting mantra might be for us — a way to remember God, a method of centering, a way to stay connected to the source. Perhaps the mother cat initiates them into their mantra? I say that

because, as has been observed, many kittens that are taken from their mother too soon after birth grow up to be cats that don't purr.

192. 2012 *Subject: Nature*

Bird Speak

I feed the birds
                each morning
When is morning?
                sometimes early
Sometimes late
                the birds wait
They look at me
                and I can see
They are patient and thankful and thoughtful
                this I know
What is their language?
                this I don't know
They know I don't
                possess the subtlety
Of comprehension
                to hear the tones they sing
And yet they don't
                judge me harshly
These dinosaurs with hollow bones
                who stand on twig legs
Tolerant and humble never flouting
                their powers of flight
It is auspicious to watch the birds
                they can teach us to see
What is good and what comes next

192. *Notes*: Dinosaurs have not totally vanished from planet Earth, they are still amongst us, but now appear in a more diminutive form, as birds.

The first thing I do when I get up in the morning when I am staying in my apartment on 7th street in New York City is to feed the birds. I make sure that I always have bird food in the apartment — sunflower seeds, millet, cracked corn, and thistle seed. It is quite an ordeal to open the window and take off the screen and put the birdseed out on the fire escape. I put the food in a large pan and also in a cage-like bird feeder. Then I have to deftly slide the screen back into its track and clap it shut. It is not like just simply opening the window and scattering some seeds on the ground. But it is worth it to be able to see the birds fly over to my window. Pigeons, mourning doves, sparrows, chickadees and also the colorful migrating birds that come when it is warm like the red cardinals and yellow finches. They are so talkative when they are eating and their eyes so penetrating when they look at me.

It must be very challenging to be a wild bird in a city like New York where most of the human beings either have a distaste for, or are totally unaware of the world of birds. It wasn't always so — in ancient Rome special people, endowed with the gift of divination could read the future by studying the ways of the birds. These people, who watched birds were revered as oracles. The word auspicious, which we use to denote something really good actually comes from a Latin word, which means bird watcher (avis=bird +specere=to see).

193. *2012 Subject: Nature*

A Fish Who Can Walk

I know a fish who can walk
Believe me yes
His name is Lawrence
I call him from the shore
Swimming to greet me
We take a walk
Me placing one foot
In front of the other
On the grassy ground

He swishes along
Keeping pace
Right there
Beside me in the water

193. *Notes*: There are two large ponds on the land where I live. Lawrence is a fish, known to most as a trout, who has lived in the "upper" pond for at least as long as we have lived in this forest. At first, I didn't notice him. But then when I started to take regular walks along the pond towards the forest where the Grandmother Oak tree lives, I noticed him. He was unmistakably the same fish. As soon as I come to the pond and call him, he swims over to me, then as I walk alongside the pond he swims beside me, keeping pace with me until the pond curves and we have to go our separate ways — me into the forest and he, I suppose, back to whatever he is involved with in the pond. When I first met him, I whimsically called him by the name Lawrence, after the actor Lawrence Fishburne who played Morpheus in the Matrix trilogy of films. Over the years he has responded to that name every time I call him to walk with me.

194. 2012 *Subject: Nature*

Ground of Being

Venture out on a clear morning
Dressed and hoping to be

Walking through a sparse forest
So sure of your identity

You can smell the rotting leaves
Insuring there'll be ground eternally

194. *Notes*: A walk through the forest, can put one back on track — reminding us that as long as there are trees, we will have some soil and that means a ground of being from which to grow.

Cruel Senseless Things

Who says trees can't walk
And birds can't talk
And fishes are cold blooded
Cruel senseless things

Who says rocks don't smell
And pigs can't tell
And fishes are cold blooded
Cruel senseless things

Who says rivers don't die
And flowers can't lie
And fishes are cold blooded
Cruel senseless things

Who says that only men are people
endowed with souls, minds and
feelings, who can think, speak,
reflect, remember and aspire
while all the rest
are dumb and stupid
put here to be acquired
as if we were separate
from the world
and that the world would be a
better place if only men
inhabited every space

They say fishes are cold blooded
Cruel senseless things
But what about a man
Who says such things?

195. *Notes:* It is no longer defensible to arbitrarily divide the world into categories based on a false hierarchy with humans at the top and all other lifeforms below. It is purely an exercise in egoism that has caused humans to see other species of beings as less, and to defend to the death these disturbing blind spots. The same ego-centeredness that makes it easy for a white man to relegate women or people of color to a lesser position also allows the prejudices that most humans hold against non-human animals, the forest, the fungi, and the Earth herself. In our world where self-esteem and power accumulation are based in how many lives you control, all humans are guilty of discrimination that erodes the spiritual essence of being and diminishes the life force in all of creation. Prejudice can be a strong disease that eats away from the inside out, like a virus that is able to disguise itself and appear as being the same as its host. The good news is that these prejudices are not hard-wired in us, they are learned and what is learned can be unlearned. It is possible that we can wake up from our ignorant delusion and see the world through enlightened eyes, and when we do, we will recognize that all of life is alive.

196. 2012 *Subject: Portrait*

Madame Lazonga

Birds, fish and other curving things swim close
Enraptured by your oceanic celestial body
You are a queen Ms. Bean
Porcelain skin red haired bewitching Vyvyn
With a sense of wonder and surety of beauty
Never a doubt never out of step
Hands steady as a surgeon
A heart as radiant and clear as a diamond
So self-assured from years of discipline
I remember the first moment I met you
There you were sitting at a sewing machine
Under a slanted roof
In a room smelling of roses and incense

Wearing a silky Japanese kimono
Tapestries covered the walls
Paisley scarves draped the lamps
When introduced
Your turquoise blue eyes lifted to catch my gaze
But your hands never left your stitching
A voice so musical and sweet
Each word chosen carefully
As if you were buying peaches in the market

196. *Notes:* This is a poem to my friend, the Seattle based, tattoo artist, Vyvyn Lazonga. I received an invitation to her surprise birthday party and was in awe of the photograph on the invite. I had not seen her in a few years and she looked absolutely incredible — no one would guess her age. Looking at that photo I was flooded with memories of the first time I met her, before she had any tattoos and her name was Beverly Bean. I was in high school, and she must have been in her twenties. A friend of mine was talking on and on about an incredible girl he had met and fell in love with. He wanted me to meet her, so he took me to her attic apartment at the top of a Victorian house on Capitol Hill. When we walked in, she was elegantly sitting at a sewing machine sewing. I was in awe of her: not just how she looked, which was beautiful, but by her aura and the atmosphere in her place, created no doubt by her intense ability to concentrate her mind on what she was doing. Many years later, after she became Madame Lazonga, famous tattoo artist, I shared a house with her, which also was her tattoo parlor. Often times I would have the privilege of watching her at work, creating tattoo art on human bodies. Nothing could distract her. She had the one-pointed focus of a yogi, the steady hands of a surgeon and the impassioned skill of an artist.

197. 2010 *Subject: Culture*

Bitumen

sticky viscous bitumen
glues the linen robes

wrapped around and around
a lifeless corpse disposed
for burial in the sands of eternity

sticky viscous bitumen
stains the linen robes
wrapped around and around
the mummies for sale
arriving by the boat full

sticky viscous bitumen
remains on the linen robes
even when the bandages
have been boiled for hours
into pulp to make rag paper

sticky viscous bitumen
colors the paper
the butcher wraps around meat
can't get that embalming fluid
out no matter how we entreat

sticky viscous bitumen
three cents a pound buys a dark dead
shriveled Egyptian
covered in stained linen with
resins and oils from toe to head

sticky viscous bitumen
preserved the body from decay
but not from being sold as fuel
many an engineer stoked the locomotive's
furnace with many an ancient Egyptian

we will never know who they were —

those through their burning
helped us reach our destination on time
name-less, dehydrated dead, shipped
by the ton-loads

from Cairo to New York
a queen, a cat or a basket maker
who's that?
all hardly recognizable covered with
sticky viscous bitumen

197. *Notes*: Bitumen (pronounced bi-two-men) is a naturally occurring black, oily, viscous resin also known as tar. Because it is a sealer and preserver it was valued by the ancient Egyptians in the wrapping used for their embalming procedures to mummify a corpse. After the body was wrapped in linen it was covered in bitumen before burial.

      I took a trip to Cairo in 2009 and visited the Cairo Museum, where I saw mummies close up and had the opportunity to study a bit about the ancient Egyptian culture. I was shocked to learn how Egyptian mummies were used during the American Civil War to make paper. During that time there was a shortage of paper in America due to the shortage of rags. Cloth rags, not just wood pulp, were an ingredient used in the making of paper. But during the Civil War, the cotton fields went untended, of course, so there was not much cotton available, resulting in a shortage of cloth and thus a shortage of paper. Isaac Stanwood, an enterprising paper manufacturer, had the idea of importing mummies from Egypt for their cloth wrappings. He was able to buy and ship them cheaply — three cents a pound — and he bought tons. He unwrapped the mummies and used their linen bandages to make paper. But because the bandages had been covered in bitumen they were a dark brown color that he wasn't able to bleach out, so the paper that Stanwood made was used mostly to wrap meat, and to this day dark brown paper is used as butcher paper. Once the linen was unwrapped Stanwood had no need of the mummies. He sold most of those mummies to the railroad companies which used them like firewood to fuel the trains, which was cheaper than using coal or wood at the time. There is a passage in the 1869 story by Mark Twain, *The Innocents Abroad*, where he references mummies being burned as firewood on a train. He describes seeing a railroad engineer feeding the furnace and trying to increase the train's speed who says, "Damn those plebeians, they don't burn worth a cent, pass me a King."

Green Snake

yellow table a
top a green snake silently
listens and awaits

198. *Notes*: I wanted to write a Haiku. I know that to make a haiku you need to have 17 syllables (known in Japanese as *morae*) in the form of 3 lines, which follow a 5-7-5 formula. I think I have that if you count the syllables in each line like this:

> yel(1) low(2) ta(3) ble(4) a(5)
> top(1) a (2) green(3) snake(4) si(5) lent(6) ly(7)
> lis(1) tens(2) and(3) a(4) waits(5)

In traditional Haiku, there also has to be a juxtaposing idea (in Japanese described as *kiru* or *kireji*, which means cutting) and a seasonal reference (*kigo*), and the images used should be every day, ordinary objects or occurrences found in this world. I have designated the words "a top" as the juxtaposing idea because the reader is not sure if the yellow table is atop of the snake or the snake is atop of the table — it could be either way. If the snake is atop the table he/she might be sunning their self, being a green snake, who would appear most likely in the summer (seasonal reference). Then again, the table may be atop the snake — the table may have fallen on or was purposely placed on the snake, killing it. So either way, whether the snake is alive and sunning herself or dead, they can be seen as silent and waiting.

Fox

Nina a Russian
baby fox on my doorstep
in a cardboard box

199. Notes: Another attempt at a 17-syllable haiku, in 3 lines following the 5-7-5 formula:

> ni(1) na(2) a(3) Rus(4) sian(5)
> ba(1) by(2) fox(3) on(4) my(5) door(6) step (7)
> in(1) a(2) card(3) board(4) box(5)

The sad story behind this poem comes from a National Public Radio show I heard about how a group of Russian scientists have been selectively breeding foxes to create a domesticated, human-friendly fox, whose personality resembles a loyal and affectionate lapdog. Apparently, they have succeeded, if one can use a term like "succeed" to describe such a cruel venture as the genetic manipulation of a fellow living being to make them easier to exploit. But with the demand for fur declining and a surplus of affectionate baby foxes, to maximize their capital investment, the scientists have partnered with entrepreneurial businesspeople to launch the next must-have fetish: pet foxes! Why give a second look to a cockapoo or yorkie when you can order your very own foxie and have her delivered, shipping included? The radio reporter traveled to Russia to visit one of these warehouses, which are pretty similar to puppy mills and factory farms, where all the animals are kept in cages. You can hear the poor foxes crying and whimpering in the background, while the reporter narrates. At one point in the story, the reporter remarks that she can't believe that the foxes are wagging their tails! Then she pokes her hands through a cage and laughs with surprise and delight, to have her hands licked enthusiastically by many cute little foxes dying for affection and human contact.

Why I Read Poetry

I read poems so that I can write poems
Opening my brain admitting the words of the poets inside of me
to mingle intimately with the mess of my mind and the
ache of my heart
gives me something to stand upon — a solid place to step off from
into possibility if I want to

Fleeing fragments unfinished sentences can speak
more truth than volumes
of clearly constructed essays or instruction manuals
I love the feeling of being washed over and through with poems
Unspeakable unspeakables teasing and tempting the unquenchable
yearning of my body, my soul my self

There is nothing more inspiring to a poet than to listen to poetry
Yes, other people's poems can push a poet deeper into the inarticulate
bogged down hard to get at places, allowing the poet to catch a glimpse
which they will naturally and unapologetically devour, digest,
and like a fungus will transform alchemically
into words that will mushroom as their own

I am in awe of poems, I am in awe of written words
conveying the mystery that can never be completely fathomed
the bottomless pit that is abstract and so empty
Poems are desperate and who can pass up desperation?
it is immensely attractive
and begs to be paid attention to

200. *Notes:* When I am looking for inspiration to encourage me to write a
poem. I often read poems written by other poets.

Maha Laxmi

I opened the heavy wooden door and there she was
dressed only in sparkles,
tiny dancing electric lights

And so it came to pass that we were walking
in golden circles with neat
invisible busy buzzing bugs

Through a grass floored cathedral
with diamond windows
where singing angels were
silenced by dropping tears

Last night the ducks returned to the pond
feathers fluttering green
tails a smiling twitching

In the morning a vanished wilderness
of bewitching where love had loved
on a nest of blue

I don't know much but I have decided that
she can melt the pain of others
and refresh a heart anew

201. *Notes:* I have a friend who is the embodiment of Laxmi — the Hindu goddess of beauty, grace and prosperity. My Laxmi is a real-life practical person who lives a committed life of activism. The more she gives the more beautiful and capable she becomes. She seems to derive her dazzling beauty and enchanting charms from the joy of making other people happy by helping them to fulfill their dreams. I wrote this poem after we had visited a mysterious crop circle that came to be known as the "Cathedral of Lamenting Angels" that had appeared near her home in England.

Written Words

In a dream you cannot read words
Written on a page in a book, unless you are a poet
Only when awake can most do such things
If you dare you will drink
Underneath the faucet
And so will come to think
These photos are not me or you they
Are only fleeting images of bodies caught
On the patient pages of samsara
These sounds and sights
Wait with words of forgiveness, written in
Their hearts, there are no mistakes
Asleep or awake, yes you can come too
You said you lived on seventh or eleventh street
Is it true
That you are so close and yet so far?
The father is remote
The brother like a bird flies and sings
Who am I but a spattering,
Small like thing?

202. *Notes:* Most people take a break while they sleep and don't dream of the three Rs (reading, writing and arithmetic). When we sleep, the language area of the brain is less active, making reading and writing very rare in dreams. Scientists who study dream consciousness say that most people can't read in their dreams, but research has revealed that poets are an exception to this rule. Poems don't have to make tight logical sense. Reading and other rational, cognitive skills are generally functions of the left hemisphere of the brain, while intuitive, artistic and creative skills are governed by the right. Some people, like poets share language processing ability across both hemispheres. "Seventh or eleventh" is a reference to the daytime waking state between 7 a.m. and 11 p.m.

Happiness

Emptiness is bent into infinity
Black hole absorption
No way out
The color of love is blue
Blue black music
Attracts you to you
You are me and I am you
Happiness is circular not relative
Up down over under sideways through
Anyone who thinks they are too small
To make a difference
Has never been bitten by a mosquito
You got rid of my girlfriend,
moved into my house and are driving my car
I should have a heart attack more often
I'll thank the monkey and ask the
Cat who came for Christmas if this is really
Going to be the golden apple
That shakes the peaches from the tree

"I've found something I really like to do,
I figure that puts me ahead of most folks.
Making others happy is what I've found
I really like to do," so you said.
The best way to uplift our own lives is to do
all we can to uplift the lives of others
How we treat others will determine
how others treat us
How others treat us will determine how we see ourselves
How we see ourselves will determine who we are
Happiness comes to those who bring happiness to others

It all sounds unsound and impossible because everyone knows
That you can't make another person happy
And why is that true?
Because happiness is inside of you — It is you
Yeah but that doesn't mean that it isn't
inside of me too
The fact is — not only is happiness inside of me too,
But so are you — inside me too.

203. *Notes:* Can we make someone happy? Can we share our own happiness? These are things we try to do, but in the process find out it is not possible. Each of us is happiness. When we try to bring "it" out in another it is brought out in us. Why is this so? Because "it" is not relative, it is who we are. When we are happy, we become like a black hole attracting all others and we begin to recognize the innate happiness in all. The gold the silver, the apple the peach, the blue, the black, we start with difference but search out unity; happiness is the essence of life.

204. 2012 *Subject: Mysticism*

The Balloons

The balloons, the balloons, the balloons, loons, loons
The balloons, the balloons, the balloons, loons, loons

Light, light, lighter
Nothing is lighter than air
Only helium does dare
The Self never will forsake
Still, floating does awake

A momentary hubble
Smiling safe inside the shuffle
Walk the miles in cold and snow

To the museum with laughter to know
Outside the reality without
Inside the reality no doubt

Still so close to what is alright
Took a while to get through the night
Now with day urging on
I awake but remain in my bed so warm
Like a cloud tossed about
Oft succumbing to countless routes

Slip away, come quietly
Allow me to roam in this reverie —
In this brief musing with eternity
The sheets so smooth and even on
'tis the ecstasy that hope brings with the dawn

The balloons, the balloons, the balloons, loons, loons
The balloons, the balloons, the balloons, loons, loons

204. *Notes:* Waking up in the morning is a time filled with potential — perhaps because that time has newly emerged from the peace of deep sleep. I never feel more comfortable in my skin than at this time. The reference to balloons in the poem primarily comes from one morning when I was recollecting about a time when David and I would walk from the Lower East Side of New York City to the Natural History Museum uptown to see all of the helium balloons being filled up the night before the annual Thanksgiving Day parade. The walk through the city took a long time and was cold, and sometimes the first snowfall would come. We would arrive to a small crowd of people just standing around while the balloons would be resuscitated from their folded-up sleep in a Macy's warehouse all year. It was a bit of an off-beat thing to do, I admit, and when asked by friends why we would do such a thing, I really had no good answer for them other than it was very uplifting to be in a crowd of people in a large city where the only motivation for being there was to watch balloons be blown up. In other words, there was no sports event happening, no celebrity appearance, no burning building or terrible accident, just a lot of

helium being pumped into these ridiculous balloons who would then come alive filled with the gas, floating above the crowd, much to the delight of onlookers, no doubt themselves inflated by the helium to some degree. To those of you who are fellow fans of the poetry of Edgar Allen Poe, I am sure you will hear a resonance to his bells, bells, bells, in my balloons, loons, loons. The word "hubble" in the third verse means, hubbub.

205. 2012 *Subject: Mysticism, Time*

What Remains

What is given
Falls away
Eventually
It is inevitable
For things to go
We all know
This
What remains
Is that which
Is
And cannot be taken
Or given away

205. *Notes:* All things are temporary and pass away eventually. Anything that can be given or taken is impermanent. What remains is never a tangible thing that can be given or taken away.

206. 2012 *Subject: Perception, Yoga*

When the End of the World Comes

When the end of the world comes
As we have come to know it

And time can be no longer
We will have to move into space
There was always more to this
Then what could be contained
In 3 dimensions
There is an Earth above the Earth
A soul place, a musical mathematical space
extra-terrestrials live there — in Fairyland
extra hyper just out of sight and reach
can't be held with hands, claws nor teeth
E.T.s after all,
are what we used to call, fairies
If our planet is destroyed
It is true that we will not
Be able to live as we do — now
The world will end as we have come to know it
No substance to stand on,
no temporary matter to speak of or care for

Why not nurture the immortal soul
The blueprint for joy?
Let us start now and create
A spaceship, musical and fine —
able to navigate
through the matter-less reality
of transcendent time
Yoga practice was never designed
solely for a fragile body and mind
Yoga practice strengthens one's astral vehicle — the spacecraft

So when the blood stops and the
skin and bones dissolve
you will have no legs to stand on
But you won't fall
you will live on, as spirit

as the thoughts, words and songs
that move within and without you
So what are you thinking these days?
What are you singing, what do you say?

206. *Notes:* The poem touches on many subjects: crop circles, the end of the world prophesies, fairies, E.T.s, spaceships, astral bodies and yoga sadhana. E.T.s might actually be the same beings that we used to call fairies. The descriptions of both are certainly similar — ethereal creatures with pointed chins, large slanted eyes and elongated limbs. There are many old stories about human beings falling in love or being abducted by fairies or accidentally stumbling into the fairy realm beyond this mortal one.

    The night before I wrote this poem, I watched a documentary film about two crop circles that had appeared in southern England. These crop circles depicted our galaxy. The first one showed the sun surrounded by all of the planets, as we know them, in orbit. The second showed the same except that planet Earth was missing. The narrator explained it as a prophecy foretelling of the disappearance of planet Earth. There were many speculations about what may happen on December 21st, 2012. Some said it would be the end of the world — that Earth would be destroyed, either by a meteorite or perhaps by our own human weapons of mass destruction. Some said that it would be the end of the world *as we know it,* implying that there will be a massive shift in consciousness, and we will evolve beyond the narrow limits of our ego-driven perception and become kinder more compassionate beings able to cooperate with nature so as to mutually enhance rather than compete. None of these predictions have come to pass, yet.

    In the 2008 remake of the film, *The Day the Earth Stood Still,* Klaatu, the alien visitor to Earth, played by the actor Keanu Reeves, is asked by a scientist, "Are you a friend?," and he replies, "I am a friend to the Earth," implying that he and the others he represents may not be a friend to human beings who themselves don't seem to be too friendly to the planet Earth. I see a connection implied here between fairies and E.T.s. Fairies are friends to the Earth, they nurture, defend and support nature, assisting plants, trees other forms of life. Maybe visitors from outer space, like Klaatu in the film, want to help the Earth survive the environmental destruction orchestrated by humans, even if it may mean taking the animals to another world for a while, or into another dimension, or perhaps giving them new bodies. There is a scene in that film where a spacecraft lands in the woods, many animals become aware of its presence, fearlessly move toward it and enter into this ark. I saw this scene as a possible metaphor for what may be happening on our planet to billions of animals and plant life forms. We human beings are destroying them — their physical bodies that is. But we are not destroying their subtle astral bodies, which contain their immortal souls. The spaceship could symbolize a force from another world or dimension that is rescuing the souls of these animals and providing a new place for them to manifest.

The mass animal extinction that is occurring now is not an extinction of the souls of these beings but a destruction of their physical, earthly forms. Perhaps all of life as we know it on planet Earth will disappear, meaning the physical forms. Physical bodies are temporary vehicles and die in time. But the soul that animates each physical body is eternal and continues its journey in whatever subtle form it is able to manifest.

It seemed obvious by the year 2012 that we human beings have not been able to live on planet Earth without destroying the environment and many other bodies in the process. But nonetheless, where we are going next depends on how we treat others now. Physical bodies might be temporary and souls eternal, but that doesn't mean that we should callously destroy the bodies of others. Cruelty pollutes our souls and disconnects us from remembering who we are as part of the greater body of the planet.

If the planet were to disappear, our souls would not, so it is important to become involved in activities that increase the health of the soul; activities that allow us to experience our connection to the whole. Most of us don't even know how to make contact with our souls. We live on the surface of imprints from the internet, television, newspapers, magazines and other media, never delving deeper to experience who we might be beyond the sights and sounds of our culture. Music, mathematics and Sanskrit might be subjects to try to embrace and master at this time, because they provide a bridge to the world of spirit. Performing acts of kindness towards others is also powerful because it can nurture the subtle astral body within, neutralize emotional toxins such as anger and heal internal corruption. The yogic sadhanas are other means to strengthen the astral body.

The practices of yamas, niyamas, pranayama, prayers, mantras, chanting, meditation and even asana practice is not limited to the enhancement of the physical body (the *annamayakosha*). It is actually the subtle body that receives the greatest benefit from these practices, that peel away layers of ignorance, enabling a person to come into closer contact with the soul. At the time of death of the physical body, the yogi, who had prepared by strengthening the subtle astral body, would have a means to continue their existence in other dimensions with a purified subtle vehicle — a light body able to travel the cosmos. This is why, perhaps, the yogic scriptures say that it is through regular and consistent practice that the self is purified and the soul is able to shine through the denser forms of matter that cover it.

Why Not Sing?

Apocalypse let it come
Standing in the yard
Winds ripping off my clothes
Forget about rebuilding the house
Picking up the pieces
Let's let it all go
Crawling stumbling and falling
Let's say we have had enough
Put down the phone
Stop trying to find what you
Think is lost
You know
We have always been here
How about if we started to live now
How do we spend the precious
Remaining moments of our day
What to do what to say?
While we are trying to decide
Why not sing —
Hare Krishna Hare Krishna
Krishna Krishna Hare Hare
Hare Rama Hare Rama
Rama Rama Hare Hare
Each utterance a victory
For the Self
Finding refuge in the sound
Through letting go the
World comes 'round

207. *Notes:* The last line is a reference to a George Harrison song, "The Day the World Gets 'Round." *Apocalypse* is a Greek word meaning "to uncover, to

reveal," and so perhaps it could in some context mean "to stand naked." Krishna stole the gopis' clothes so that they were forced to stand naked before Him. When He did this, the story goes, they were bathing — that's a good sign. We could look at this to mean that they, like us, were already engaged in ways to purify themselves. To the Krishna bhakta, the gopis are already enlightened beings, not needing any purification whatsoever; anything that happens to them is all part of the *lila*: the play of God. For us unenlightened beings, we can use this story as a way to reflect upon ourselves. In that case we could say that God knew they needed some really deep cleaning so he took away their clothes, the habitual coverings they had been using to distinguish themselves from each other. Like the Old Testament Adam and Eve, they had become ashamed and clothed their nakedness. Krishna's message is one of exaltation. He invites the soul to step out of cultural conditioning, to let it go, as he beckons, "Come to me as you are, let me hear your natural voice — sing. Through singing you will build a new body, an eternal body of light, made of celestial vibration, a musical body, beautifully proportioned according to the mathematics of sacred geometry. You will not need to wear clothes; you will not need to cover over your soul. You will lose the need to distance yourself from me. You will wear the clothes of song."

208. 2012 *Subject: Portrait*

Liz

So beautiful you are
today I saw you golden
with yellow roses on your breast
they say you are jaundiced
due to a failure of your liver
but we see you with a golden
complexion like Radha —
illuminated from the giver
within — a soul aligned with the brightness
of a thousand suns radiant one

You are not so far away
you shine upon us like a star
with dancing eyes
streaming full pouring forth serenity and wit
no doubt 'tis by means of eternity you are lit
So beautiful you are
gracefully willing and able to die
to this world without a regretful sigh
to let go and let God move you
to walk laughing into the mystery
of the night journey
You have no reason to fear,
for you do not go forth stumbling in the dark
your joy and sense of adventure
for sure guides your way
Fortune smiles on the brave they say
As you go you leave us forever touched
overwhelmed by your wisdom and goodness —
oh my goodness
So beautiful you are

208. *Notes:* David and I went to the hospital to see our friend and devoted student, Liz Roberts as she lay dying. We had brought her yellow roses not knowing beforehand that her liver had failed her, leaving her skin yellow. When I saw her, I thought of Radha, Krishna's beloved consort who was said to have a golden complexion. Radha was luminous, the reason being that she was reflecting her beloved Krishna — she was lit up by the brilliance of love. Liz had been diagnosed with cancer a year before and now she was nearing the end of her journey. What we encountered when we saw her was a soul so fearlessly beautiful and bright that goodness and grace radiated from every pore and tissue of her physical body as she was rapidly etherealizing. Her body was golden, heart and mind serene and her speech still clear, clever and quite witty. When we told her she looked beautiful, she looked at us with a sparkle in her eyes and said, "That seems to be the general consensus." She seemed so ready willing and able to go — to let go and let God move her to the next chapter of her journey. What a joy and honor to be in the presence of

such an accomplished yogini. All in the room by her bedside were overwhelmed by her laughter, goodness and wisdom. We chanted the mantra *Shri Krishna Sharanam Mama* together round after round, in celebration of her most beautiful soul, so completely emerged in love — in God's love more brilliant than a million suns.

209. 2013 *Subject: Portrait*

Shyam

Hearing the flute they flew
what else could they do
but drop their cumbersome aspirations,
commitments, dramas
and all the stuff
they thought they had to do?

Floating warm in a watery pool
soft caresses like little fish biting
lotuses
opening into perfume
eyes closed vision igniting
no reason to go or do anything else

Radharani's side-long glances break his heart
how can that be how can we
take refuge swinging
in the name
over and over again

Holding up a mountain
still always time to eat
corn on the cob, dhokla, quinoa

smoothies sweet
the path of grace bowing at your feet

Peddling through the country on a bike
discussing conflicts and romantic trysts
in a boat while the sun sets down
chanting the name
walking barefoot the parikrama 'round

Reckless in a green jaguar
heart stopper shopping in the price-chopper
dhoti in a whirl all minds melting
talking about aunt Shirl

Napping with his arm held high
precious one resting on a thigh
to embrace his revealed heart I sigh
Then I dreamt of sounds and songs and
all that I thought went wrong

Every moment your invitation sent
every moment
my ignorance went out to infect my worldview anew
how could I have known it was always
you, you, you?

Surrender to your name
I have known you forever
Through all ripples, all the change
taking shelter in the forest, in the river,
the pond the lake — as all take your shape

But what of me waiting with the crying peacocks
in a Belvan tree by the river's sandy edge

like the golden dog frantic because she
could not swim across to be with you
on the other side

My dark one I have put love
off for too long and now I am
alone without your song
of sweetness
without your lips your arms and all
of your adorable contradictions

I can't get across can't get through
what to do
but yearn and yearn
and yearn
for you...

209. Notes: My beloved friend Shyamdas was killed in a motorcycle accident in Goa, India in January of 2013. Krishna no doubt, pulled him out of this world and into His eternal lila. On hearing of the disappearance of his physical form my mind with all of its petty aspirations was shattered and my heart, left exposed, pulsated with a one-pointed focus bent on yearning and certain of nothing. Shyam is a name for God appearing as the Dark Lord — Krishna whose complexion is dark blue/black. Shyamdas was a devotee of this Hari. He awakened in me devotion to Hari. To see, to hear, to be with Shyamdas was to be reminded of God. I would often say to him, "You remind me of God." He would always respond, "Don't say that. Oh Padma, I am a das, I strive only to become a better das, a servant of other bhaktas — I am actually your servant — your das." And so it was, but it took me a long time to even begin to comprehend his guru wisdom and the power of his embrace. Even so, in his presence all of our talk, all of our interactions all of our experiences became elevated and I was able to remember God. To be reminded, to remember, these are potent words, they convey a profound occurrence. To remember that you in truth are a part of God. To be re-minded of God is to allow your mind and heart to remember. This remembrance contains only thoughts of the most exalted nature. Shyamdas is my beloved heart Guru. Shyamdas introduced me to the Pushti Marg teachings of Shri Vallabhacharya. He taught me the refuge mantra, "Shri Krishna Sharanam Mama" and how to cultivate bhava, the divine mood of loving devotion to God. After Shyamdas's passing and perhaps because of it, I was compelled not to lose any more time in unrelated worldly pursuits and to devote whole heartedly, in the time I had remaining, to commit to the most important pursuit in life — the realization of God. Shyamdas opened the door for me to a magical realm and bid me to cross over, he would say, "What to do? Look at the gopis of Vrindavan, who dropped everything when they heard His flute, why not drop your dharmas, dramas, karmas and try coming over here for a while?" It took me some time to embrace his message and to step through, but now I live in the forest and worship Shri Krishna, daily perform His seva and take refuge in His name. I see the form of Shyamdas, Shyam's servant and friend, my ears hear his words, my whole being continues to yearn toward its highest potential — to be with the dark Lord. I was and am still blessed by my association with Shyamdas, a powerful guru — a saint incognito. This poem has many references to times we spent together. It is a loving tribute to him.

210. 2013 *Subject: Portrait*

Shyamdas Remembered

A conundrum of contradictions
Like Puck, Pan, Peter Pan, Govinda and Gopal
Mischief in mind love in heart
Wings on his heels a modern-day mercury
Here today and gone tomorrow — but always
Showing up again and again on your doorstep,
in a waiting car outside or in your dreams at night.
Trying to get through the ringing telephone
Jai Shri Krishna are you at home?
Who could keep up with this mercurial whiz?
Certainly not me
Like most of us we were only able to
Imbibe him in small doses

But oh how potent those doses were,
they could set you reeling in a daze

A shape shifter from the outside for those
Who judge books by their covers he may have appeared crazy,
unsophisticated and unkempt,
Loveable yes — but not someone you'd bring home to mama —
Or give a prime spot as the headliner act...
And yet he was more accomplished in all the arts of heaven and earth
then anyone around—he was truly a holy being-complete and
profound

An unquenchable thirst for adventure and fun
He hardly slept — preferred a short nap
A brilliant cook — could whip up a meal in a snap
Always the first to credit others and bestow praise
By disappointments and insults he was hardly fazed

His body a disguise — chubby and undone
But his hands gave way to the truth of his soul
When you looked at his palms
You'd see the lines of heart and head
Wedded together in a single thread
Who do you know with hands like that?
One in a billion and eight I'm sure is a fact

Born in February on the eleventh day — a magical number
for karmic resolving
His vast knowledge like water falling
His talk sometimes stuttered
His mercury mind so lucid his tongue had trouble keeping up

There have been five great Vedantic acharyas
Since the 8th century

All of them having been translated
into languages for us
But the final teachings of Vallabha's pushti marg
the path of grace has been drunk and digested
by one clad in a flowered bundhi

This brave man has shared with ease and delight
the *Nine Jewels of Wisdom, 252, Subodhini* and more...
so masterly and free
We hardly noticed as his bhav enraptured us
The blur of our senses the rush the must the ras...
This happened so fast this phenomenon known as Shyamdas

A mutual friend when hearing the news said,
"This doesn't make sense that he would die in a motorcycle crash —
sounds so mundane.
I would have expected a more dignified exit,
like while singing kirtan or in the midst of seva
or buried under mounds of translations."

But Hari never makes a mistake
He left us so perfectly moving so fast
with a beautiful gopi
around his round waist
chanting the name savoring the taste
Heading full on into that he flew

But what of us?
What to do? What to do? What to do?

We must continue to yearn and yearn
For what he knew what he was pointing too
Our days might be numbered but we have been blessed

By one who lived reminding us
by his living adorable example
to go for truth consciousness and mostly bliss
Radhe Radhe

210. *Notes:* A poem written to be read at a public memorial to Shyamdas held
at the Omega Institute, NY Sept 2013.

211. 2014 *Subject: Culture, Yoga*

Naked Tyagi

Take off the clothes
Sky clad disrobe
Nothing but skin
Gone the
Feathers, fur, hair and fin

Are you naked then?
In your birthday suit
Have you been
revealed
Are you stripped and nude?

Really now, so shy
ashamed shaking in
Your modesty
Look you still have five bodies
covering your soul

The washing will take more
then this

It will take nothing less, I mean
Then a samsaric apocalypse
For you to come clean

One who has let go of everything
and more
gives it to one's eternal heart's desire
That one only is free,
a naked Tyagi

211. *Notes:* *Tyagah* is a Sanskrit word, which means to abandon. It is used to express yogic renunciation. When one has let go of all attachments and lives without expectations, exposed, surrendered to God they are referred to as a *tyagi* (tee-a-ghee). I have often contemplated our cultural obsession with clothes and our uncomfortableness with nakedness. We even have laws against it. A person who does not cover themselves out of modesty and social etiquette can be put in jail. For us nakedness is all bound up in sexuality, and sexuality, as we know is a valuable commodity that is highly regulated. In the yogic tradition renouncing clothes and all possessions is seen as a step toward freedom from vanity and self-obsession. A yogi wishes to approach God devoid of artifice. They don't want to allow any self-identifying covering to stand between them and God. The word apocalypse comes from a Greek root meaning to uncover, to reveal and so I use it here in that sense. To stand naked implies revealing an inner essence devoid of artifice and hankering after temporary material satisfaction.

    Samsara is a Sanskrit word that literally translates to mean same agitation (sam=same + sara=to agitate or wash). It is used to describe life. The soul is reborn lifetime after lifetime in the samsaric world making the same mistakes over and over again eventually becoming enlightened or purified of false identification or ignorance, which is basically the same thing. In the yogic tradition the only "dirt" is ignorance and the only ignorance is falsely thinking that you are your body and mind. Life (samsaric existence) can be thought of like a washing machine that gets the laundry clean by means of agitation, so one can become clean, naked and free of all delusion.

Eat Crow

When I had nothing
  I was kind to you

You took the kindness
  as if it was my privilege
  to be so

When others began
  to overwhelm me with their gifts of gratitude
  it threw you into a jealous rage

Tossed about
  in a sea of mean

Your long arms with blade like fingers
  thrashing about
  wounding anyone and everyone

Even innocent flowers and flying insects
  were not spared by your wrath

As you cut off curious heads
  and ripped through hopeful wings

I heard from someone
  once a mutual friend
  that you are sick now

And I wonder
  if anyone will visit you
  and held up as an insult, as not enough

Of course I suppose
        I will come to see you as I ought
        but don't expect flowers to be brought

As you know all their heads are lying
        lifeless on the floor

Maybe I will decide not to come
        hospitals are smelly places after all

Perhaps with some solitude the well
        will begin to spring and bubble up
        through your spidery body, crow

212. *Notes:* Bitterness is a vile disease. Sometimes when people are infected with it, it is best to keep your distance so as not to provoke them, but still hold them lovingly in your heart and mind and continue to send prayers and blessings mentally.

213. *2014 Subject: Portrait, Time*

The Time Returns

Columbina Columbina
Magdalina my little dove
thus spoke, Lorenzo the magnificent
her one true love

Simonetta Simonetta
Magdalina my dying bird
laments Sandro the Botticelli
without so much as a word

My arms wrap around you for a moment
just a moment
His brush strokes her as a feather
ever wanting always yearning
for the time to be returning

Even when he painted twin winds
who blew so gently nothing could,
inspire or protect her freckled body
as fate is so unrelenting

They saw her soul flutter
as it lingered for a moment
just a moment
Then with a sigh flew as an apricot
inflamed
to where but heaven knows

Those who have eyes to see
and ears to hear
draw near draw near
just a moment
and let me whisper in your ear
the names of the one
whose time will be returning

Hope makes the body bold and
time the heart to sing
let many seasons come and go
in the remembrance
of Spring

It is said that truth is beauty and
beauty is truth
but what of
purity, pleasure and bliss
surely something must come of this.

213. *Notes:* Have you ever studied a figurative painting and wondered who the models were and what kind of life they lived and what was their relationship to the painter? The painting, *Primavera* by the great Renaissance painter, Alessandro Botticelli, and the women who might have provided his inspiration, inspired this poem. This is an allegorical painting, which has caused many to speculate it's meaning, I am certainly not the first nor am I an art historian (or *her*storian). But due to my Catholic background, I have been interested in the teachings of Jesus and have done my best to research anything I could find that might give me clues about the actual man, his life, family and friends. This research has led me to investigate Mary Magdalene and the mysteries and theories that surround her. One such theory put forth by Kathleen McGowan in her book, *The Poet Prince*, involves the Medici family and how they might have been members of a secret society, which recognized Mary Magdalene as the wife of Jesus and a teacher in her own right. Certainly holding a belief that Jesus and Mary were married and had children challenges the power of the Catholic Church and its emphasis on celibacy. To honor the Earth as a goddess is considered heresy to the Church that holds a negative view of nature, as well as being speciesist and misogynistic. But many believe that in the art that was commissioned by the Medici family there are nuanced teachings, which support a positive view of Mother Nature as well as Mary Magadalene. Lorenzo de' Medici, called by the people of Florence, Lorenzo the Magnificent was the friend as well as the benefactor of Botticelli and he commissioned the *Primavera* painting.

In my poem I reference John Keats's line, "Truth is Beauty and Beauty is Truth" and investigate how this could be so by playing with the idea of beauty being not just a fleeting physical attribute that fades with time but as eternal truth, which returns over and over again. Spring is evidence of this — with spring we have the manifestation of beauty as truth — the expression of undying love and of time ever renewing. Interestingly, this concept is expressed in the yogic teachings found in the *Bhagavad Gita* as well as the *Yoga Sutra*, which cite Om as the name of God and call it the *pranava*, meaning that which forever renews itself. The poem focuses on four characters: Lorenzo de' Medici, Sandro Botticelli, Lucrezia Donati and Simonetta Vespucci. Lucrezia and Simonetta who both appear in the painting were models in many of Botticelli's paintings that were commissioned by Lorenzo de' Medici. All knew each other and may have shared and explored heretical ideas regarding the relationship between Jesus and Mary Magdalene. Lucrezia Donati depicted as Venus, the Goddess of beauty and love, is the central figure of the *Primavera* painting. She appears pregnant and draped with a red shawl, which for adherents to the heretical teachings of the Magdalene and Jesus followers can be interpreted to mean that she is the wife of Jesus. Lucrezia was affectionately called Columbina, which means little dove, by the poet prince, Lorenzo de' Medici who dedicated many of his poems to her and was most likely her lover, and she, his muse. The dove is the holy spirit in the Catholic trinity. But dove is also a code word for Mary Magdalena. Some consider the holy spirit of the trinity to be a female force, a goddess, akin to *shakti*, the Sanskrit word that denotes the animator of life, the one who brings forth life, as Spring certainly does. *Primavera* means Spring and the poem refers to Spring as the eternal time returning. Some art historians say that *Le Temps Revient* (The Time Returns) was actually the original title of the painting, *Primavera*.

The other woman referred to in the poem is Simonetta Vespucci who is depicted in the painting as Flora the incarnate goddess of Spring — Her flower filled body being breathed into existence by the twin winds. She also appears as one of the three graces. At the time she was considered the most beautiful woman in the world, at least in the world of Florence. She is described as having apricot colored hair, and translucent skin showered with delicate star-like freckles. It was rumored that the painter was in love with her as were most of the citizens of Florence. She died at twenty-two, probably of tuberculosis and Botticelli requested that when he died, he was to be buried at her feet, which did happen. Whether or not he was in love with her or with the ideal of her, as Beauty and Truth — that which is eternal and ever returning and renewing itself is certainly up for speculation. I'd like to give additional credit for the lines "draw near draw near and let me whisper in your ear" — which are paraphrased from "Draw Near", a hauntingly beautiful song by Deva Premal and Miten, based on a Rumi poem.

214. *2015 Subject: Perception*

How to succeed in Flying

Flying
For this you need
A launching device

Bicycling
Works with circles
Hardly a matter of mirrors

Magic
Is often quite practical
In its formulas

Results
Usually appear
When you least expect them

Surprise
Always being
The essential ingredient to success

Airborne
Is a swirly matter
Without a doubt

Pedaling
Is after all
Drawing circles round about.

214. *Notes:* I am an avid bicycle enthusiast. I've been riding a bike since I was 6 years old. I ride whenever I can — usually that means just about every day, at least when I am home in Woodstock, NY. I have a regular route. It takes about an hour to complete. Lots of ideas, song lyrics and poems come to me while I am riding; riding also provides me with a space for contemplation and time to organize my thoughts, and so I prefer to ride alone. The experience is much more than physical exercise — it is mystical for me — it is an immersion into the experience of time moving through space. I love riding a bicycle so much that when I moved from Seattle to New York City in 1983, becoming a bike messenger was on the top of my list of priorities. In fact I did realize my dream and did work as a New York City bike messenger, but only for a few months before I had to resign due to sexual harassment issues. At the time I

was one of only two women bike messengers working in New York City — it was pretty tough. I have always loved the freedom experienced on a bike. It is the closest thing to flying that I know. This poem expresses how riding a bike can be a launching device for flying; how the circular motion of the wheels and pedals as well as the gears and sprockets can provide a take-off for effortless motion through time and space. No physical condition can limit a committed cyclist, in fact the day I wrote this poem I was on my bike, it was January, there was snow and ice on the roads it was 18 degrees and I felt limitless.

215. 2015 *Subject: Perception, Time, Yoga*

Relentless Water

They spout they spout
Let me in let me out

Like a cat meowing at the door
water's pleas cannot be ignored

Everyone knows we are all the same
all slaves to the relentless rain

I'm fixing a hole where the rain gets in
and stops my mind from wandering

Where it will go — water
H2O can always achieve the seemingly
impossible feat of taking a fragmented
unruly consciousness and pulling it into
exact single pointed-ness

Dharana is insistent concentration
like a leaky roof or a full bladder
nagging and tugging replacing

whatever was so engrossing
with the current necessity

Demanding to be either plugged up
or allowed to run free — like
the sealed tap of a fire hydrant
wrenched opened on a summer day

Controlling the mind is a matter of
water regulation
Noah could have told you that

Your thirst for water or your need to pee
gives you a glimpse of the ever illusive
keys to eternity.

Where water runs like oil not rain
smooth and even in a roundabout way
again and again

It grabs your attention pulls you out of
the deepest sleep or the most
enthralling pursuit

Fishes aren't the only ones swimming in the sea
we all live in water bags with leaky holes
fluidly — our creativity floats upon the skill required
to regulate the flow of H_2O

Parched, dehydrated or spilling, overflowing
either one will succeed in capturing a wandering
mind and bring it back in time

215. *Notes*: I woke up one morning from a deep sleep because I had to pee. I got
out of bed and obediently went to the toilet. Coming back to bed, I reflected

upon the power of water — how it can compel one to leave the sanctity of sleep to relieve oneself of a full bladder. As I lay on my pillow I reflected also upon thirst. Thirst and the urge to pee are two of the most powerful motivators and they both involve water. When you are really thirsty or when you have to pee — nothing else is more important to you — your mind is brought from a fragmented state to a focused one. Most of us never question the powerful control that water holds over us. Like much of the natural world, we don't really notice its significance, as Jimi Hendrix pointed out, "Blue are the life giving waters taken for granted," (lyrics from Axis Bold As Love). As I was writing this poem the lyrics, "I'm fixing a hole where the rain comes in and stops my mind from wandering" (from Sgt. Pepper's Lonely Hearts Club Band), appeared to me as the song refers to the power of water and its affect upon consciousness, so I lifted the words onto my page.

Dharana, the sixth limb of Patanjali's yoga system, means concentration. Concentration is a prerequisite to meditation. Dharana is often described as pouring water while dhyana (meditation) is described as pouring oil. In order to be able to bring your mind to one-pointed meditative focus you have to first concentrate it and not allow it to wander. This poem acknowledges the relentlessness of water, H2O, the blend of two parts hydrogen and one-part oxygen, the most prevalent chemical substance in our world — and its affect upon us.

216. 2015 Subject: Perception, Yoga

Your Guru

Your guru is your most
precious resource
Do not squander their gifts
harnessing them to your plough or cart

Demanding that they plant your
fields, prepare your dinner
and sweep your floors
A lifetime is so short

and besides
you are smarter than you think
Come now
we don't have all day
so use your teacher well,
hey

216. *Notes:* Many of us, don't understand how to utilize the gifts of a teacher. We don't know how the relationship works. Instead, in our clumsiness, we reduce the teacher to just a person in our lives who we expect will do things for us. But the things we ask them to do are way below their skill set — mostly mundane stuff. Non-the less, they usually comply and patiently do as they are told for the enlightened teacher knows that it is the student who makes the teacher wise and it is the wise student who knows how to use the teacher to become wise rather than otherwise.

217. *2015 Subject: Perception*

Polka Dots

What does the universe look like?
It looks like lots of bright spots in a black sky
So if 'as above so below' is true
Then polka dots are how I must look to you

217. *Notes:* We are all looking to make sense of ourselves, life, the world, the universe, God...so we try our best to understand it all by first reflecting on what it might look like. Does how someone or something look, determine who or what they are? Physicists are trying to formulate a theory of everything and look into the sky to see what the universe looks like. Cosmologists, who are experts on universal things, tell us it looks like a bunch of bright spots on a black background — at least that is what the Milky Way Galaxy looks like and it is also what Andromeda, which is our next closest neighbor galaxy looks like too. When we bring our view more down to earth, we see that images are formed by tiny dots called pixelations — tiny bits of information — the

impressionist painters were on to this. Patanjali speaks about dots too, he calls them *kshana(s)* — dimension-less points that together make up the reality of time. Stars do appear to be poking through a black sky. Polka dots is a popular print found in fabrics that are made into clothing worn by people like Bob Dylan as well as flamenco dancers, but usually shows up on children's clothing and toys — indicating something playful. My grasp of mathematics is not well developed but non-the less I enjoy adding things up. This poem is a way to contemplate that there may be something to this polka dot way of perception.

218, 2015 *Subject: Yoga*

I AM

Who is this I am?
Is there such a one?
That one who is the in-between
That which is the connection
That who's very being
is the unification of all things
as well as the things themselves
nothing, no-thing is outside of that one
Say it if you dare:
I am the light
I am the darkness
and all the in-between
I am the crucifixion as well as the resurrection
In the sea of possibility
I am the death and the rising phoenix
I am the ashes as well
as the to and the from
in the from — ashes to ashes
in the to — to the well
I am the ascension

above all and yet
flying into the fall
where electrons explode
I am love itself
boundless and limitless joy
oh Boy! O Lord,
I am not worthy that you should come
into my heart,
speak but the word and my soul
shall be healed — my heart's desire revealed
Make me your instrument
There is nothing else worth doing for
ever and ever
Onward
stretching time then back again to the
beginning
a-gain imploding into itself
Supposing such ecstasy and repose
Who is this, that
will go on and say the words
You are mine and
I Am yours?

218. *Notes:* The beloved bhakta, Shyamdas said, "Your true wealth is the awareness of who you really are." The two mantras that are held in the highest regard in Vallabhacharya's path of grace (the Pushti Marg) are: the 8-syllable: "Shri Krishna sharanam mama" (Krishna you are mine) and the 5-syllable: "Krishna I am Yours". The first mantra purifies the heart of all selfish desires; the second intensifies devotion. To the bhakta the ultimate identity of the enigmatic "I Am" is only found in loving devotional surrender to Krishna. The bhakta has no use for the *mahavakyas,* the "great sayings" of the Upanishads that convey cognitive realizations of I am as 'I am That', Tat Twam Asi or 'I am Brahman'; the devotee of the Lord wants only to know that they belong to God, not that they are God.

Take me I am Yours

Krishna these toes, feet and legs are yours
Krishna this back is yours
Krishna this front is yours
Krishna these fingers, hands and arms are yours
Krishna this throat is yours
Krishna this face is yours
Krishna my breath, blood and bones are yours
Krishna my body is yours
Krishna my mind is yours
Krishna my heart and soul are yours
Take me I am yours

219. *Notes:* When I lie down to practice *shavasana* these are the words that I say silently. The asana practice of shavasana is a practice that prepares a person for death. *Shava* means corpse and *asana* means relationship or connection to. I have found that the practice of relating to my body as belonging to God and not to me is a good practice, as it helps to develop the awareness of the body as a temporary vehicle. In the *Bhagavad Gita*, Krishna promises His devotees that at the time of death, if they remember Him they will go to Him and not be reborn back into the material *samsaric* world.

220. 2015 *Subject: Yoga*

How to Know God

Remember God
Be kind to others
This is all I know
It's a starting place
At least

220. *Notes:* I am certainly not the first to ask big questions. You know them: Who am I? Why am I here? Why are we here? Is there a God? What does he or she or it look like? What is all of this? Does life have a purpose? How did the universe begin? What is the origin of the universe? What makes form, form? Why is it so diverse? Did time have a beginning? Will it have an end? Is happiness possible? What happens after death? Do we have souls? Do animals have souls? This poem expresses my formula for arriving at the answers to the Big questions. The formula is articulated in the first two lines, the rest of the poem is an apology, although I intended those last lines to imply that I'm working on it and can't tell you anything more at the moment.

To remember God is to know God. To remember is to reconnect. You cannot remember or reconnect to something unless you are already a part of it. You can't ask a question unless you already know the answer. The biggest obstacle to this remembrance comes in the form of our relationships with others. Unresolved issues with others can inhibit the remembrance of God. What does the practice of remembering God look like? It can look like lots of things and it is usually quite subjective — each person has their own way. Chanting God's name, thinking of God, offering everything to God. Discussing God with others, cultivating the mood of God, listening to God and hearing God. The other dictate: be kind to others — takes care of what to do with all the others we encounter in the world. Through kindness we create a conducive situation for remembering God. One cannot be kind to others in a state of forgetfulness of God. God is Love — the unifying principle.

221. *2016 Subject: Life*

Do Not Cry

And he said, if you truly love me
Then please do not cry
Your tears are felt like heavy
Boulders shattering my heart
They come crashing through my brain

And he said, if you truly love me
Then please do not cry

Shower me with offerings of gladness
Sadness only hurts and burns my heart

Happiness is a blue bird
A soul that needs to fly
Crying is like rain
Birds can't fly in a sky of rain.

221. Notes: It is customary to cry when someone we care for dies. Crying at the time of someone's death is normal. To cry when we have lost someone dear is normal. We are encouraged by therapists to allow a time for grieving. But on deeper reflection, we might see that mostly our tears are not about the one dying, they are about us. Feelings of fear, loss or guilt can induce strong emotional responses. Often our tears are shed for ourselves in feelings of disappointment. Tears could indicate feelings of resentment towards the dying person; frustration at not being able to resolve old standing issues. At the time of my brother's death (see poem #127 "Bluebird"), while I was sitting next to his bed, I would often break down, crying uncontrollably. After the second day of me crying by his bedside, he mustered up enough energy to speak to me and this poem is based on what he said at that time.

222. 2017 Subject: Yoga

A Yogi Is Someone

A yogi is someone
    who is happy
A yogi is someone
    who is kind
A yogi is someone
    who doesn't blame, complain or explain
A yogi is someone
    who doesn't think that others should do this or that
A yogi is someone
    who does their best

A yogi is someone
 who lives in harmony with the Earth
A yogi is someone
 who sees themselves in others
A yogi is someone
 who doesn't eat others
A yogi is someone
 who cares for God
A yogi is someone
 who has remembered
A yogi is someone, like you and me
 who is interested in we.

222. *Notes:* I was invited to give a talk at the United Nations on World Yoga Day, June 20, 2017. Prior to the event, one of the organizers phoned me to discuss ideas as to how activism and yoga were related. This poem came out the notes I took from that conversation.

223. *2017 Subject: Time*

Doth Speak

Doth speak doth speak
If only for a moment speak
Clementine, Udine, Time

You in your cloak of
Three colors
Enrapturing all who dare approach
You who conceal and reveal
Cause the sun, moon and stars to appear
You, for whom words have their
Meaning
And tears their meaningless streaming
Doth speak doth speak

If only for a moment speak
Clementine, Udine, Time

223. Notes: This manifested universe that appears to be made of countless individual parts — atoms, molecules, organs, elements, beings, rivers, oceans, plants, trees, insects, snakes, birds, mammals, etc., appears in many forms due to the grand illusion which is sometimes called Maya. Maya is composed of three qualities called *guna*s in Sanskrit. *Sattva* is usually translated as goodness or lightness, *rajas* as activity or passion and *tamas* as heaviness or inertia. Gunas are present in all things manifest. Maya is God's agent, sometimes known as time. Time is that wonderful gift that prevents everything from happening at once. The enlightened ones transcend the three gunas, exist in timelessness and are not bound by the limits of individual, separate forms. This poem is an invitation to Maya, asking her to speak, to come from behind her veil and reveal herself and engage in conversation.

224. *2019 Subject: Portrait*

Dr. Dee Comes to Visit

Come in, come in
so nice of you
to call...
and all
what do I owe,
for this
so fortunate
of pleasures?
If I am not
mistaken
I think I see
it is you; it is you
come to see me
is it not,
Dr. Dee?

and what are
we
to do
do you foresee?
Look here
or sit there
but please
let us not...
stare
You in your cap
me in a wrap
How about...
Dr. John, John
is it not,
Dr. Dee?

Through a glass
lightly
the angels
ah...
those ones
who have come,
come in, come in
Come closer and see
how it all,
all is to be
But it is
the future
you seek
is it not,
Dr. Dee?

Oughten we?
What ought to be
funny tis it

the square to
the pear
But how is this
what ought
to be
Shouldn't we
call...
call upon he
shouldn't it be,
the pharaoh of old
is it not,
Dr. Dee?

Oughten
Akhenaten
be the one
we should see
Bright as
the light
the sun
is the one
No need for
fright
All is all right
the queen's
delight
is it not,
Dr. Dee?

224. *Notes:* Through historical accounts we know of several people who have tried their hands at alchemy. Some apparently mastered the art quite successfully. Doctor John Dee (1527-1608 C.E.) was one of those, devoting his life to the magical arts: hermetic philosophy, divination, astrology, sorcery and communing with angels and to science: mathematics, astronomy, chemistry, biology, and medicine. He did not consider the magical arts

different from science. To him they were all valid studies to pursue, believing that to truly understand the material world, one had to look deeper into the unseen, occult forces; and try to communicate with the beings who inhabit those realms. He was much respected as a learned man reputed to have the largest library in existence at the time. He was a teacher and advisor to Queen Elizabeth I, who reportedly held him in great favor. Even though he enjoyed tremendous acclaim he managed to remain humble and curious. But who today actually knows what Dr. Dee was really like? I mean his personality. I'm more inclined to perceive him, as novelist John Crowley paints him in his *AEgypt* series, as a sort of "soul in wonder"; having the innocence of a child, insatiable curiosity, infused with love and devotion for God.

Some pursue alchemy and the magical arts to feel powerful, to try to control others — mortal or otherwise or to curse others or to baffle and shock or to flaunt superiority over us lesser mortals, whereas Dr. Dee's quest was to converse with angels and become more aligned with God so as to become God's instrument in the world. In other words, he was a nice person, someone you would like to invite to your house for tea, conversation and a walk in the garden.

I mention Pharaoh Akhenaten (1380-1336 B.C.E.) as I felt Dr. Dee would have been one of those rare Englishmen during his time who knew something of Egypt, the birthplace of alchemy and chemistry as well as many of the sciences and practices we consider now to be magical. Since I also have an affinity for the pharaoh; in the poem I am imagining inviting them both to a wondrous time-defying tea party.

At the time of writing this poem I was practicing piano every morning, trying to learn Beethoven's *Fur Elise* and there are some tricky repetitious 'tongue twister' parts that were quite challenging to me. Although it was wintertime, after piano practice I would go for a bike ride on the snowy country roads of Woodstock. The turning of the bicycle wheels and the cold air helped me to work out some of the complexities in the music. The poem arose while I was on one of these rides and after I had come home and written it, I realized that it shared, in how the stanzas are arranged, something with the Beethoven piece.

The Tree

FIRST she was itsy bitsy — her name to blame
The tree is three, gives birth to one
Into the mud the toes began to grow,
crocheting dendrite spidery connecting webs
all this underground work woke up fingers who began
to reach out and by doing so
pulled arms and neck into slender extensions

THEN the name changed again — had too
A tree was forming in the sun
Where spring has sprung certainly there is a muse at play,
wouldn't you say?
The daughter of an apsara fed with drips of
soma by the finger of the gentle moon
Strong trunk filled with many jewels and rock
locked behind a mystery miasma of bark

UNTIL by means of sound, words then song
The tree is three, gives birth to one
small pebble — her name to blame
rolling out as gravity helps
the stone gathers momentum

SOON enough becomes a boulder
can you hear the voice from the mountain
singing watcha' gonna do?

225. *Notes:* A poem inspired by my friend, the artist, and singer Anisa Romero, who when I met her was called Betsy, a diminutive of her first name, Elizabeth. Anisa in Arabic means friend and also refers to the tree of life. The poem morphs her into a tree who lives in a garden and is fed by the moon,

which is a loose reference to an ancient story found in the Sanskrit text, *The Shrimad Bhagavatam*, about the orphaned daughter of a celestial nymph who is adopted by some kind trees, but since the trees don't have hands and cannot gather food to feed a child, is cared for by Soma the moon god, who feeds the little girl nectar with his finger. There is another reference to this ancient story in poem 154: "Widening Lanes".

The ancients saw trees as people with magical powers. That actually is not so far-fetched because trees do have the power to create soil. In my poem the tree gives birth to a stone. In her real life Anisa has a daughter named Petra. The lines, "where spring has sprung" and a "voice from the mountain" are taken from lyrics by English singer/songwriter Nick Drake. The last line, "watcha gonna do? is something that Anisa says often when she is between a rock and a hard place, as a way to express her optimism and choice to always look on the bright side of life, no matter how challenging. This ability she has to shift her perception is a magical ability.

226. 2019 Subject: Nature

Two-Toned Eagle

I saw a noble bird
sitting up high
with a head all of white
wrapped in dark
wings
as a cloak folded tight
Stoic he was with
claw fingers locked 'round
Then when he should
he upped and took flight
spreading wings 'cross the light
It was then that
I saw that his body was all feathery
white
whilst the limbs were dark,
as dark as the night

226. *Notes:* As I was riding my bicycle on a very cold wintry day along a deserted road off the main highway I looked up and saw perched in a tall tree a huge bird with a white head. I thought that I was seeing a bald eagle. I stopped my bike and watched this raptor in rapture. After a minute or so, perhaps aware of my gaze, he took off to reveal that his head, body, tail and feet where snowy white, while his wings were very dark brown. I got back on the bike and tried to follow his flight pattern but lost him when he ventured deeper into the woods where no roads allowed me to follow. His sighting left me in a state of awe.

227. *2019 Subject: Portrait*

The Piano Mushrooms

She doesn't make music —
that is what the piano does
inside — the inner workings
of strings and hammers.
Mycorrhizal networks making delicate lace
fungal mycelium extravagantly, unashamedly,
pulsating their way outwardly
with one-pointed focus —
desiring to touch and talk with her.
The piano mushrooms under her fingertips
yearning to make her happy, feel her smile.
She is a fairy in gold and pink,
who holds the keys that unlock the doors to thousands of scores,
seductively causing life to quicken
— awakening what others would see,
as cold wound up metal, pieces of lacquered wood glued together —
a segregated family of sharp and flat
deaf mutes, nothing to take note of.
She sees the colorful life inside, just underneath the surface
of black and white.
They sense her approach, entangle
and start to sing, pushing through the soil before she even sits down
and flutters her wings.

227. *Notes:* Katya Grineva is a classical pianist with a rare gift. Critics have said that she has a liquid, light feathery touch on the keys; the piano comes alive when she plays. I see her as caring for the piano as an elemental fairy cares for the life of plants in the forest. Through her gentle attention music emerges out of the piano, like mushrooms popping up through the forest floor.

228. *2019 Subject: Mysticism, Nature*

Ecstasy

Awakening to ecstasy
Remembering blessedly
Piercing precisely the arrow plunges deep
Recalling wordless release
Silence enfolds in billows of soft sheets
Caressed and kissed by the lips of eternity
This body evened out smooth like a trout
rubbed the right way
Surfaces to sip the air of serenity
only to dive again and again
Piercing precisely the arrow plunges deep
Each time renewing this miracle of sleep
That velvety rapturous revelry
Awakening to ecstasy

228. *Notes:* I am blessed to wake up most days, with God's name on my lips. As soon as I'm conscious that I am awake I begin a grateful blessing meditation, where people that I know float to the surface of my awareness, so I can embrace them for a moment while bestowing a blessing. This goes on for a time until I am once again pierced by the rapture and pulled under the surface into the oceanic depths of wordlessness. One characteristic of the ecstasy is that my body and mind are free of all pain and agitation. This process can repeat itself many times in the morning before I finally step out of bed and go about the day. What could trigger this blessed gift? I am not completely sure, although a few factors may figure in, for example: a

completely dark room, no electronic devises nearby, no one in the bed with me, a long sleep of at least ten hours and the remembrance of God's name.

229. 2019 Subject: Alchemy

Good Friday

He lived reminding us of our holiness
He died trying
His body like a box, opened and bled
Laid out as a cross
spirit freed from illusionary matter
May we all die to our mediocrity
and be reborn in our entirety

229. Notes: An Easter poem invoking spring, rebirth, optimism and new beginnings. Written with the hope that the crucifixion of Jesus was not in vain and that we will awaken to our own selves as holy. I have always felt that one of the essential teachings of the Christ was how to become a holy (whole, entire) being. A holy being would feel equally confident engaged in a variety of activities: cooking a meal, washing floors, fixing a toilet, standing on their head, praying, or rescuing an injured bird.

The cross is an ancient symbol that communicates the message of spirit freed from matter (the confines of a separate limiting existence.) This can be illustrated in simple geometric terms: If you take 6 squares and fold them into a cube and then open the box out flat it forms a cross. The liberation message given by the great saints and jivanmuktas, is that separation from God (from the whole) is illusionary and false. We cannot truly exist apart from God, because all is God. Through reuniting with our wholeness we become holy beings. Christ means the christened one, who remembers who they are — who knows themselves as one with all that is. This remembrance is available to anyone who is willing to die to their mediocrity.

Epilogue

I write the closing of this book, *Magic is a Shift in Perception*, at the dawn of 2020, a new decade promising clear vision. In the Vedic tradition of ancient India it was suggested that after a person had reached a certain age and had done their best to contribute to the enhancement of society they should excuse themselves from the hustle and bustle of the city and market place and relocate to the forest turning their attention to enhancing Mother Nature, worshiping God and preparing for death. This phase of life is said to bring clear focused vision geared to spiritual development rather than material attainment. This stage of life is called in Sanskrit, *vanaprashta*, which means dwelling in the forest.

The forest is a place of wildness, not a man-made place of cultivated gardens and landscaped terrain. A wild forest is viewed by human society as undeveloped land, not useful unless commodified into timber or other resources; not valued for its own sake. A forest is home to untethered undomesticated beings, who don't follow the artificial laws and time clocks of the workplace — in other words they don't make a living out of making money and buying stuff. The world of the forest, unlike the whirling world of civilization is not concerned with buying, selling, acknowledgment, fame, appreciation, being seen, being heard, being respected, blaming, complaining, explaining and vengeance. In our present culture the inclination to retire in order to focus on one's sadhana is not understood or valued much. We celebrate the person who keeps working into their 70s or 80s, respect the elderly who feign retirement, opting to continue to work till they drop dead on the job. We have been conditioned to feel that to be useful or productive means to be out-there, making money, acquiring things and leaving a legacy. Retirement often conjures images of reclining by a swimming pool sipping martinis or sitting in front of a TV screen binging on *netflix* episodes, or the opposite end of the spectrum: a bent, lonely, wrinkled crone pushing a walker, shuffling along, no longer useful, a burden to family and society.

But what if a person, after years of engaging in the business of civilization, entered into their twilight years more hermetically, but with the same enthusiasm and purpose that they invested in public life? I am putting that question to myself after living a life of externalizing. I am now moving into the realm of internalizing, no longer feeling compelled to express or engage outwardly.

It may be true that each of us owes a debt to society and that we should spend a portion of our lives giving back. But what of the debt to Nature? What about devoting your time to getting to know God better? To enhance the lives of others is a good and perhaps noble pursuit, but besides enhancement what about the good and noble pursuit of enchantment? It is the allure and magic of Nature and the immersion into the subtle celestial realms that can provide that. Enchantment may not deliver monetary dividends and fame, but for some, there comes a time when the karmic dues are paid up and you have earned the right to step barefoot off the pavement and feel the soft moss of possibilities and leave behind the doing of things. After all to realize that you are not the doer is the realization that comes to the yogi. To facilitate this realization we have to be willing to allot some time to the possibility and that means we have to stop doing. At least let go of the incessant drive that motivates us to identify as the doer.

This book represents a body of work, time spent in the doing of writing. With its completion, I am not saying that I will never write another poem. But perhaps, in the time to come if I am visited by a poem, rather than write it down in black and white for those who read, maybe I'll send it as a colorful whisper into the air to the illiterate trees and let them hear it as ubiquitous molecules dissolving and falling like leaves into the ground of space and the arrangement of time. And may those etheric poems remain in the privacy of the forest.

Acknowledgments

Thank you to **David Life**, the biggest fan of my poetry, who in 1979 founded the Life Café, giving a place for poets to write and read their work. Without David's love, blessings, patience, encouragement, practical support, grammar expertise and technical know-how in the preparation of the manuscript, I could not have brought this project to completion. Thank you to my old poet friend **John Rogers** for encouraging me to read and write poetry fifty years ago. Thank you to **Karoline Straubinger** who helped me prepare the early version of the manuscript for presentation. Thank you to my friend **Joshua M. Greene** for his friendship and generous foreword which reveals his accomplished ability to perceive gold inside a murky stream. I am indebted to **Gopal (Paul) Steinberg**, my editor, who sat by my side for countless hours, listening to me try to explain the many obscurities and abstractions in the poems and then providing constructive rewrite directions so as to render this book more readable for others.

Poems aren't written without inspiration nor is a life lived void of relationships with others. Some poems in this collection identify people by name, but most do not. I hope that all of the people who have enriched my life and found a way into my heart find themselves in these poems and realize how grateful I am for their presence.

Most importantly, all glories to my beloved **Shri Krishna**, the one who pulls the strings.

About the Author

Sharon Gannon has been described as a modern-day Renaissance woman, a polymath, excelling in many arts: painting, music, dance, cooking and writing as well as an animal rights vegan activist. She is best known as the co-founder, along with David Life of the Jivamukti Yoga method. www.jivamuktiyoga.com

Index of poems by Title

References are to page numbers

Index of First Lines

References are to page numbers.

Index of Subjects

References are to page numbers

CPSIA information can be obtained
at www.ICGtesting.com
Printed in the USA
LVHW021246131020
668666LV00001B/50